Liberal Languages

LIBERAL LANGUAGES

Ideological Imaginations
and Twentieth-Century
Progressive Thought

Michael Freeden

PRINCETON UNIVERSITY PRESS
PRINCETON AND OXFORD

Copyright © 2005 by Princeton University Press
Published by Princeton University Press, 41 William Street,
Princeton, New Jersey 08540
In the United Kingdom: Princeton University Press, 3 Market Place,
Woodstock, Oxfordshire OX20 1SY

Library of Congress Cataloging-in-Publication Data

Freeden, Michael.
Liberal languages : ideological imaginations and twentieth-century
progressive thought / Michael Freeden
p. cm.
Includes bibliographical references and index

ISBN 0-691-11677-6 (alk. paper) — ISBN 0-691-11678-4 (pbk. : alk. paper)
1. Liberalism. 2. Political science—History—20th century. 3. Ideology. I. Title.

JC574.F595 2005
320.51'09'04—dc22   2004041463

British Library Cataloging in Publication Data is available

This book has been composed in Sabon
Printed on acid-free paper. ∞
pup.princeton.edu
Printed in the United States of America
10 9 8 7 6 5 4 3 2 1

_To the memory of my mother, Dr. Marianne Freeden,
and of my father, Dr. Herbert Freeden_

Contents

Acknowledgments

THIS COLLECTION IS the product of many years of reading, talking, listening and thinking about both liberalism and ideology with colleagues, authors past and present, students, friends and family. H.-G. Gadamer famously wrote about "the conversation that we ourselves are," and I can only concur. Specific thanks to Ian Malcolm of Princeton University Press for his support and encouragement.

I would like to express my thanks for permission to reprint articles and chapters previously published in the following books or journals:

"Twentieth-Century Liberal Thought: Development or Transformation?" in M. Evans, ed., *The Edinburgh Companion to Contemporary Liberalism* (Edinburgh University Press, 2001).

"Liberal Community: An Essay in Retrieval," in A. Simhony and D. Weinstein, eds., *The New Liberalism: Reconciling Liberty and Community* (Cambridge University Press, 2001).

"The Concept of Poverty and Progressive Liberalism" was published in French in F.-X. Merrien, ed., *Face à la Pauvreté* (Paris: Les Éditions de l'Atelier, 1994).

The seeds of "Layers of Legitimacy: Consent, Dissent and Power in Left-Liberal Languages" were planted in an article entitled "Liberalismo, Potere ed Élites in Gran Bretagna 1890–1930," *Ricerche di Storia Politica* 7 (1992). The chapter loosely builds on that article and on a lecture given at the University of Bologna in 2002 to develop a different set of arguments.

"J. A. Hobson as a Political Theorist," in J. Pheby, ed., *J. A. Hobson after Fifty Years: Freethinker of the Social Sciences* (Macmillan, London, 1994), reproduced with permission of Palgrave Macmillan.

"Hobson's Evolving Conceptions of Human Nature," in M. Freeden, ed., *Reappraising J.A. Hobson: Humanism and Welfare* (Unwin Hyman, London, 1990), reproduced with permission of HarperCollins Publishers Ltd., (c) 1990 Michael Freeden.

"Eugenics and Progressive Thought: A Study in Ideological Affinity," *Historical Journal* 22 (1979).

"True Blood or False Genealogy: New Labour and British Social Democratic Thought," in A. Gamble and T. Wright, eds., *The New Social Democracy* (Blackwell, 1999).

"The Ideology of New Labour," *Political Quarterly* 70 (1999): 42–51.

"Is Nationalism a Distinct Ideology?" *Political Studies* 46 (1998).

"Political Theory and the Environment: Nurturing a Sustainable Relationship," in A. Light and A. de-Shalit, eds., *Moral and Political Reasoning in Environmental Practice* (M.I.T. Press, 2003).

"Practising Ideology and Ideological Practices" in "Political Ideas and Political Action," ed. R. Barker, special issue, *Political Studies* 48 (2000).

Irene, Jonathan, and Daniella have ensured that my labours are labours of love.

PART ONE

LIBERALISM RESARTUS

The term "liberalism" has always enjoyed a separate existence away from the constricting, formal, and austere world of political concepts and theories. To be liberal evokes generosity, tolerance, compassion, being fired up with the promise of open, unbounded spaces within which the free play of personality can be aired. Yet the clues to liberalism's political nature are not hard to detect. Generosity suggests the dispensing of bounties beyond the call of duty—to prioritise justice as the first liberal virtue is unnecessarily reductionist. Tolerance suggests a flexibility, a movement, a diversity—of ideas, of language, and of conceptual content—that sets liberalism aside from most of its ideological rivals, whose declared aspiration is to finalise their control over the political imagination. Compassion suggests an empathy, a sociability, an altruism, that pays homage to the human networks in which individualism is integrally and beneficially enmeshed, as well as an ardent desire to alleviate human suffering. And openness suggests that the permutations of human conduct and thought are unfathomable and wonderfully unpredictable. Lest we forget, those are liberalism's most remarkable qualities.

Just over a century ago, something significant happened to liberalism that brought those qualities into particular prominence. It underwent a series of transformations that changed the nature of Western politics, while altering the internal balance of liberal political thought itself. Many factors contributed to that change. Among those were the growing reach of democratised politics; the (re)discovery of social relations as partly constituting the individual; the popularisation of evolutionary theory grafted on to theories of progress; a new attentiveness to the psychology of human vitality; the identification of additional barriers to human action and development that required novel conceptions of liberty; and, not least, a reconceptualisation of politics as a responsible, responsive, and facilitating communal activity. That process occurred in a number of cultural locations: in France, in the Antipodes, in the United States, in Italy. But above all it took place in Britain, and Britain—then still a net exporter of political ideas—persevered in its nineteenth-century role as the leading producer and disseminator of cutting-edge liberal theory and of the practices that accompanied such thinking. The chapters in this first section are intended both to illustrate the potential that is always available in liberal theory and ideology, and to emphasise the actual importance and impact of a body of ideas that grew over time and across space.

That British movement of ideas, known as the "new liberalism," was no chimera or historical oddity, no flash in the pan, no geographical eccentricity. Rather, it teased out of liberalism implicit and underplayed features that created an ideological turn. This juncture lies at the basis of the welfare state—probably the most important domestic institutional achievement of Western political systems in the twentieth century. Two of the central figures of the new liberalism, Leonard Trelawny Hobhouse and John Atkinson Hobson—who figure prominently in the following pages—deserve that salience because they epitomise that ideological turn in their fecund writings and in their innovative methodology. We can, indeed, employ them to unlock much of the liberal potential that has become hidden, or has been overlooked, in many of the philosophical liberal discourses that dominated the period between the 1970s and the 1990s. As befits a broadly based intellectual tradition, the two British thinkers are equally important for who they were as for the trend they so brilliantly and efficiently symbolised, for their ability to optimise liberalism's humanist promise, and for the distinctive liberal language they developed. Nonetheless, the story of the new, progressive liberalism of the twentieth century is a far more extensive and subtle one, involving individuals, groups, and institutions that through their synergies moulded an intricate and pervasive modern Weltanschauung, employing a range of liberal languages. And it is a story that should on no account be displaced by the political remoteness, specialised interests, and hypothetical thought-experiments characteristic of recent academic liberal debates.

In addressing the issues raised by those liberal currents and rearticulations of liberal principles, we are inevitably drawn to a profound set of concerns. What is liberalism? How does one go about attempting to answer that most seductive and elusive question? In particular, which of the features that typify the liberal tradition should we take note of from the vantage point of the present? Can we use our knowledge of liberalism, as it has developed over the past century or so, to decode some of its more recent manifestations, as well as to appreciate the complexity of that ideological movement over time and space? And, simply but importantly, where should we look for liberal thinking?

Extending the Search

In the broadest sense, three fundamental perspectives on liberalism exist side by side and it may help to set them out.

First, liberalism—as history—can be understood as a narrative about the emergence of a belief system, contextualised and temporalised. That narrative has focused primarily on the liberation of individuals and groups from oppression and discrimination. Second, liberalism—as ideology—can be understood as an actually identifiable configuration of specified political concepts, such as liberty, progress, and individuality, that adopts a distinct pattern, or a series of family resemblances, to which the name "liberal" is designated. Third, liberalism—as philosophy—can be understood as a modelling device in which universal ground rules are drawn up for a just and free society, rules that permit in particular a fair and equal pursuit of the chosen life plan of every person.

These are some of the questions and approaches that the essays in this book, especially in its first part, address. But if Hegel's owl of Minerva has any say in the matter, my own journey through liberalism has been accompanied by a permanent flapping of her wings. There is no end of day at which understanding descends. Comprehension is incremental and insight changes with accruing perspectives. When I first embarked on exploring aspects of the liberal tradition, my aim was specific: to understand what had happened to liberalism between the mature John Stuart Mill— at the time appropriated by liberal minimalists and "self-regarders"—and the Beveridge Report of almost a century later. Even given the impact of the more holistic and other-regarding philosophical idealism that emerged in the post-Millian late nineteenth century, what occurred inside the liberal "black box" to transform a tract such as T. H. Green's *Liberal Legislation and Freedom of Contract* of 1881 into a policy document such as the Beveridge Report of 1942—William Beveridge's *Social Insurance and Allied Services*—still remained something of a mystery. Aside from some general awareness of Hobhouse as a worthy but secondary figure in the modern liberal canon, there were few accounts, and fewer analyses, of the complex movement of liberalism from an assumedly individualistic, even atomistic, theory of human nature and social structure towards something at the heart of welfare-state thinking. What accounted for that leap? *Was* it a leap, or was it an oversight of both participants and scholars in failing to recognise a more sustained and steady process that had been happening under their eyes? And if so, why did that failure in recognition happen?

Failure to recognize is not tantamount to a failure to get it right. It means that cultural and ideological causes obscure certain interpretations, certain points of view; that they deliberately conceal or underestimate them, or, more accurately and frequently, that the conceptual apparatus for their formulation and recognition is simply unavailable; and that the methodology employed by students of political thought is designed to extract and illuminate certain kinds of information but not others. The study of liberalism suffered from all these characteristics, so that by the mid-twentieth-century research into the liberal tradition had become a highly constricted and stylised approximation of the evidence and perspectives that were potentially available to its students. But there has been another major impediment to the scholarly retrieval, mapping, and appraisal of liberalism. For the past forty years, its philosophical exploration has drifted apart from the thinking, the theorising, and the debates that have constituted liberalism as a broad political movement, both intellectual and political. Gone are the days when a John Stuart Mill could produce a text that would serve as reference point to political leaders as well as philosophers, a text that could be grasped by a reasonably educated individual. The specialized language of late-twentieth-century liberal philosophers, directed mainly at their colleagues rather than at the thinking public,[1] has been accompanied by a partial reconstruction of the liberal enterprise, a reconstruction that runs counter to many—though far from all—of the assumptions, beliefs, and prescriptions that have typified Western liberalism.

The loss is a double one: to historians of ideas and students of ideology because they no longer are as keenly in touch with the critical and reflexive testing of liberal principles; and to political philosophers because they no longer are significantly in touch with the political and cultural constraints that ensure the viable flexibility liberalism requires, as it competes in the real-world arena of policymaking, of reform, of social inspiration, and of political mobilisation. These diverging fields of analysis have to develop a common language and to begin to reconnect, to intersect, and to overlap in their concerns, in order for the members of the liberal family to be recognised as possessing a common ideational pool, however different the actual drawing out of political languages from that pool may be. There are only three modes of going about this. First, one of the discourses can be eliminated—an unlikely as well as a most undesirable possibility. Second, the disparate discourses can be reconciled, if each is prepared to learn the language of the others and make some serious mutual methodological concessions. Third, new discourses may be constructed that offer alternative sites for developing the study of liberalism, or that re-evaluate the existing discourses so that common, hitherto nontransparent, organising motifs and conceptual patterns are unveiled. My own forays into liberal theory, increasingly propelled by frustration with the current nonconversation among the disciplines, have attempted to establish small beachheads, initially for the second mode and more recently for the third.

---

[1] In part the pressures on an increasingly beleaguered and specialised academic profession have brought about the need for philosophers to impress their scholarly peers long before they convey their thoughts to the public; in part liberalism has in their hands again become

This book has a second theme, though. It concerns the application of recent theories of ideology, my own included, in order to obtain a clearer view of the components of liberalism and their internal flexibility and substantive indeterminacy. It also assists in comprehending the boundaries of liberalism, their permeability, and the structures that exist outside them. At what points in a discursive field do we begin to move out of the liberal domain? Which conceptual mutations have to occur for us to decide that the configuration of arguments before us is no longer liberal? Finally, it examines some features of ideological morphology I have explored since completing my *Ideologies and Political Theory: A Conceptual Approach*.[2] That second theme is a minor one in some of the chapters of the first part, whereas the first theme, likewise, is a lesser thread present in most chapters of the second. I shall address the second theme more specifically in a chapter linking the two parts.

ALTERNATIVE RECONSTRUCTIONS

The historical study of liberalism has become increasingly and healthily diversified over the past quarter-century. Some of it still follows canonical convention in setting out the qualitative criteria of the liberal political thinking it is prepared to take seriously, even as it has moved to extend somewhat the range of theorists that form part of the classical liberal canon. An example of that approach is that of Stefan Collini, who channelled the 1960s–1970s Cambridge focus on high politics into the scrutiny of high-minded political thinking among a broader cross-section of the liberal intelligentsia, while insisting that less structured or less sophisticated forms of political thought could not be subject to the same standards of analysis.[3] Other branches of historical research have illuminated the populist sources of issues that intellectuals later raised to the levels of properly articulated discourses. Thus, some liberal conceptions of communal identity and fraternity could be traced to working-class cultures that percolated into mainstream political thinking and that pressed on liberalism a need to develop greater social inclusiveness. An example of that is the work of Eugenio Biagini, who has also argued that continuities with earlier, "older" liberal strands should not be underestimated.[4] Fur-

---

the élitist enterprise it used to be before democratic practice softened the overly rational and insular garb liberalism once donned.

[2] M. Freeden, *Ideologies and Political Theory: A Conceptual Approach* (Oxford, 1996).

[3] See, e.g., S. Collini, *Liberalism and Sociology: L. T. Hobhouse and Political Argument in England, 1880–1914* (Cambridge, 1979).

[4] E. F. Biagini and A. J. Reid, *Currents of Radicalism: Popular Radicalism, Organised Labour and Party Politics in Britain, 1850–1914* (Cambridge, 1991), pp. 9, 15.

ther recent developments have yet to figure prominently: the continental, German-led development of conceptual history, investigating competing and changing vocabularies, and linguistic and conceptual adaptability in crucial historical bridging periods, has so far had little resonance in the study of liberalism.[5] Similar issues have arisen through the work of J. G. A. Pocock on political language and vocabulary—again insufficiently cashed out in existing research on the nineteenth and twentieth centuries, on which the essays in this book focus.[6] Ultimately, it has to be said, liberalism has a far broader multidisciplinary genealogy than that assumed by canon-led historians of political thought: politics, psychology, sociology, management, biology. It is not just a philosophy but a sophisticated cultural compound. And its sources are manifold: liberalism is a discourse that surfaces at countless levels of written and oral expression.

When I first started work on *The New Liberalism*,[7] conceptual history was in its infancy, the focus on authorial intentions had just commenced, while discourse analysis and the linguistic turn had hardly begun to be applied to the study of political thought. I was convinced that the activity of creating socially significant and historically important political theory was a far broader one than what was represented through the traditional apostolic successions of the "great thinkers." My aim was to extend the range of subject matter that came under the legitimate scrutiny of political theory and to examine thinking that was located closer to the coal face of political activity. In so doing I tried to apply some of the analytical questions that concerned political theorists to the archival materials at the disposal of historians.

By the time *Liberalism Divided* had been completed,[8] I was beginning to make the first inroads into the approach I believed was needed to understand and decipher the political thinking produced by broader groups of intellectuals and activists. The opening sections of that book adumbrate some general thoughts about the forms in which that thinking appears to us. Curiously, some historians urged me to drop those methodological musings, which a decade later had been transformed into my theory of ideological structure (which I later termed ideological morphology in order to distinguish between that theory and the various currents under the general heading of "structuralism").

---

[5] R. Koselleck, *Futures Past* (Cambridge, MA, 1985); idem, *The Practice of Conceptual History: Timing History, Spacing Concepts* (Palo Alto, CA, 2002); M. Richter, *The History of Social and Political Concepts* (New York, 1995).

[6] But for an illuminating recent study on liberal vocabularies see R. A. Primus, *The American Language of Rights* (Cambridge, 1999).

[7] M. Freeden, *The New Liberalism: An Ideology of Social Reform* (Oxford, 1978).

[8] M. Freeden, *Liberalism Divided: A Study in British Political Thought, 1914–1939* (Oxford, 1986).

Ideologies and Political Theory enabled me to revisit British new liberalism—while exploring other forms of liberalism as well as different ideological families—and re-examine the ideas I had already studied. This time, however, the emphasis was on their decontestations and their configurations, and on investigating how specific conceptual arrangements created determinate fields of meaning from the raw material available to the formulators of liberalism—indeed, of political thought in general. An interest in methodology no longer seemed to me—as it still does to quite a few scholars—merely to be the overindulgent preliminary to talking about what really matters. Rather, it was the key to deciphering the secrets contained in written texts and oral utterances. It offered solutions to the central question I now knew had to be asked: what has to hold for this sentence, that paragraph, this narrative, to make sense to its author, and what has to hold for it to make sense to its consumers, be they the intended audiences at the time, or the audiences of the future? How are the sense and the meaning that should interest students of politics produced, formed, and extracted from the thoughts and practices available to a society? Which options are opened and which foreclosed, both for political thought and for political practices, when a particular cultural map is superimposed on a virtual infinity of logical conceptual possibilities?

But whereas part 2 concentrates on alternative modes of analysing ideologies, part 1 is concerned with alternative reconstructions of the history of liberal thought. While historians of liberalism in the past generation have approached their chosen subject through the prisms of high or of low politics, and while questions of genesis and lines of influence still have a strong hold on their academic imaginations, most of the essays in part 1 follow a different trajectory. They reshuffle the priorities accorded to questions asked of the liberal tradition, and they legitimate and respect the thought-artefacts themselves—the debates, discourses, conflicting renderings, shifting grounds, everyday discussions and concrete grapplings with liberalism on a number of levels of articulation that I hold to be informative, even illuminating.

The first two essays nevertheless also reflect the need of most academics to keep abreast of intellectual fashions—in this case the explosion of liberal political philosophy that made most of the running in the agendas of political theorists during the last quarter of the twentieth century—and to react to dominant paradigms of analysis. To forestall potential wrath from the ranks of political philosophers, I cannot stress too strongly how important that discipline is, and how crucial its analytical insights, critical appraisals, and ethical sensitivities have been to the refinement of political thought. There is, indeed, overlap between the study of political thinking in its broader scope and the types of arguments and perspectives that political philosophers have developed. But political philosophy is nevertheless a different enterprise, and in recent decades it has become very distanced from those who wish—through the analysis of actual or possible patterns of political thought—to understand better the nature of the political itself and to return some of the concerns of political theory to the sphere of the social sciences. This is particularly true of enquiries into liberalism, for not only has the language of liberalism changed, but some of its defining features have as well. Here is an example.

For John Rawls, liberalism—through its conception of justice—"protects the familiar basic rights and assigns them a special priority; it also includes measures to insure that all citizens have sufficient material means to make effective use of those basic rights . . . a liberal view removes from the political agenda the most divisive issues, serious contention about which must undermine the bases of social cooperation." And again, "liberal principles meet the urgent political requirement to fix, once and for all, the content of certain political basic rights and liberties, and to assign them special priority. Doing this takes those guarantees off the political agenda and puts them beyond the calculus of social interests."[9]

Contrast this with Hobhouse, for whom

> liberalism is the belief that society can safely be founded on [the] self-directing power of personality, that it is only on this foundation that a true community can be built . . . we have come to look for the effect of liberty in the firmer establishment of social solidarity . . . in the organic conception of society each of the leading ideas of historic Liberalism has its part to play. The ideal society is conceived as a whole which lives and flourishes by the harmonious growth of its parts, each of which in developing on its own lines and in accordance with its own nature tends on the whole to further the development of others.[10]

And on the role of the liberal state Hobhouse wrote,

> the conscience of the community has its rights just as much as the conscience of the individual. . . . Liberty and compulsion have complementary functions, and the self-governing State is at once the product and the condition of the self-governing individual. Thus there is no difficulty in understanding why the extension of state control goes along with determined resistance to encroachments on another. It is a question not of increasing or diminishing, but of reorganizing, restraints.[11]

The ahistoricity of arrested time versus historical development, depoliticisation versus the regulatory role of a democratic state representing the communal interest, justice through individual rights versus well-being and

---

[9] J. Rawls, *Political Liberalism* (New York, 1993), pp. 156–57, 161.
[10] L. T. Hobhouse, *Liberalism* (London, 1911), pp. 66–67, 72.
[11] Ibid., pp. 79, 81.

flourishing through the recognition of social solidarity—these are some of the varying, and even irreconcilable, differences that open up between those twentieth-century notions of liberalism.

THE EVIDENCE FOR LIBERALISM

In chapter 1, I seek to offer an account of liberalism not from the external and critical perspective of analytical political philosophers, nor from the usual focus of historians of political thought on mainstream liberalism that tends to operate within the conventional garbs of individuals versus collectivities, nor even from the themes of freedom versus welfare that have been at the heart of some of my own studies. Rather, it is a tentative attempt to look at a number of alternative and insufficiently valued features of liberalism that, in retrospect, shed light on its under-researched twentieth-century manifestations. Those are then related to the Rawlsian phenomenon—phenomenon being the operative word!—as itself a particular historical occurrence, one liberal conversation among many. On the microlevel, I argue that concepts such as civilisation, movement, and vitality turn out to be inextricably linked to liberal discourse and the liberal frame of mind. Liberals are partis pris about their beliefs; they spread them not in terms of rationally and morally irresistible ground rules for a fair society prior to its establishment, but rather as the apex of a long process of a civilising mission—of becoming, not being—during which societies mature and propagate constantly evolving and spatially proliferating views of the good life. For liberals, civil society immediately assumes the dual meanings of gracious urbanity and of voluntarism, but it is assisted by an enabling and visionary state. The recent fixation of philosophical liberalism with neutrality is alien to a liberal tradition that has held to its non-negotiable beliefs and ideas as strong preferences for certain values and activities over others, and that has even advocated a limited exercise of duress in order to protect liberal values when those come under serious threat.

One of my contentions has been that the study of liberalism is enriched when we enlist different forms of evidence. That involves a challenge to the distinctions that many political philosophers—and some historians, too—make between primary and secondary texts in investigating political thought. A chief merit of the hermeneutic approach has been to identify a constantly changing set of horizons from which the past and the present are viewed and interpreted. When applied to the study of liberalism, that approach decrees that any secondary text, any commentary on a "great work," may itself be a worthy object of study. It is therefore perfectly possible to move seamlessly between texts designated as "primary" or "secondary," when we appreciate that "primary" and "secondary," and even occasionally "first order" and "second order" are the products of a world of absolutes, a world of statics where "nothing flows" and time stands still, or the products of a scholarly paradigm in which original thoughts are merely revised and, occasionally, corrupted. This signals the absence of narrative and the absence of constructive change.

By contrast, liberal thought is not only a narrative, but should be savoured as a *collective* narrative that is formed by conversations, reactions, and ripple-effects within large groups, allows the introduction of impermanence within constraining family resemblances, and concurrently enables the idea of development, and of potential evolutionary improvement, to occupy centre stage. For that reason alone such methods of analysis are particularly adept at capturing the features of the liberal tradition, as both the notion of development and the notion of conceptual flexibility—often reconstructed ethically as a plea for tolerance—are situated at its core. In addition, to portray liberal thought as a configuration of conceptual decontestations that take on a specific, if fluid, profile allows us to conceive of it as a confluence between long-standing values and shifting cultural contexts. The outcome of all this is to reinforce the insight that, if we are to acknowledge that something significant did happen to liberalism, it can only become evident through new perspectives that embrace narrative as well as ideological morphology, and through engaging pluralism not only as a liberal value evoking tolerance, or the moral and value diversity of human life,[12] but as a structural feature that invariably reveals many liberalisms.

At the same time, evidence must remain empirical. The existence of liberal views has to be validated, even though interpretation may direct us to specific sites and may select circumscribed information from a larger field. The studies in this collection are strongly informed by the contention that liberalism is a pliant tradition subscribed to by identifiable groups, and that the scholar ought to reascertain periodically what those generally held beliefs are. Only then should they be subjected to the kind of critical appraisal necessary to locate them in this, rather than that, segment of the liberal family (and occasionally outside it). Of course, ideologies usually endeavour to anchor themselves in scientific foundations. But that is a different matter involving legitimacy, not scholarly plausibility. The scramble for the mantle of scientific authority is frequently a facile and flawed route to legitimacy pursued by the ideological producers themselves. The scholar of political thought, to the contrary, needs to abide by conventions of authentication and validation acceptable in the social sciences.

---

[12] On this standpoint see recently W. A. Galston, *Liberal Pluralism* (Cambridge, 2002).

All too often, however, proponents of philosophical liberalism have moved in a secluded and artificial world of perfectionism and neutrality. When they model a universal ethics, they call it liberalism because it is reflexive, and because it entertains some idea of rational equality as well as one of equal liberty. Nevertheless, philosophical liberalism is partially insulated from the practices and complex discourses that have made up the family of liberalisms. This was already the case in the past,[13] but it has now become more pronounced. Modelling frequently involves the substitution of name tags for complex theoretical positions, and the tendency of some Anglo-American philosophy is to simplify for reasons of brevity and for heuristic purposes. The return to dichotomies (e.g., perfectionist-neutral; individual-communitarian) and to ideal types (liberalism as grounded on single foundational ideas such as equality or autonomy) may serve as "extreme-case" or "pure-case" constructs through which to test the viability and coherence of arguments and explore their raw logical paths. Nonetheless, the contemporary mass-appeal nature of the political cannot be understood by reference only, or even predominantly, to philosophical texts—that would cause us to go seriously astray as political theorists and political scientists. The bulk of political thinking in a society does not take place in such texts. The ethical and epistemological motifs of liberal thought have always been carried also by authors and articulators who are not academically proficient, using less demanding forms of expression. This is true also of the strong American liberal tradition in the twentieth century, whose features—encompassing community, a common good, planning, and populism, as well as specific understandings of liberty—are rather different from those propounded by those who now speak in the name of liberal justice. Although not central to my own research,[14] that tradition, too, is beginning to receive the kind of serious scholarly attention it deserves.[15]

Thinkers such as Hobhouse and Hobson are different kinds of political theorists, though not less important for that difference. For in order to understand liberalism as a living ideology, we have to look in new places. Many liberals are not public intellectuals as conventionally understood,

---

[13] Cf. M. Stears, *Progressives, Pluralists, and the Problems of the State: Ideologies of Reform in the United States and Britain, 1909–1926* (Oxford, 2002), p. 28, on nineteenth-century idealism as a form of liberalism.

[14] I have offered brief comparative comments on American progressive liberalism in *Ideologies and Political Theory*, chap. 6.

[15] For representative writings of the times see H. Croly, *The Promise of American Life* (New York, 1909); J. Dewey, *Liberalism and Social Action* (New York, 1935). For current analysis, see, e.g., Stears, *Progressives, Pluralists, and the Problems of the State*; D. T. Rodgers, *Atlantic Crossings: Social Politics in a Progressive Age* (Cambridge, MA, 1998); L. Williams, *American Liberalism and Ideological Change* (DeKalb, IL, 1997).

in the sense of contributing to an authoritative ethic that is publicly available for others to dilute—though obviously they may be. They are typically ideologically active intellectuals who—whatever else they write and say—need to adopt an optimal ideological language, a language that has general appeal and is geared to maximising public support. Public intellectuals are therefore not only those concerned with public affairs but those that address mass publics. It is no accident that Hobhouse's more abstract works and his evening editorial writing for the famous liberal newspaper, the *Manchester Guardian*, sustained each other. Ideological, as distinct from philosophical or scholarly, quality relates to communication, to mobilisation, and, not least, to the deftness with which ideologies weave short-term issues and a changing political landscape into a loose and periphery-sensitive morphological framework. By "periphery-sensitive" we refer to the interface between ideological structures and the concrete and specific practices and events that serve either to translate them into political action or, conversely, to redefine the meanings attached to the ideological cores. Intellectuals as ideologists are nearer to Gramsci's understanding of their role, explored in the final chapter of this book. Hobson, in particular, has been regarded by some technicians of political philosophy as far too woolly to be taken seriously—a judgment that he was destined, ironically, to suffer from economists during his lifetime. That misses the point. Not even Rousseau, let alone Hobson, would pass the stringent deliberative and logical tests that current philosophy constructs. Without the shadow of a doubt, Hobson was a pivotal liberal political thinker. His input into liberal thought (quite apart from his impact on economics and on theories of imperialism) was outstanding, and if we—as scholars— decode him correctly, that input is revealed for the pervasive, multifaceted, and inventive contemplation that it was.

PLURALISM AS A DEFAULT POSITION

One curious effect of philosophical liberalism has been to present pluralism as problematic. It has demonstrated a dual tendency to extol diversity—as an expression both of individual autonomy and of multicultural identity—while insisting on the unity of the moral foundations of a well-ordered society. That latter constraint restricts the ontological possibilities contained in liberalism: ethical evolution or mutual dependence, for instance, are excluded as normal possibilities on that moral map. If this view of morality continues to prioritise autonomy and identity over other features of human existence and conduct, it will desensitise its proponents to the awareness of the ideological and semantic complexity embraced in political thinking. I refer to one manifestation of this issue in chapter 2:

the role of community in liberal thought. The new liberals accessed the concept of community through their strong organicism, predicated on biological views of the interdependence of living entities and on Idealist and classical notions of harmony. Although the organic analogy has gone out of fashion (though see chapter 8, below), its philosophical anthropology and reliance on social theory represented a departure from the nineteenth-century liberal individualist iconography in which heroic entrepreneurs, such as inventors, were seen to propel society forwards. It also represented a holistic view of society quite in tune with more recent hermeneutic perspectives. That holism requires a nonliteral reading to extract from it the idea of an interrelated and intermeshed semantic field and an appreciation of the consequent knock-on effect that a change in a political practice will have on the equilibrium of that field.

There is, however, a further consideration. If we postulate the existence of communities as valuable social entities—something that even philosophical liberals enamoured of individual cultural identities do—that will have a bearing on the conception of rights a society employs. I have argued elsewhere that rights are devices for first identifying and then prioritising crucial attributes and requirements of the rights-bearing entity, and as a consequence they require action or inaction by others to protect those attributes and requirements.[16] As such, rights are not substantively exclusive to liberalism. But they are procedurally highly salient in liberalism, for they postulate either or both of the following: the insulation of social spaces from external control because of the high premium put on self-determination or, to the contrary, the social obligation—that occasionally is a structural necessity—to enter such spaces in order to secure a range of *additional* liberal ends such as self-development, individuality, and rational action. It is only through appreciating the compound conceptual morphology of liberalism that we can account for the dual possibility of intervention and nonintervention in the liberal tradition as permanent and parallel features, depending on the liberal good/concept that needs to be protected. If we then ask, as so many do, how successful were the new liberals in reconciling individualism and collectivism, I believe that question to be somewhat off the mark. The question should rather be: Of the many forms of (imperfect reconciliation) of those two ideas that liberals adopted, how did each of them work, what did they resolve, and what did they leave unsettled? Such reconciliation can neither be a clear and final undertaking, nor one that requires a single blueprint.

To reiterate in a different way a point already made: One can never understand liberalism if one assumes that it is a monolith in its postulates, assumptions, and values. Liberalism is a cluster of concepts and goods,

---

[16] M. Freeden, *Rights* (Milton Keynes, 1991).

some of which can only be attained by social initiative, others by its absence and by reliance on individual judgment and virtue. A right is then not an attribute or a foundational feature of individuals; it is not something that people are born with, nor is it the basic building block of liberal theory. Rather, it is a symbolic conceptual act *building on* elements of the world that are coopted into a social construct. It identifies crucial features of human well-being (or those considered to be crucial) and offers them a fortified conceptual defence, quite irrespective of the normative arguments it enlists. Using the terminology of rights transforms a social and analytical interpretation concerning the components of valued humanity into compelling political language. And it can be attached to whichever social units are identified as the main incarnations of the human condition. When liberalism abandoned the theory of natural rights, it replaced them with a more flexible understanding of rights. That understanding avoided the built-in brittleness that causes natural, universal rights to snap under the pressure of a single contrary instance; instead, it contextualised them while retaining certain limits as to what they could signify. The right to liberty, for example, became the right to the release from dehumanising socioeconomic as well as physical or legal hindrances, hindrances that were not universal but the product of imperfect social orders such as untrammelled capitalism. The limits imposed on rights were simple: the protection of any core liberal value only as long as its pursuit did not begin to impinge fatally on other core liberal values. Thus, liberty had to be constrained at the point where it began to undermine individuality or progress. That approach permitted the continued renegotiation of liberal values in the light of changing cultural paradigms concerning what was important about human beings and how best that could be furthered.

Through an acquaintance with the peculiar features of liberalism, we can modify our conception of rights, proceeding beyond the list of rights usually provided by liberals and scholars of liberalism, and beyond the deontological theories of moral philosophers. Rather, to entertain a rights discourse is to articulate and reflect a particular liberal *method*, one of ordering human demands and values in a politically sustainable and legitimate manner. Rights are the liberal device of ensuring that vital social goods are accorded special protection and respect and that the possibility of arbitrary conduct by states, groups, and individuals is sharply reduced. Because liberalism is sensitive to expressing human voices, and sympathetic to periodic reassessments of the relative positioning of human values, rights—not just as a legal or constitutional procedure but as an anchor of conceptual arrangements—need to embody the suppleness of conceptual reconfigurations that is at the heart of liberal tolerance and openness.

The Responsible Liberal Community

In chapter 3 I offer an historical case study of the ideological climate in which progressive thinking about poverty was moulded. It is intended to demonstrate the broad spectrum of ideological producers within the liberal family, and the importance of sources such as parliamentary debates for reconstructing liberal political thought. It should also give pause for thought about current progressive debates. The question of poverty, of absolute and relative disadvantage in both material and nonmaterial goods, has recently been sidelined at the expense of another question: that of adequately representing the plethora of cultures within a society. The challenge of halting the marginalisation of individuals and of ethnicities by revaluing their self-identity has edged out the parallel challenge of diminishing the marginalisation of people's welfare by recognising indispensable physical, mental, and emotional needs that demand satisfaction. Even issues of citizenship are understood to refer to participation and formal access rather than to the substantive enjoyment of and sharing in the ample array of goods a society has to offer. In a largely North American–led debate, that is not too surprising; ethnic identity is a far more potent social issue there than the social provision of welfare to the genuinely needy. But the poor are still with us and, moreover, political theorists as well as policymakers need to appreciate that at critical moments in our lives every one of us will become genuinely needy and dependent on the good will of others.

Poverty was one area through which the state was repossessed by liberals to assist in discharging the responsibilities that a body of citizens owed to one another. Debates over the role of the regulatory state, itself regulated by a strong democratic accountability, were numerous. The challenge of what constituted a legitimate state underwent a thorough reexamination, as will be explored in chapter 4. New tests of a social and ethical, as well as a legal, nature were devised. The question of dissent was linked to the liberal investment in social experimentation and difference, as well as to traditional liberal individualism, but it was also limited by the awareness that civilised standards of conduct had to be imposed on those unwilling to abide by them. And once again, these conceptual transformations, and the novel practices associated with them, yield abundant evidence for charting the overt and covert metamorphoses of liberal ideology.

Part 1 ends with two detailed studies of Hobson, the epitome of the Gramscian, socially engaged intellectual. In that guise he articulated a rising social liberal culture, and tied abstract concepts such as liberty to a concrete set of activities and understandings. His impact on later liberal and social democratic traditions has been considerable on two fronts. The one has been the underconsumptionism elaborated on by Keynes, which bestowed theoretical validity on the redistribution of economic resources to the disadvantaged, thus increasing their consumption power to the benefit of all. The other has been the transmutation of Hobson's organicism into the wider, if less specific, notions of community, mutual responsibility, and interdependence that nourished much British political thinking after the Second World War, when the apparatus of the modern welfare state was extended in scope and in reach.

Particularly evident, also, was the flexibility, even generosity, with which Hobson approached human nature. His endorsement of experimentation meant the relaxation of the strict criteria that moralists had imposed on human conduct. It allowed for errors, for play and leisure activities—all from an organic, wholesome, view of the fullness of human existence. Experimentation, critically, played a dual and ambiguous role. It upheld the scientific method and the establishment of objective standards of welfare, thus producing temporary uniformities of understanding, but it also allowed the human will to discover the mutations and innovations that perpetuated differences and underwrote liberal pluralism. The ensuing tension revolves around the relationship between perceived social facts and the values that attach to them. The value of encouraging individual lifestyles, given the fact that each person is unique, confronts the belief in the power of collective and concerted decision making to improve the quality of life of the community, given the fact of social interdependence. Both are crucial liberal themes and the endeavour to establish a balance between the two was the main challenge of twentieth-century liberalism. In the struggle between liberal universalism and liberal pluralism in the early twentieth-century, the latter had the upper hand. The alleged human costs of, and philosophical reaction to, that ascendant intellectual paradigm have been heralded, however, since the totalitarian disasters of mid-century, often accompanied by misconstruals or reinventions of liberalism's modern trail. That thought returns us to some of the considerations raised in the first chapter of this book.

CHAPTER ONE

Twentieth-Century Liberal Thought:
Development or Transformation?

IN THIS CHAPTER I seek to investigate how liberalism was portrayed throughout the twentieth century in dedicated liberal literature, that is, works primarily devoted to an exposition of the basic tenets of liberalism. On the surface many, though not all, of these works present themselves as "second-order" overviews of liberal theory and ideology. Sometimes, as with the Rawlsian family of arguments, they intend both to offer a novel interpretation of liberal principles and, in parallel, reflect given cultural understandings unconsciously and unintentionally. On the whole, though, writers about liberalism have tended to elucidate a tradition rather than depart from it. But this raises a fundamental methodological problem: When does a "secondary" text become a "primary" one? The response to that is: When we interpret it as itself an act of interpretation, and when we acknowledge that the role of the political theorist incorporates not only prescription and its investigation, but also interpretation and its investigation. The analysts, chroniclers, and popularisers of liberalism become pivotal to our understanding when we query its status as a transcendent moral position and explore it instead as a diverse and flexible set of readings concerning the epistemology of the political.

Whatever else liberalism is, it is a cultural artefact, consciously intended to be adopted by large social groups. But rather than explore the *Ideengeschichte* of liberalism in time-honoured conventional manner on a unidimensional sequence, we need to draw conclusions from the variable presentation of historical liberal narratives, or from their juxtaposition with non-narrative justifications of liberalism. The history of liberalism this century, and indeed in previous centuries, is not merely the reflection of its development, or evolution, or change, or perchance regression. It is not a single story to be told. We now recognise that all current theories are located in time as well as in space. But when we say that, we are not engaging in the simplistic assertion that "context counts." Contexts are multitemporal and multispatial even with respect to one family of beliefs such as liberalism, and they generate both deliberate and unintentional meta-assumptions quite irrespective of whether liberalism itself contains views on universalism or relativism or, as we have now come to appreciate, multiculturalism. Moreover, individual liberals, and conventional social norms concerning what liberalism is, exercise choice over what constitutes a context and over which contexts to select among the many contexts—existing or yet to be discovered or invented—in which liberalism may be located. A context, like an historical narrative, is not a reflection of events out there. It is an act of private or public imagination superimposed upon a set of perceived, if fragmented, facts. This chapter will attempt to identify more precisely not why and when liberalism changes in terms of objective contexts, but what it is that has changed in the imaginative presentation of liberalism, and how different emphases on various aspects of liberalism reflect and transform the political understandings of some of its more salient, or representative, purveyors.

Far too often, recent scholars of liberalism have confidently and stipulatively approached it as if that theory or ideology represented a clear and unitary moral position encompassing knowable and objective, or at least reasonable, standards of justice and human rights: a homogeneous model that could then be incisively contrasted with alternative "monolithic" theories such as communitarianism. This is not the issue under discussion here, or the most challenging and rewarding question when examining liberalism. Rather, liberalism is that semantic field in which the political understandings of people who regard themselves as liberals, or whom others regard as liberals, may be investigated. It is a plastic, changing thing, shaped and reshaped by the thought-practices of individuals and groups; and though it needs to have a roughly identifiable pattern for us to call it consistently by the same name, "liberalism," it also presents myriad variations that reflect the questions posed, and positions adopted, by various liberals.

In the space available, some samples will be provided of the conceptualisations of liberalism during this century, through examining a number of books on liberalism that were written as central textbooks, introductions, surveys, statements, or critiques. The assumption adhered to is that these books mirrored, moulded, and disseminated broad understandings of what liberalism was, as well as carrying some unintentional baggage that has been left for us to unpack. Ultimately, in order for liberalism to be comprehended we must observe it "at thought" by exploring the mindsets of some of its typical agents. The result, one would hope, would be an enriched and rather more subtle view than can be provided by attempting to construct a philosophically "ideal" or "best-practice" liberal moral theory. Those philosophical approaches necessarily lose in breadth and political applicability what they gain in internal cohesion and ethical persuasiveness. Nor is this chapter about "mere" history, not even "mere" intellectual history. Behind it stands a broader agenda, whose task it is to provide an analysis of a family of political theories and ideologies. To do so we ought to come to terms with liberalism as a complex and elusive tradition of thinking about politics, and we may gain from locating the analysis on offer here squarely among the activities in which political theorists engage.

LIBERAL MOVEMENT: EVOLUTION AND ENERGY

The twentieth century has witnessed three main modes of writing about liberalism: as a development of political thought over time; as a political manifesto against extremism, authoritarianism, or conservative complacency; and as a philosophical view of the rational and moral relationship between the individually unique and the socially common. In intricate and concrete argumentation, these modes often overlap. When in 1911 L. T. Hobhouse wrote his famous volume entitled *Liberalism*, he was writing a tract for the times, forged out of the successful battles fought by the new liberals, but it was a tract with a moral purpose: that of consolidating the reforms liberalism had undertaken from within. He did so by emphasising above all one aspect of liberalism, offering it as an evolutionary body of thought that not only advocated progress as a social ideal, but was itself controlled by that same evolutionary law. This was not a particular liberal view of history, such as the much-mooted Whig interpretation of history, but rather a particular historical view of liberalism, which regarded it as a set of beliefs itself, crucially, subject to historical processes. In other words, one defining feature of liberalism, in sharp contrast to current philosophical liberalism, was that its theorists held to a specific interpretation of time as a central conceptual component of liberal ideology. Time was not strictly sequential in its trajectory of human and social improvement, nor totally open-ended in accompanying human and social maturation, but it nevertheless dictated that liberalism itself had to undergo steady transformation. In the past liberalism had experienced a process of growth that was now reaching its apotheosis by aligning itself with the development of a newly emerging social rationality, embodied in an integrated and organic society and regulated by a benevolent and emphatically non-neutral agency—the state.

Like Mill, and many previous liberals, Hobhouse's story about liberalism begins as an historical-anthropological narrative. It is one of social harmony and community undermined by later authoritarian political arrangements. Liberalism dawns as a "destructive criticism," a project of release in order to enable free, and natural, order and progress. Here then are some of the recognisable liberal core concepts of the nineteenth and twentieth centuries. But there is a deeper and ulterior ontology of liberalism in operation. Hobhouse endows the idea of release with a specific complexion: "a movement of liberation, a clearance of obstructions . . .

for the flow of free, vital, spontaneous activity."[1] The idea of "movement" is subtly and only half-consciously recruited to underpin this specific understanding of liberalism. First, liberalism *is* a movement, to be sure: it is an organised body with, in J. A. Hobson's words, an "active mission" directed towards the attainment of political objectives.[2] Second, however, liberalism is a carrier of truth, which moves for Hobhouse in "an expanding circle of ideas."[3] When in chapter 2 Hobhouse lists the types of liberty embraced by liberals, he conceives them as spatial, embracing parallel activities such as the civil, fiscal, economic, and social, and located in arenas such as the personal, domestic, local, national, and international.[4] Similarly, Hobson could assert that "Liberalism will come more definitely to concern itself with the liberation and utilisation of the faculties and potencies of a nation and a municipality, as well as with those of individuals and voluntary groups of citizens."[5] The liberty at the core of liberalism is hence conceptualised as undergoing movement both through space and through time, and is aligned with the concept of spreading and contagious progress. Thus it contains seeds of universalism, not in an analytical or intrinsic sense, but a historically and spatially contingent universalism, called forth "by the special circumstances of Western Europe."[6]

Third, as the initial quotation suggests, movement suggests vital activity. We arrive now at the semantic kernel. Hobhouse instructs us that "The Liberal movement . . . is coextensive with life"; "Liberalism is an all-penetrating element of the life-structure of the modern world."[7] Movement in the first two senses, as "an effective historical force" is sustained by movement in this third, animated, living sense. Liberalism is the release of dynamic biological and spiritual energy, a view reiterated by Guido de Ruggiero in his seminal *The History of European Liberalism*, when he identified liberalism as concerned with the free play of individual forces which have "*vital* importance and *energizing* power."[8] The world is naturally active and vigorous and liberalism is above all an instrument for freeing this flowing human essence. This is no mere "exercise concept" in Charles Taylor's phrase,[9] but the setting free of organic, nonstatic life that

---

[1] L. T. Hobhouse, *Liberalism* (London, 1911), p. 47.

[2] J. A. Hobson, *The Crisis of Liberalism* (London, 1909), p. 91.

[3] Hobhouse, *Liberalism*, p. 110.

[4] Ibid., pp. 21–49.

[5] Hobson, *The Crisis of Liberalism*, p. 95.

[6] Hobhouse, *Liberalism*, p. 19.

[7] Ibid., pp. 46–47.

[8] G. de Ruggiero, *A History of European Liberalism* (London, 1927), p. 359 (italics added).

[9] See C. Taylor, "What's Wrong with Negative Liberty?" in A. Ryan, ed., *The Idea of Freedom* (Oxford, 1979), pp. 175–93.

will otherwise be suppressed. Unsurprisingly, for Hobhouse well-being is as important as liberty. Moreover, the identification of processes as "natural" indicates the typical ideological device of insulating fundamental ontological claims from the sphere of debate and contention. In adhering to that thought-practice, liberalism is no different from other ideological families. Furthermore, although an understanding of twentieth-century liberalism should not be determined merely by the yardstick of some of its later manifestations, the contrast with Rawls here is striking. For if liberalism is "all-penetrating," it provides both the common element enabling the expression of all human cooperative activity, a function allocated by Rawls to narrow political liberalism, *and* the comprehensive liberalism that Rawls firmly detaches from the political.

LIBERAL EMOTIONALISM

Hobhouse unequivocally relates liberalism to human emotion on two levels. On the one he observes that "the philosophies that have driving force behind them are those that arise . . . out of the practical demands of human feeling. The philosophies that remain ineffectual and academic are those that are formed by abstract reflection without relation to the thirsty souls of human kind."[10] Liberalism opens the door by means of the rational method "to the appeal of reason, of imagination, of social feeling."[11] It is not only that human beings have emotions and imagination that demand respect in social arrangements, but that expressivism and spontaneity are defining features of life, and hence of the liberalism that enables life. Liberalism contains core rational attributes, but is nonetheless irreducible to the contemplative faculty. Reason and emotion coexist and support each other in a manner ruled out of court by most current manifestations of philosophical liberalism. Hence Hobhouse's support for forms of nationalism, for "inasmuch as the true social harmony rests on feeling and makes use of all the natural ties of kinship, of neighbourliness, of congruity of character and belief, and of language and mode of life, the best, healthiest and most vigorous political unit is that to which men are by their own feelings strongly drawn."[12] In addition, if "rational" may be contrasted with "emotional," it may also be contrasted with "unreflective." Hobhouse also drew attention to these latter components of liberalism when he contended that "human progress, on whatever side we consider it, is found to be in the main social progress, the work of

[10] Hobhouse, *Liberalism*, p. 51.
[11] Ibid., p. 123.
[12] Ibid., p. 135.

conscious or unconscious co-operation."[13] Indeed, in his later work Hobhouse was to associate the emergence of the ethical precepts of liberalism with fundamental psychological processes.[14] Similar views on the evolution of liberalism were expressed by Laski, for whom it was "never direct and rarely conscious."[15]

From another perspective, most twentieth-century liberals adopt an emotive idiom when *addressing* liberalism. For Hobhouse, liberalism aims at "a spirit of comradeship"; its vision of justice "kindles a passion that may not flare up into moments of dramatic scintillation, but burns with the enduring glow of the central heat"[16]—hardly the predominant phraseology of current Anglo-American philosophy. De Ruggiero put this similarly: "Liberalism possesses that kind of tact or flair . . . which in its highest manifestations is true political sensitiveness, and serves to recognize everything that is human—human strength and human weakness, human reason and human passion, human interest and human morality—in the relations between rulers and ruled; and is able to turn this experience to the ends of the elevation of human society."[17] The liberal spirit is possessed of a "lofty impartiality."[18] A mid-century American review of liberalism refers to the liberal who "likes to preen himself on the triumphs of human intelligence and virtue," and to the liberal tradition as a "call to adventure: the adventure of growing up, becoming autonomous, living spontaneously" (and note, incidentally, the constructive tension between development, freedom, and unreflectiveness).[19] In describing liberalism as a mood, Laski identified a "flavour of romanticism" in its temper. It tended to be "zealous" for individual action, "subjective and anarchist, to be eager for the change which comes from individual initiative, to be insistent that this initiative contains within itself some necessary seed of social good."[20] Zeal, eagerness, insistence—these features of liberalism are necessarily the attributes of an ideology whose reforming, even revolutionary, ardour is part and parcel of its appeal. For the overcritical Laski, the energising power of liberalism had become exhausted.[21] It may be the case that the fervour of liberalism diminished upon attaining many of its initial goals, though the emotional aspects of its beliefs have never quite disappeared.

[13] Ibid., p. 133. See also chap. 10 below.

[14] See M. Freeden, *Liberalism Divided: A Study in British Political Thought, 1914–1939* (Oxford, 1986), pp. 234–37.

[15] H. J. Laski, *The Rise of European Liberalism* (London, 1936), p. 11.

[16] Hobhouse, *Liberalism*, pp. 172, 251.

[17] de Ruggiero, *European Liberalism*, p. 390.

[18] Ibid., p. 437.

[19] W. A. Orton, *The Liberal Tradition* (New Haven, 1945), pp. 78, 303.

[20] Laski, *Rise of European Liberalism*, p. 14.

[21] Ibid., p. 171.

LIBERAL COHERENCE AND LIBERAL DIVERSITY

Throughout the twentieth century there has been a curious tension between the static and dynamic facets of liberalism. This problematic of liberalism may be redefined by asking whether it is a pliable structure or heavily rule-bound. The editors of *The Liberal Tradition*, published in 1956, stated that "At first sight, the most striking thing about the Liberal tradition is its intellectual incoherence. . . . This is the strongest argument in favour of treating Liberalism historically." Considering liberalism as developing and changing allows such differences to fall into place.[22] Coherence, however, is not the product of a narrative alone, because invented narratives are contingent and selective. It is importantly the product either of the formulation of directive rules or the discovery of unintended patterns (a discovery that itself may then be fashioned into a set of directive rules).

If liberal history is not accidental or contingent, if liberalism is not a mathematical aggregate of its historical parts, that is because history is understood as constituting the ineluctable design of liberalism. To write about liberalism is for Hobhouse, and no less so for de Ruggiero, always and necessarily to write about its history. They both conceptualise liberalism as the vehicle best encompassing the dynamic of individual and social life. Liberalism is a process and it evokes an activity, the activity of being self-directively spontaneous, inventive, and imaginative. Process *entails* history; history *is* the intellectual coherence of liberalism, rather than being superimposed to account for it.

By contrast, the liberal projects of Rawls or Ronald Dworkin prioritise rules as stasis, equilibrium and consensus over rules of change. The idea of a liberal constitution, to which they are wedded, is precisely such a device, creating inviolable space, such as a Bill of Rights or the two principles of justice, removed from the ravages of social time. From a slightly different perspective, the liberalism of foundational rules privileges mechanics, whereas the liberalism of creative expressivism privileges organics, both as growth and as human interrelationship. Hobhouse summed up his position as follows: "The heart of liberalism is the understanding that progress is not a matter of mechanical contrivance, but of the liberation of living spiritual energy. Good mechanism is that which provides the channels wherein such energy can flow unimpeded, unobstructed by its own exuberance of output, vivifying the social structure, expanding and ennobling the life of mind."[23] Current philosophical liberals tend to

---

[22] A. Bullock and M. Shock, eds., *The Liberal Tradition from Fox to Keynes* (London, 1956), p. xix.

[23] Hobhouse, *Liberalism*, p. 137.

concentrate on the channels while professing to have no view on the consequences of providing them, other than the tautological attainment of justice that has already been furnished by the very construction of the mechanical channels themselves. Hobhouse's agenda consisted rather in attaching liberalism to an idea-environment formed through concepts such as release, movement, energy, and vitality. That is *his* "thin" theory of the good, which informs the core liberal concepts of liberty, rationality, progress, individuality, sociability, a common good, limited and responsible power—in other words, a theory that, according to Hobhouse, undergirds every version of liberalism.

De Ruggiero's notion of history rested on similar conceptions of liberal movement, but his Hegelian historical scheme reshaped the liberal time-space relationship into a different pattern of coherence. His comparative treatment of liberalism permitted the postulation of multiple, interacting liberalisms, but his reading of the logic of liberalism was not, as with Hobhouse, through its *diffusion* in ever-expanding circles but through *convergence* and conciliation of opposite liberal currents. Liberalism has to be understood "in the diversity of its national forms and the unity of its historical organism."[24] The progress that is liberalism's lifeblood is not Hobhouse's nonteleological "onward course." For Hobhouse, a release of energy is not necessarily self-realisation. For de Ruggiero, "a more comprehensive Liberalism would recognize the dialectical ground of the antithesis and would see resistance and movement, conservation and progress, justified and validated in a higher synthesis which is political life in its concreteness."[25] The end result for de Ruggiero is thus a single liberalism that can be retrospectively accounted for as the diachronic emergence of a civilising strain in modern societies, the "irresistible operation of civil society."[26] Its political persuasiveness crowds out rival arguments and secures victory in a multi-ideational world of really existing competing viewpoints. "The study of the historical forms of European Liberalism has shown us, through all the differences of the various national minds, a process of mutual assimilation, gradually building up a European Liberal consciousness pervading its particular manifestations without destroying their differences."[27] Without such reconciliation, the liberal enterprise would be undermined by the damaging potential of its disparate currents.

That argument was taken even further by Benedetto Croce. In a chapter revealingly titled "Liberalism as a concept of life" he, too, combined developmentalism with a view of liberalism as coinciding "with a complete idea of the world and of reality," beginning in the world but going "beyond the

---

[24] de Ruggiero, *European Liberalism*, p. 90.
[25] Ibid., p. 361.
[26] Ibid., p. 437.
[27] Ibid., p. 347.

formal theory of politics." The very tolerance built into liberalism located it as the framework doctrine within which a dialectic competition among ideas could be resolved. It was characterised above all by this immanent process, which removed it from the authoritarian fiat of otherworldly, externally imposed, transcendental beliefs. History as struggle was endemic to liberalism, and struggle encompassed impulse and spontaneity.[28] Nevertheless Croce was drawn into joining to that profoundly secular doctrine an extrarational, quasi-religious understanding of liberty, attached to human "vocations" and "missions." He believed that "the liberal mind regards the withdrawing of liberty and the times of reaction as illnesses and critical stages of growth, as incidents and steps in the eternal life of liberty." As with Hegel, timelessness engulfed and superseded time in the last resort; moreover, this afforded a standpoint from which history manifested pathologies as well as normalities. The transcendental status of liberty returned to do the work of faith and underlying essential meaning, justifying the course taken by a nontranscendental history. That such liberal histories attained impartiality, as Croce claimed, is hardly borne out by the language in which that claim is expressed.[29]

A similar viewpoint, with different conclusions, is evident in Louis Hartz's modern classic *The Liberal Tradition in America*. Liberalism has multiple facets, crucially situated not above politics but in it: "We know the European liberal, as it were, by the enemies he has made."[30] Whereas European liberals experienced social diversity and conflict, the American variant acquired noncontentious invisibility through a cultural and ideological uniformity, "on the basis of a submerged and absolute liberal faith." Hartz identified a central ideological feature at work in the manner American liberalism decontested its basic premises, one involving "silent omissions as well as explicit inclusions."[31] Hence while American liberalism pre-empted political and ideational competition, European liberalism had to fight its ground within a culturally and historically disputed space. As Hobson noted, reviewing de Ruggiero's book, "in each country the spirit of liberalism was largely formed by the practical tasks which the needs and interests of the dominant classes incited them to undertake."[32]

Both Hobhouse and de Ruggiero subscribed to a concrete spatial universalism that is a function of time (as of course does Marxism) rather than a transcendental and spaceless universalism that is a function of atemporal reason. But de Ruggiero removed internal pluralism and un-

[28] B. Croce, *Politics and Morals* (London, 1946), pp. 79–81.

[29] Ibid., pp. 84–85.

[30] L. Hartz, *The Liberal Tradition in America* (New York, 1955), p. 16.

[31] Ibid., pp. 7, 10.

[32] J. A. Hobson, review of G. de Ruggiero, *The History of European Liberalism*, in *Journal of Philosophical Studies* 3 (1928): 378–80.

structured open-endedness from liberalism as it emerged as a teleological worldview in a very real, and irreversible, sense. Hobhouse, to the contrary, voiced an increasing postwar despair concerning the future of liberalism when he identified "arrest, retrogression or decay" as part of the historic course of change and concluded: "Hence if progress means the gradual realisation of an ethical ideal no continuous progress is revealed by the course of history."[33] There is none of that pessimism concerning the evolution of the human mind in de Ruggiero's 1927 deluded prognosis that "one may conclude that the omens are favourable towards the capacity of the German people to win for itself that liberal education in politics which the old regime denied it."[34] Consequently, de Ruggiero was epistemologically unable to criticise liberal practices and beliefs in their current form because of liberalism's inherent evolutionary capacity of self-development and improvement. Those distinctions aside, the liberalism of Hobhouse and de Ruggiero is primarily about individual and social expression and development, and only secondarily about pluralism and difference, especially in view of its allegiance to the nation-state.

By contrast, current liberal pluralism, in some of its multicultural forms, applies a preformed, ahistorical, singular liberal morality to concrete societies comprised of many components. It regards structural variety as a service concept for autonomy, rather than regarding temporal development as a service concept for individuality, sociability, or welfare. What de Ruggiero noted about liberty and liberties ought to be said about the tension between liberalism conceived of as universal philosophy and as situated ideology. The one is "an abstraction, a concept intended to express the essence of human personality, exalted above all historical and empirical contingency," the other a complex of features "acquired one by one as circumstances dictate." Each on its own is, tellingly, totally dispossessed of the liberal spirit.[35]

THE RENEWED SEARCH FOR CERTAINTY

The experience of totalitarianism in the 1930s and 1940s dramatically changed some interpretative liberal paradigms. One of the most striking reformulations of liberalism to emerge from the Second World War was John Hallowell's *The Decline of Liberalism as an Ideology*. His analysis constitutes a watershed in twentieth-century liberal self-conceptualisation mainly through its disentangling and counterposing of the historical and the ahistorical mode of liberalism. If for Hobhouse and de Ruggiero liber-

---

[33] L. T. Hobhouse, *Social Development: Its Nature and Conditions* (London, 1924), p. 90.
[34] de Ruggiero, *European Liberalism*, p. 274.
[35] Ibid., p. 348.

alism embodies a vital growth impetus, Hallowell reversed this historical tendency to identify a move from something live and vigorous to something decadent and degenerate. Growth may also imply regression, especially once de Ruggiero's Hegelian dialectic of progress is abandoned. "As a political ideology born of a particular historical period in a specific sociological environment [liberalism] is subject, like all such systems of ideas, to development, decline, and death."[36] Significantly, and in contradistinction to Hobhouse's anxieties concerning *external* impediments to liberalism, Hallowell attributed the death of liberal ideology to liberals themselves, for a man-made belief system is subject to human fallibility. That fallibility has revealed itself in the forsaking of a parallel but morally and intellectually superior liberalism, "integral" liberalism, couched in the language of absolutes that would have prevented the intellectual perversion of liberalism, particularly by nazism. Hallowell's version of liberalism embodied the typical disillusionment of postwar scholars with the fickle impermanence of legal systems, unless anchored in dictates of objective reason. The rediscovery of normative foundationalism became prominent in the American legal tradition, in its renewed antipositivist appeal to natural law and its consequent revival of the notion of universal human rights during the 1940s and 1950s.[37] Liberal ontology therefore sought refuge in invoking new variants of traditional certitudes: the absolute value and dignity of human personality, and the construction of impenetrable boundaries that the state may not pervade. Liberal principles are, or ought to be, untouched by history, even by the experimental reason that many liberals see fit to encourage in people. Instead, they are to be secured to transcendental standards and eternal truths, beyond the contaminating reach of untrustworthy human judgment.

Hallowell occupies a strange position—both regressive and progressive—in relation to the liberal epistemology of the twentieth century. The notion of progress, so central to liberal values,[38] had in his view become attached to a theory of evolution that, when applied to liberalism itself, undermined the absolute moral value of the individual. It did so by legitimating humanly directed change, especially through the German construct of the *Rechtsstaat*, which established positive law—a law that was made and not found—as the guarantor of equality. One of Hallowell's

---

[36] J. Hallowell, *The Decline of Liberalism as an Ideology* (London, 1946), p. 1.

[37] For a discussion of these developments within the American legal profession, see R. A. Primus, *The American Language of Rights* (Cambridge, 1999), pp. 177–97.

[38] In the extreme case, progress is seen as the central structural principle of liberalism: "Progressivism is indeed a better term than liberalism for the opposition to conservatism. For if conservatism is, as its name indicates, aversion to change or distrust of change, its opposite should be identified with the opposite posture toward change, and not with something substantive like liberty or liberality" (L. Strauss, *Liberalism Ancient and Modern* [New York, 1968], p. vii).

inputs into the liberal debate was to re-emphasize not its polysemic but its static character. Another was to distinguish between liberalism as philosophy and as ideology, a move of importance associated with the mid-century decline in prestige of the concept of ideology. The decline of ideology is not, however, articulated in terms of the postwar debate over undesirable dogmatism versus commended pragmatism, but in terms of undesirable pragmatism versus incontrovertible truth. Hallowell approvingly quoted C.E.M. Joad, for whom pragmatism ministered "to human complacency by assuring human beings that right and wrong, beauty and ugliness, reality and unreality, are not external facts, features of the universe to which human beings must in the long run subject themselves, but are the products of human consciousness and, therefore, amenable to human desires."[39]

Hallowell proposed the following ideational compound as liberalism's epistemological base: first, a humanist doctrine that relinquishes anthropocentrism and rejects intuitive judgment; second, a theory of human freedom that dismisses the view of individuals as autonomously capable of exercising their subjectively free wills; third, a conception of rationality that subjugates individuals to the "dictates of reason" and the external criteria of justice as obligation to transcendental law, accessed through an inner conscience. For a liberal, Hallowell imposed a particularly stringent limitation on value pluralism, for liberalism relies on "a common knowledge, or recognition, of values transcending individuals."[40] Nevertheless all this is a "theory of political order based upon individualism," and it is identified as a "comprehensive Weltanschauung."[41]

Contrast this with the Rawlsian view of rationality emerging volitionally from individuals and expressed in a reasonable, overlapping, and public consensus over principles of justice; and moreover a view that now relegates individualism to a feature of comprehensive liberalism, a liberalism that is no longer specifically endorsed as necessary to a just social order. And contrast this with the Hobhousian faith in the evolution of social understandings of valued practices that release the potential and sustain the well-being of a community as well as those of its members.

ONTOLOGICAL MINIMALISM AND THE SUPRAPOLITICAL

Works such as Hallowell's that began as manifestos against totalitarianism have been transformed into a richer and deeper philosophical position. The heritage and motivation are plainly visible in late-twentieth-

---

[39] Hallowell, *The Decline of Liberalism as an Ideology*, p. 88.
[40] Ibid., p. 109.
[41] Ibid., pp. 21, 108–9.

century liberal theorising, but so are the epistemological and conceptual modifications. One of the residues of this mode of thinking has been to reduce liberalism once again to a form of ontological minimalism, captured in the loose use of the indeterminate word "thin." But one of the modifications it has undergone is the rediscovery of a Kantian-inspired autonomy, an autonomy unavailable or decentred in early- and mid-century liberal language. The two have combined in the revival of the private/public dichotomy as a moral statement about the inherent but socially indifferent good sense of individuals, detached from the impact of sustaining groups, the latter now perceived as more dangerous than formative.[42] In addition liberalism has been absorbed into the dominant Anglo-American philosophical practice of model building and counterfactual thought-experiments that translate the requirements of coherence and procedure, rather than growth and energy, into structural fundamentals of liberalism. Is this, intriguingly, a parallel tendency to what Orton describes as "the queer double strain in nineteenth-century liberalism. The rationalistic, system-making tradition in laissez-faire theory never found common ground with the personalistic and humanitarian impulse"—an inspirational, empathetic, and energy-liberating humanism?[43] Hobson, in fact, denied that "coldness and placidity of purpose belong essentially to Liberalism," rather than "organic purpose" and "free enthusiasm."[44]

Is it also the case that what some feminists term the colder philosophical liberalism is a product of the Cold War that never got round to thawing? Not for nothing has the end of the Cold War witnessed a reheating of liberalism under the impact of nationalism and the accompanying revalorization of the emotional resonances that have always existed within liberal discourse: the language of bonds, allegiance, sympathy. What nonetheless sustains the current philosophical variant is the predominant and overwhelmingly shared image of the U.S. Constitution as mediating between the presumption of the reasonableness emanating from human beings and the requirement of permanent, suprapolitical standards. This avoids the language of transcendentalism while attaining some of its ends. It is hence unsurprising to find Rawls describing the Supreme Court as "the exemplar of public reason."[45] Is that another way of asserting, as Hartz did, that "the absence of 'opposing principles,' the fact that beneath its political heroics the nation was of the 'same mind' on the liberal for-

---

[42] W. Kymlicka attempts to attach the (cultural) properties of groups to the promotion of individual identity-cum-autonomy alone. See W. Kymlicka, *Multicultural Citizenship: A Liberal Theory of Minority Rights* (Oxford, 1995).

[43] Orton, *The Liberal Tradition*, p. 308.

[44] Hobson, *The Crisis of Liberalism*, p. 92.

[45] J. Rawls, *Political Liberalism* (New York, 1993), pp. 231–40.

mula, settled in advance the philosophic question"?[46] Only instead of the nation are we not referring to the academic community, sustained by its justices with their presumption of expressing the vox populi? Indeed, Hartz had given the role of the Supreme Court, and the liberalism it sustained, a totally different and more persuasive gloss: "the Supreme Court had always been the Hebraic expositor of the American general will, building on the irrational acceptance of Locke the Talmudic rationality involved in his application to specific cases."[47] Moreover, Hartz was deeply cognizant of the emotive aspect of concrete liberalisms. The American version, he argued, possessed "the ideologic power of the national irrational liberalism" that, in the case of the New Deal, "was responsible for its whole pragmatic orientation, for its whole aversion to systematic social thought."[48]

In view of the above, Croce's reaction to critics of liberalism, who labelled it as "formalistic," "empty," "sceptical," and "antagonistic" is edifying. Rather than see these terms as referring to foundational categories whose generality enables the integration of all reasonable ways of life, Croce welcomed them as liberal attributes that embody the essence of nondogmatism in the spirit of modern philosophy. The liberal conception thus denied "first place to laws, casuistry and charts of duties and virtues, and places the moral conscience at its centre." This was "like modern aesthetics, which refuses models, categories and rules, and places at its centre the genius that is good taste, both sensitive and very strict." That approach was formalistic only in the sense that it shied away from imposing philosophical formulae and principles. The end result was strongly emotive and parti pris: "the liberal conception is not meant for the timid, the indolent and the pacifist, but wishes to interpret the aspirations and the works of courageous and patient, of belligerent and generous spirits." No wonder that Croce could refer to Hobhouse's opus as "a beautiful English eulogy and apology for liberalism"—language more apposite for a work of art than for the mechanics of a system of rules.[49]

THE RAWLSIAN PROJECT: A PARADIGMATIC SHIFT

Looking back at liberalism from our vantage point, the unity of the Rawlsian project is conspicuous. In the early years of the twentieth century, as in much of the nineteenth, the growth model central to liberal conceptions of human nature was applied to liberalism itself. The development

---

[46] Hartz, *Liberal Tradition In America*, p. 141.
[47] Ibid., pp. 208–9.
[48] Ibid., pp. 249, 307.
[49] Croce, *Politics and Morals*, pp. 87, 106.

of liberalism was tantamount to the development of civilisation. After the Second World War that very capacity for change, with its newly high-lighted contingency, lost its attractiveness, and was increasingly replaced with an appeal to independent, immutable standards. Rawls himself com-menced his argument in *Political Liberalism* with that problematic: "Po-litical liberalism assumes that, for political purposes, a plurality of rea-sonable yet incompatible comprehensive doctrines is the normal result of the exercise of human reason within the framework of the free institu-tions of a constitutional regime"—a philosophical anthropology diamet-rically opposed to Hobhouse's. Rawls's overriding aim is for a political liberalism that provides not only justice but unity in what would other-wise be a fissiparous, even Hobbesian, society. The difficulty with the core liberal concept of non-necessitarian development was that it had to allow for a choice that could include error. The risky model of develop-ment, even riskier when "irreconcilable conflict" is assumed to be socially latent,[50] was replaced with a more advantageous model of justice, stabil-ity, and autonomy that would eliminate unpredictable choice.[51] De Rug-giero, too, had attempted to eliminate choice on a grander, supraindivid-ual scale by positing a Hegelian necessitarianism, but that variety had been extinguished as a fashionable archetype under onslaughts such as Karl Popper's.

Nor was Hallowell's transcendentalism acceptable to 1960s and 1970s Anglo-American philosophy. Hence the foundational assumptions of Rawls's system were couched in anthropocentric terms of empirically at-tainable reasonableness, even though the outcome of this process was to all effects and purposes equally invariable. Like the contract model, Rawls's theory simulated open-ended liberal choice without, of course, offering it, through assuming both a prediscursive rationality (the veil of ignorance) and a convergent reasonableness (the overlapping consensus). Rawls's political liberalism was presented as a Western paradigm, but one whose *rightness* would gain it universal recognition, moving from historicity to ahistoricity. Its universal appeal would not be forged out of competition over legitimacy with other ideological arrangements—the manner through which most liberals have measured their successes, earn-ing their spurs on the battlefield of ideas—but as a nonpluralist proce-dural and moral necessity.

Put differently, this liberalism employed a second-order argument not over substantive goods, but over justifiable rules. Justification depended

---

[50] J. Rawls, *Political Liberalism*, p. xxvi.

[51] Rawls (ibid., pp. 72–78) attempts to distinguish between various types of autonomy in a discussion that is highly contentious. Suffice it to observe that his notions of rational and political autonomy, as distinct from full ethical autonomy, are posited on an untenable

not on the nature of the political benefits available, but—and here lay its novelty—on the shared acceptance of those rules by all the members of the polity.[52] Locke's liberalism, by contrast, had sought only a limited general acceptability as a prior arrangement to establishing relations of mutual and substantive trust, anchored in the norms of natural rights. Late-twentieth-century liberalism has, however, been characterised as being that system of ideas that requires and attains general acceptance, even prior to the political implementation of those ideas. The only ideas that comply with this scheme are those concerning the public rules of moral engagement and interaction. In earlier versions of liberalism, acceptance had to be won through the substantive benefits that would accrue from the liberal way of life in struggle with other political options.

Moreover, the Rawlsian procedure was constructed to create boundaries and hence moral spaces in which individuals were responsibly reflective. Intentionally or otherwise, that accomplished three ends. First, it restored liberalism's emphasis on the inviolability of individual space, rather than on the controlled permeability of space that organicist, communitarian liberals had encouraged. This was closely linked to a thinning of the sociability component of liberalism and a resurrection of individualism as an attribute of separate personal existence.[53]

Second, it focused on equality—a concept to which evolutionary liberal traditions could not fully subscribe because of the unpredictable dynamics of human relationships. The a priori rule-following of Rawlsian liberalism had to assume not only temporal stasis but relational stasis: equality as the participation of each and every member in decision making and hence in justifiable and responsible action. Strikingly, this limited notion of equality was a nonvoluntarist view of participation. Participation and sharing in responsibility had become the be-all and end-all of liberalism, rather than adjacent concepts that could be put into practice by those who wished to participate.[54] As an ethical exercise, this liberalism offers no space to opt out or to refrain from opting in. Obtaining the considered and unconstrained consent of all—a mechanical view of politics—becomes the heart of the liberal process, rather than the attainment of a package of values.

---

divide between political and comprehensive liberalism, and on a blindness to the thickness of his notion of an autonomous person in the space occupied by political liberalism.

[52] See M. Evans, "Is Public Justification Central to Liberalism?" *Journal of Political Ideologies* 4 (1999): 117–36.

[53] See chap. 2 below.

[54] This is notably the case for Locke, who, in a little-noted comment on the transition from the state of nature to civil society, states: "This any number of Men may do, because it injures not the Freedom of the rest; they are left as they were in the Liberty of the State of Nature" (J. Locke, *Two Treatises of Government*, ed. P. Laslett [New York, 1965], Second

The extreme view of this position, outside current exemplars of the liberal family, was expressed by nonliberals such as Leo Strauss in his book *Liberalism Ancient and Modern*: "Liberal education is the necessary endeavour to found an aristocracy within democratic mass society." The point, however, as Mill recognized, was that liberalism was shaped by a few and then disseminated to the many. Some of its substantive values might precede the full evolution of democratic consent and might not be entirely sustained by that evolution. As is the case with all ideologies, liberals wish to protect the values they most cherish. The problem with liberalism is that some of those values (such as self-determination or participation) are intrinsically dependent on the exercise of choice by all, and may be catered to instantly, whereas others (such as individuality or progress) are dependent on the exercise of good choices by as many as possible, but by less than all if unavoidable, and are time-sensitive.

Third, it disposed of change in the arena of political liberalism. Gone was the experimental attitude of Hobhouse and his colleague Hobson towards some of the decontestations of liberal values.[55] Rawls assumed coherence rather than tentativeness. "We may," he writes, "reaffirm our more particular judgments and decide instead to modify the proposed conception of justice until judgments at all levels of generality are at last in line on due reflection."[56] If there is experimentation, it is in order to iron out kinks in the overlapping public reasonableness of political liberalism, not experimentation that can provide different and contrasting views of liberalism's values. Compare this with another mid-century appraisal of liberalism: "as a form of social thought Liberalism has been empirical, scientific, mundane, and more or less skeptical-minded."[57] The sense of paradigmatic shift is palpable.

Gone also were Hobhouse's and Hobson's anxieties concerning an unknown liberal future.[58] Rawlsian liberalism is curiously unperturbed, not only because logic, procedure, and coherence are by definition emotionally neutered (though their outcomes are hardly value-neutral), but also because moral conflicts are presented as politically soluble. Certainty allows one to dispense with some of the affective language in which liberalism has usually indulged. How can that nontranscendental certainty be sustained? Because the precarious nature of progress based on human

---

Treatise, ¶96). This historically astute nonuniversalism is inconceivable in the Rawlsian project.

[55] See J. A. Hobson, "Character and Society," in P. L. Parker ed., *Character and Life* (London, 1912), p. 96.

[56] Rawls, *Political Liberalism*, p. 45.

[57] T. P. Neill, *The Rise and Decline of Liberalism* (Milwaukee, 1953), p. 18.

[58] Hobhouse, *Liberalism*, pp. 226–28; J. A. Hobson, *The Crisis of Liberalism*, passim.

reason is eliminated at a stroke by removing liberalism from the impact of a temporal perspective.[59]

One pre-eminent consequence of this paradigmatic change has been the drastic contraction of the natural habitat of liberalism, the political arena.[60] The bulk of the liberal conceptual configuration now spills over into a politics-free area, as Dworkin has reminded us,[61] and individuals are literally abandoned to their own fates in the names of autonomy and self-determination. The result is a political liberalism that claims to be compatible with an indeterminate variety of reasonable comprehensive social and political beliefs, as long as they accept the procedural "minimum-kit" of democratic constitutionalism. This has significant repercussions for liberalism. For in universalising political liberalism, the specific appeal of other doctrines is undercut either by excluding them as unreasonable or by reducing them—through revealing them as congruous with political liberalism. Political liberalism thus becomes a particularly potent weapon that can outbid the attractions of other doctrines/ideologies by subsuming aspects of them into itself. The shrinkage of the political is thus both very modest and highly ambitious. To judge this enterprise as successful depends on whether one thinks such formulae work, or on whether one can demonstrate that such philosophical liberals are unaware, or in denial, of their own surpluses of meaning. As I have argued elsewhere, Rawls's political liberalism contains almost all of the crucial attributions of meaning that typify the family of liberal concepts. His political liberalism has gone so far down the road towards a comprehensive liberalism that there is no turning back, no fork in the road that could lead on to a comprehensive socialism, conservatism, or reasonable religious doctrine.[62] It is therefore instructive to find Rawls's later utterances redefining his theory of justice as fairness—hitherto understood to be a general theory—as a comprehensive doctrine, and hence bereft of the reasonable pluralism that a narrower political liberalism requires.[63]

Other theorists, as we have seen, have distinguished between good and bad forms of liberalism, but no one prior to Rawls proposed to regard liberalism as a two-tier edifice. What has this done to liberalism? It has

---

[59] That precariousness is noted in Neill, *The Rise and Decline of Liberalism*, p. 21.

[60] Contrast this with Laski's complaint that liberalism has been far too political, in the sense of espousing the ends of political, but not economic, democracy. For Laski, "it was inherent in the Liberal idea that men should use their political power for the improvement of their material position" (Laski, *The Rise of European Liberalism*, pp. 158–59).

[61] R. Dworkin, 'Liberalism,' in *A Matter of Principle* (Oxford, 1985), pp. 181–204.

[62] See M. Freeden, *Ideologies and Political Theory: A Conceptual Approach* (Oxford, 1996), chap. 6.

[63] J. Rawls, "The Idea of Public Reason Revisited," in Rawls, *The Law of Peoples* (Cambridge, 1999), p. 179.

injected into it a spurious neutrality and dissociated it from gathering the fruits of the political process, hitherto a central aim of the liberal agenda. It has upset the delicate balance between essence and contingency so typical of liberal argument. And it has emaciated liberalism by relegating its comprehensive values to the status of equal contenders with other socio-political doctrines, thus undercutting the specific ideological appeal of liberalism that its other proponents have been so eager to advance. That is another way of arguing that what are now termed the liberal virtues are excluded from the static preconditions concerning justice and pluralism. Maybe we should take Rawls at his word and stop calling his project liberal in a doctrinal sense altogether?

Of course, liberalism continues to exist as a developmental and humanist theory. While universities have over the past two decades sent liberalism on a confusing trajectory, the ideology called liberalism is still a comprehensive and culture-bound set of conceptual decontestations that operates, like any ideology, to compete over the legitimate meanings of political language. Philosophical notions of liberalism have not replaced historical, concrete, polysemic, and hence ideological understandings. The former, too, may be seen in that latter light and simply serve as further evidence of the contingent and manifold guises liberalism adopts within the broad constraints of shared family resemblances.

CHAPTER TWO

Liberal Community: An Essay in Retrieval

THE LIBERAL/COMMUNITARIAN debate, that intellectual companion and topological vade mecum of Anglo-American political philosophers in the 1980s and early 1990s, has left a residue that is still difficult to expunge. At its worst, it has created a new generation of students unable to think about liberalism in a manner that escapes the contrast in which the terms are presented, and a contingent of politicians who have eagerly assimilated communitarianism or anticommunitarianism to their shortlist of sound bites. At best, it has encouraged professional philosophers to reengage with issues of social responsibility, respect for individuals, and the quasianthropology of human nature. But facile dichotomies, however attractive to the pedagogue and categoriser, are the bane of understanding social life in its complexities; monolithic interpretations assigned to political concepts obfuscate the varied indeterminacy of the meanings they contain; and abstractions from concrete human conduct are a hindrance to the moralist who is also a social reformer, as well as a hindrance to the political theorist who is also an analyst of the actual political thought of a society and its key thinkers.

The purpose of this chapter is hence manifold. It attempts to put recent philosophical discussion in a comparative historical perspective. It endeavours to suggest that other conversations about liberalism existed before the current ahistorical and asocial version and that to ignore those conversations is not only to turn a blind eye to a cumulative ideational discourse but to impoverish our comprehension of current issues. And it proposes that the concept of community—an intricate, polysemic term possessed of multiple and not necessarily compatible meanings—was, and perhaps still should be, central to the mature liberal traditions of the West, rather than external to them. This latter viewpoint is now more in evidence among political theorists who have entered the debate.[1] As yet, however, the discussants have not engaged in detailed textual examinations of the structures of arguments employed diachronically, in particular at the point when the relationship between liberalism and communitari-

---

[1] For some instances see C. Taylor, "Cross-Purposes: The Liberal-Communitarian Debate," in N. Rosenblum, ed., *Liberalism and the Moral Life* (Cambridge, MA, 1989), pp. 159–82; A. Ryan, "The Liberal Community," in J. W. Chapman and I. Shapiro eds., *Democratic Community, Nomos XXXV* (New York, 1993), pp. 91–114.

anism became central to the liberal tradition. In what follows, that relationship is therefore not (re)invented but retrieved through an examination of some key British liberal theorists of the late-nineteenth and early-twentieth centuries. Nor is the intention to suggest that the moral theory behind contemporary philosophical liberalism is superior or inferior to the one underpinning British new liberal theory. Rather, it is claimed that the former is not wholly or even mainly representative of what earlier liberals included in their creed, of what they believed they were talking about, or of what they bequeathed to mainstream liberal thinking.

I have contended elsewhere that conceptions of sociability, some stronger, others weaker, are to be found in the writings of the main shapers of British liberalism, in the utterances of Locke, Mill, and T. H. Green; indeed, that a total absence of the concept of sociability must raise serious doubts as to whether the theory before us is liberal.[2] Here I shall examine in greater detail how, in the writings of key new liberals, sociability appears in the form of community. Community, however, did not embrace a single meaning for new liberals, and its diverse nuances were attached to other core liberal concepts in such a way as to produce variations within the new liberal family of political thinking. In order to understand these variations, we need to appreciate on which dimensions of meaning "community" underwent changes. And in order to understand why these dimensions played an important role, we need to recognize that the ontological assumptions and methodological concerns of the new liberals differed considerably from those adopted by contemporary American East Coast philosophical liberals.

Hence a brief reference is necessary to current theories of community within the mainstream of those who have attempted to address the problems of contemporary philosophical liberalism. The most central feature of those theories is that community—if liberals can speak of it at all—is the consequence, not the cause, of social arrangements, that it is largely (and for some, entirely) the product of human volition, and that its role is to augment the autonomy of the individual, now understood as related to group culture. The heuristic intention of philosophical liberals has been to construct reasonable and persuasive arguments in favour of specific conceptions of justice and distribution, of autonomy and identity, of self-expression and rights-protection, and of resolving potential conflict among groups, through the modelling of logical possibilities and their alternatives.[3] They have addressed these issues by establishing framework

---

[2] M. Freeden, *Ideologies and Political Theory: A Conceptual Approach* (Oxford, 1996), chaps. 4, 5.

[3] I exclude conservative theories of community such as A. MacIntyre's from the current discussion.

rules through which solutions incorporating principles of fairness and equality are mooted.

The project of the new liberals, however, was importantly different, but these differences only become clearly focused if we are prepared to recognize that liberalism is not only a philosophical enterprise but also an ideological one, that it not only equips us with reasonable or valuable ways of approaching complex social problems but also contains conscious and unconscious cultural and ideational assumptions that respond to, and seek to shape, salient concerns of individuals and groups at particular times and in particular spaces. Needless to say, these ideologies help in understanding why some ethical solutions to the questions that have preoccupied both contemporary philosophical and new liberals are preferred to others, namely, because they assist us in appreciating why specific questions were asked.

Many of the considerations new liberals brought to bear on their political theories were forged in an era that, while sharing some of the aims of current philosophical liberals, differed on many others. The new liberals came to political thinking equipped with a strong sense of beneficial historical change. They attached to rationality a confidence not only in its survival value, but also in its continuous enhancement. They believed in the power of politics to improve human lives. They claimed to discover that the social costs of human immiseration through subscribing to unfettered laws of supply, demand, and individual initiative were intolerable. And on that edifice they constructed their various views of community, because they believed that human beings prospered best when socially benign interaction was permitted full rein.

But contemporary liberals live in a rather different world. They take as given that encouraging individual life plans is the aim of a civilized society, and that people differ sufficiently in such plans, preferences, and capacities to install pluralism as a fact of social life, and a desirable one at that. They believe that choice making is not merely an essential, but a dominant, feature of human nature, and that the multiplication of opportunities for choices in current societies carries with it enormous potential for human self-expression. Many of these liberals, through the power and mystique of the U.S. Constitution, believe that suprapolitical and largely suprahistorical constructs are not only in evidence, but also offer the best hope for reducing, if not overcoming, the discord present in pluralism. And even when such liberals are concerned with groups, at least with the cultural groups that have dominated the sociopolitical landscape of North America (because those groups are believed to be crucial carriers of pluralism), they are concerned because they question the monopoly of ethical legitimacy of the group on which many individuals still bestow emotional allegiance—the national community.

COMMUNITY IN CURRENT DEBATE

The multilayered concept of "community" may benefit from an analytical perspective that addresses both its historical and structural dimensions. These have been notably absent, on the conscious, intentional level, in recent characterisations of community. Instead, conceptions of community have been constructed so as to exclude compatibilities with many of the *ethical* ends attributed to liberalism, but they also are selective about certain *ideological* assumptions. "Philosophical" communitarianism is thus seen by its critics to blur the distinction between the political and the civil; it is seen to uphold an untenable majoritarianism against the justified claims of minorities; it is seen as a homogeneous and exclusivist structure through which a common good is sought and the basis of individual identity is furnished, often by recognising the cohesive force of existing practices and traditions; and, of course, it is seen as introducing considerations irrelevant to liberal argument.[4] Again and again, we find a tendency to speak of "the communitarians" as one entity. Unsurprisingly, one theorist asserts: "Examining community from the perspective of American constitutional theory is highly instructive. . . . the longing for community is a chimera—romantic, naive, and, in the end, illiberal and dangerous."[5] Community is thus constructed out of what liberalism is not.

Many communitarians, on the other hand, proffer conceptualisations that establish the paucity of liberalism both as an ethical and a social theory, and they notably fashion communitarianism as a counterproject to liberalism. For Sandel, membership in a community is a constituent of individual identity, and it is an attachment that shapes, at least in part, the ends of the self, prior to the exercise of choice by that self. A "community must be constitutive of the shared self-understandings of the participants."[6] In his most recent book, Sandel reiterates the view that liberalism purports to be neutral towards particular visions of the good life, substituting fair procedures for specific ends. But he does invite the reader to distinguish between two meanings of liberalism. The first is liberalism in "common parlance" (what others might term "liberal ideology"): "the outlook of those who favour a more generous welfare state and a greater measure of social and economic equality." The second refers to the historical tradition of thought of liberalism that "runs from John Locke, Imman-

---

[4] For an example of the latter point, see A. Gutmann, "Communitarian Critics of Liberalism," *Philosophy and Public Affairs* 14 (1985): 316.

[5] H. N. Hirsch, "The Threnody of Liberalism: Constitutional Liberalism and the Renewal of Community," *Political Theory* 14 (1986): 424.

[6] M. Sandel, *Liberalism and the Limits of Justice* (Cambridge, 1982), pp. 149–50, 173.

uel Kant, and John Stuart Mill to John Rawls."[7] Having thus made an important distinction, Sandel immediately renders it ineffectual. For "common parlance" liberalism is merely contemporary, its historical development having been overlooked, while the historical tradition Sandel traces is highly selective and, one might add, ahistorical. Any acquaintance with the new liberals demonstrates that "common parlance" had clear historical roots. On the other hand, the sequence from Locke to Kant to Mill to Rawls is a particular historical construction adapted to the United States, but while Locke and Mill are arguably major players in forming the basic ideology of contemporary American politics, both Kant and Rawls are relative newcomers, if not rank outsiders.[8] Moreover, when we look at alternative horizons of the European liberalism that inspired its American counterpart, chosen from multiple readings of liberalism's history, another sequence could equally, if not more, persuasively be rerouted from Locke to Bentham to Mill to Green to Hobhouse, and result in a very different interpretation of liberalism's features.

As a counter to a liberalism based on a largely negative conception of liberty, assuming the ultimate capacity of the individual as choice-maker, Sandel posits a republican communitarian theory that, he argues, has been replaced with liberalism. One can understand why, on Sandel's account, that dichotomisation is a necessary outcome of his particular interpretation of historical traditions. For republican communitarianism is not only participatory but also engages civic virtues: "a sense of belonging, a concern for the whole, a moral bond with the community." This version is to be distinguished from "the liberalism that conceives persons as free and independent selves," manifesting a voluntarism that casts them "as the authors of the only obligations that constrain."[9] Moreover, Sandel promotes the case for strong communal obligation and a conception of the common good that, in his view, is not part of the liberal case for the welfare state. That case, according to Sandel—drawing almost entirely on the writings of Rawls—depends "on the rights we would agree to respect if we could abstract from our interests and ends."[10]

Walzer's communitarianism is conspicuously different from Sandel's. Sandel employs community in order to re-establish the source of the ethical ends individuals invariably carry with them, and in focusing on that aspect of deontology he reintroduces the political into our understanding of individual identity, which a neutral liberalism ostensibly eliminated.

---

[7] M. Sandel, *Democracy's Discontent: America in Search of a Public Policy* (Cambridge, MA, 1996), p. 4.

[8] Cf. Freeden, *Ideologies and Political Theory*, pp. 236–41.

[9] Sandel, *Democracy's Discontent*, pp. 5–6, 12.

[10] Ibid., p. 16.

Walzer's sympathetic approach to communitarianism is distinguished by its readiness to examine, and to dispute, not a disembedded liberal neutralism, but an older and more historically authenticated liberalism. He locates that liberalism on two dimensions: first, the model of fragmented free choice supposedly representing liberalism; second—and more significant—the actual social and political practices that liberalism purports to embody. Walzer's focus is thus not on community as the basis of individual identity but on communi*ties* as the expression of social networks. His communitarianism is not a challenge to liberalism's assumed estrangement from the political but a challenge to the social unit of analysis employed by political theorists, an attempt to move away from the individual to "patterns of relationship, networks of power, and communities of meaning."[11] In recognizing the social power and political reality of the liberal fragmented model, Walzer shifts the debate onto the level of concrete ideological and sociological practices. And in so doing, unlike the more extreme antiliberals, he acknowledges that much of the language of liberalism is "inescapable": rights, voluntarism, pluralism, toleration, privacy. His solution—a more realistic and historically more accurate one than Sandel's—is a liberal communitarianism. Walzer sums up his view in a plea: "It would be a good thing . . . if we could teach those [liberal] selves to know themselves as social beings, the historical products of, and in part the embodiments of, liberal values."[12] That is precisely what the new liberals had already achieved in their own manner.

REALLY EXISTING LIBERALISMS: ALTERNATIVE COMMUNITIES AND NATURALIST ONTOLOGY

Many of the above communitarian or republican attributes are central features of British social liberalism (and of many of its continental counterparts). In claiming this it will of course be necessary to argue that those European doctrines were still liberal on any reasonable understanding that does not narrowly equate liberalism with a spurious atomistic model of human conduct that—as we know from historical evidence—mainstream liberalism did not espouse,[13] or with the opus of Rawls and his intellectual

[11] M. Walzer, "The Communitarian Critique of Liberalism," *Political Theory* 18 (1990): 10.

[12] Ibid., p. 15.

[13] Thomas A. Spragens Jr., while recognising the importance of sympathy, benevolence, mutual obligations, and social solidarity in developing a liberal sense of community in the period stretching from Locke to J. S. Mill, unfortunately vitiates his argument by remarking that the picture began, in the late nineteenth century, to change away from community, totally ignoring the developments in liberal thought in that latter period (T. A. Spragens Jr., "Communitarian Liberalism," in A. Etzioni, ed., New *Communitarian Thinking: Persons, Virtues, Institutions, and Communities* [Charlottesville, 1995], pp. 37–51).

circle.[14] Specifically, by insisting on drawing a line between political and comprehensive liberalism, Rawls removes any notion of community from ontological assumptions linked to human nature, replacing them with a willed cooperation as an option reflecting a rational but contrived overlapping consensus. Instead, community is relegated to a feature of a comprehensive doctrine, that is, to a position of adjacency to the core features of political liberalism.[15] For the new liberals, a notion of community was, to the contrary, one of the fundamental constraints within which choice would be exercised. It is, however, also the case that, within the new liberal family, frames of reference that were partly different engendered disparate conceptualisations of a liberal communitarianism.

To maintain that the new liberalism was a communitarian body of thought is not necessarily to adopt recent characterisations of community, let alone the role of "community" in promoting certain kinds of political argument. To begin with, the new liberals' view of community was constructed on the basis of historical and scientific theories about the structure and growth of societies. At the historical level, they subscribed to quasi-naturalistic accounts of social relations and social development, which served as the cause of, and hence genetic explanation for, certain attributes of human conduct in society. At the structural level, they subscribed to theories concerning the primacy and intensity of social bonds that offered an interpretative framework for their human and social values. Each particular theorist might have had a somewhat different understanding of the components of these theories but nevertheless operated within a recognisably shared discourse. Beyond that, on a heuristic level, the new liberals assumed that a viable political theory should achieve two aims. First, it should be grounded on empirical evidence. Second, it should foster and enhance the moral conduct that, in their view, could be deduced from an evolutionary and, occasionally, psychologically based explication of a well-functioning society. Human will was neither antagonistic to nature, nor was it to dominate nature.

Those aims of political theory were superimposed on—though the new liberals professed to derive them from—accounts of the empirically ascertainable structure of society and, in particular, the identification of the social unit as one of crucial and constitutive importance in fashioning human ends. But the new liberals, far from adhering to the homogeneous conception of community apparently detected by contemporary critics of

---

[14] Another argument that cannot be ignored, but which is beyond the remit of this chapter, is that the "procedural," neutralist liberalism that Sandel identifies as at the heart of American public philosophy is an illusory stance based on myths and self-deception as well as on a bracketing out of crucial aspects of the American liberal tradition. See Freeden, *Ideologies and Political Theory*, chap. 6.

[15] J. Rawls, *Political Liberalism* (New York, 1993), pp. 40, 201.

communitarianism, subscribed to a broad range of communitarian positions and identified a variety of attributes of community, some mutually compatible, others not. Moreover, all of these were tenable within the family of late-modern British liberalisms.

One of the more sophisticated versions of community may be found in the mature thought of L. T. Hobhouse, particularly in his postwar trilogy.[16] Hobhouse approached human societies as predicated on psychological impulses that evolved into more complex expressions of feeling and eventually into a rational consciousness. Dismissing, as did his contemporary new liberals, any suggestion of a society-forming contract, and hence of society as a voluntary association, he explained a community as an initially unconscious elaboration of sexual, parental, and sociable impulses. Human development was hence tantamount to the development of a nexus of social relations. This naturalistic explanation of the social impulse ("society grows out of human nature") took, however, an interesting turn. Although the community and its organising rules grew unconsciously, the natural social development of human beings culminated in the emergence of a "common sentiment" and a "common interest," in which "the development that each man can achieve is conditioned in kind and degree by the development of others."[17] This was brought about by the appearance, at an advanced evolutionary stage, of rational consciousness, conscious effort and, above all, deliberate purpose.

COMMUNITY AS INTERACTIVE STRUCTURE

At this point, the second feature of community entered the picture. The naturalness of sociability and of group membership was joined by the specific input of human rationality into social behaviour. Human rationality was a "thick" rationality, closely associated with the adjacent concepts of harmony, commonality, and welfare. It would be far too simplistic to explain these links as a particular kind of biological or psychological or moral theory. The interconnections among these disciplinary perspectives were the defining feature of Hobhouse's new liberalism, and this epistemology itself separates it from current concerns. He viewed rationality as the property of exercising self-consistent judgments. Such judgments were based on subjective grounds tested against other subjective judgments in terms of their mutual consistency. That process accorded them objective

---

[16] L. T. Hobhouse, *The Rational Good* (London, 1921); *The Elements of Social Justice* (London, 1922); *Social Development: Its Nature and Conditions* (London, 1924). Many of these themes are to be found in Hobhouse's prewar writings as well, though they are more developed and more carefully argued in the later work.

[17] Hobhouse, *The Rational Good*, p. 90.

rational status. The crux of that intersubjectivity was, in effect, a particular notion of consistency as harmony, namely, the mutual support of a system composed of component judgments. This complete system of interconnecting parts supplied the rational self-evidence of a system of complementary truths, which would otherwise be partial. Put differently, and crucially for Hobhouse's conception of community, reason was "an organic principle in thought," incomplete but progressive. The reality that this reason identified and reflected was likewise an organic whole.

In sum, the ethical principle of the good involved a harmony between feeling and action, reflected both in the internal make-up of an individual and in social relationships. Rationality entailed the attainment of balance, which for Hobhouse meant both fundamental similarity and a single system of purposes that held human diversity in check, thus minimising conflict. Finally, this ethical principle of organic, interrelated complementarity was both embedded in experience and superimposed on it. It emanated from knowledge of the world and directed it as well, for to say that something is good was both a judgment of value and an assertion of fact.[18] That, ultimately, was the optimistic lesson the new liberals drew from evolution. Community was a sociological reality in a strong sense completely absent from recent debate, but it was also an ethical partnership if accompanied by a rational respect for individuality and for cooperation.

Central to rationality were its social implications, "the conclusion that the belief that we owe allegiance to a wider life than our own is justified in reason." These implications had at an earlier evolutionary stage been present in the social instincts of mutual forbearance and mutual aid. Now, however, the rational good could be attached to sociability as a direct consequence of its interpretation as "one in which all persons share in proportion to the capacity of their social personality."[19] The result was a complex conception of community, explored by Hobhouse at the developmental stage of modern societies, and one that allowed for both individuation and integration, precisely the elements that late-twentieth-century political philosophers have allocated either to liberalism or to communitarianism or, when combined, have held up as a project political theory may take on board *in future*. A community informed by an organic harmony among its parts led inevitably to a carving out of that element of harmony as the common good. Specifically, the organic relation was one of mutual service, constituting a harmony in which each part assisted the fulfilment of the others. Hence a community was, in Durkheimian fashion, "a system of parts maintaining themselves by their interactions."[20]

[18] Ibid., pp. 65–66.
[19] Hobhouse, *Elements of Social Justice*, p. 117.
[20] Hobhouse, *Social Development*, p. 70.

Whether or not a community was merely the dynamic interaction of individuals in their social, structurally interdependent mode or a distinct social entity was a matter of some difference, even altercation, among new liberals. Hobhouse tended to subscribe to the former, Hobson, as we shall see, to the latter. But the implications of Hobhouse's preference of the attribute "organic" to the entity "organism" were nevertheless considerable. It supplied a sufficient basis to identify the community as a rights-bearer, and consequently required individual liberty to be limited by the rights of the community. The shared element of the common good took on an identity of its own, an identity absent in most late-twentieth-century versions of communitarianism. But this constraining communitarianism was far from being repressive. Methodologically, its constraints need to be appreciated as a general recognition of the limits of permissible ranges of political values and the conduct that embodied them. An unlimited liberty had long been rejected by all except extreme individualist anarchists. What had changed, however, was the constraining object, and what requires scrutiny is the extent to which liberalism could place its faith in the rational self-limitation of a community, having preached as a matter of course the rational self-limitation of the individual. Undoubtedly, individual constraint could more easily be secured through the power of a collective body, in particular the state. Could liberals rely on parallel and sufficient constraints on the community? Their response was a compound based on the ethics of commonalities, social self-interest, social utility, the democratic alertness of the individual members of a society, and an appeal to the facts of social structure and evolution.

On the first criterion, referring to the nature of social ethics, Hobhouse was confidently optimistic:

> A rational ethics starting with the web of human impulses is forced to discard those which are blind or contradictory, and retain as reasonable those only which form a consistent whole. . . . It cannot confine the good to any section of humanity . . . it sets the consistent body of human purposes before each individual as the good, which he as a rational being must recognise and support, and within which alone can his own good be reasonably sought. The good of all others enters into his own, and by the same logic his good enters into theirs. Thus the rational system in the end is one of mutual furtherance, or what we have called harmony . . . social development and ethical development are at the end the same.

Crucially, this ethics did not ignore the centrifugal tendencies of individual existence. Hobhouse insisted that, though human beings were social animals, they "did not see social life steadily and see it whole." Human interests were "fragmentary and often inconsistent," and their harmonisation could never be total. Yet Hobhouse vested so much value in the individual that, in a strong echo of hermeneutic holism, he could claim that in "his social potentialities each constituent individual holds the germ of the whole social order."[21] Here individuality was endowed with the entire human potential, while concurrently human sociability was elevated to a supreme attribute. But to assert this was not to insist that the individual was complete in itself. Quite the contrary: because each individual member of a society was incomplete, yet also endowed with the capacity of self-direction, a state of organic interdependence was a conscious aspiration in an individual's quest for self-development *through* community. To consider people apart from the society that they formed was a false view of social development.

Similar arguments are of course integral to socialist ideologies, yet Hobhouse was no socialist. At most, he saw himself as a liberal who incorporated some socialist perspectives in articulating his beliefs.[22] Occasionally he even extended his purview. A rational social order had to assimilate three philosophical principles: philosophic conservatism required a communal system that could actually sustain itself and offer a semblance of continuity; philosophic liberalism required the liberation of vital impulses so that personalities could grow; and philosophic socialism required the principle of similars because of the importance of sharing significant goods. Hence equal treatment of individuals and groups applied, unless essential differences could be produced. This was a recognition both of human equality and, as a lesser constraint, of the diverse claims of groups.[23]

For Hobhouse a community was neither a single, nor a static, entity. Communities developed on four different levels: population size; the efficient coordination and discharge of their functions; freedom for thought, character, and initiative of their members; and participation in mutual services. These developments did not occur at the same pace, allowing for a range of configurations of the conceptions constituting community, only a few of which carried Hobhouse's seal of approval.[24] In his more pessimistic moments he was unable to ignore the divide between the ethical and the sociological. For although a notion of complete ethical development could be conceived as form rather than specific content—as the fulfilment of the mutually compatible aspects of personality—the historical process, according to Hobhouse, shuddered and stumbled. Hobhouse was after all no Hegelian, neither in his assessment of the political consequences of Idealist theory nor in his personal, war-induced abhorrence of

---

[21] Ibid., p. 67.
[22] Hobhouse, *Liberalism* (London, 1911), p. 165.
[23] Hobhouse, *The Rational Good*, pp. 132–34.
[24] Hobhouse, *Social Development*, pp. 78–79.

German philosophy. As he commented, "while social development in its completeness corresponds to the ideal of a rational ethics, partial development may diverge from it, and . . . the historic course of change includes what from either point of view is mere arrest, retrogression or decay."[25] This was a far more subtle position than the crude perfectionism now often attributed to teleological political theories.

According to Kymlicka, reinforcing commonly held views of what constitutes liberalism, "there seems to be no room within the moral ontology of liberalism for the idea of collective rights . . . . Individual and collective rights cannot compete for the same moral space, in liberal theory, since the value of the collective derives from its contribution to the value of individual lives."[26] If that schematic and dichotomising feature is intended to characterise actually existing liberalisms, it must be conclusively rejected, if only because self-described and other-recognised liberals such as Hobson and Hobhouse persuasively argued the contrary. They could do so because they identified both the individual and the group-cum-nation (and occasionally the nation as separate from the group) as coequal units, capable of harmonious coexistence and mutual sustenance. Hobson, in an early piece entitled "Rights of Property," argued concurrently for the requirement of individual property in order to underpin what was necessary to express the vitality and developmental nature of human beings, and for the requirement of social property in order to service the cooperative needs of a society. As both the individual and society had a share in the bestowal of value on individual productivity, they both had a claim on the product.[27] Hobhouse echoed this argument: "if private property is of value . . . to the fulfilment of personality, common property is equally of value for the expression and development of social life."[28]

Hobson's conception of community differed from Hobhouse's, and it is arguably the case that on occasion Hobson transcended the boundaries of liberal debate in his firm adherence to the analogy between society and an organism.[29] Though he incorporated elements of Hobhouse's empiricist and developmental approach to social interdependence, Hobson focused on the existential structural features of human societies. Thus, an organic community was one in which the activity of each part had, in holistic fashion, an important bearing on society in its totality. Hobson,

[25] Ibid., p. 90.

[26] W. Kymlicka, *Liberalism, Community, and Culture* (Oxford, 1989), p. 140.

[27] J. A. Hobson, "Rights of Property," *Free Review* (Nov. 1893): 130–49.

[28] L. T. Hobhouse, "The Historical Evolution of Property, in Fact and in Idea" in C. Gore, ed., *Property, its Duties and Rights* (London, 1913), pp. 30–31. See M. Freeden, *The New Liberalism* (Oxford, 1978), pp. 45–46.

[29] See especially J. A. Hobson, "The Re-Statement of Democracy," in Hobson, *The Crisis of Liberalism* (London, 1909), pp. 71–87.

however, assigned a separately discernible identity to society in a strong version of organicism that plainly exceeded Hobhouse's, and that was an attempt to harness scientific knowledge in a bid to redefine the boundaries of a viable social ethics: "this organic treatment of Society is . . . still more essential, if we consider society not merely as a number of men and women with social instincts and social aspects of their individual lives, but as a group life with a collective body, a collective consciousness and will, and capable of realising a collective vital end. . . .The study of the social value of individual men no more constitutes sociology than the study of cell life constitutes human physiology."[30]

JUSTICE AS A GOOD

What then of justice, that mainstay of recent philosophical theories of liberalism? For Hobhouse, justice occupied a complex position adjacent to and derivative from the core concept of the common good, yet concurrently playing a part in constituting it. If it still is necessary to persuade contemporary political theorists that, historically, liberalism has not been neutral among different conceptions of the good, Hobhouse provides one of many clinching examples. Demonstrating that there are useful distinctions between neutrality and impartiality, Hobhouse declared that "justice . . . is the impartial application of a rule founded on the common good." Rather than holding to a Rawlsian assertion of just rules that precede the good, Hobhouse commented: "Now the rules (applied by a state) themselves may be wise or unwise, just or unjust. If they are such to serve the common good . . . they are wise and good." The good preceded the right, but one aspect of the right helped in determining the good. That aspect was a conception of equality that may be described as impartiality in the application of rules. So the structure of the argument runs as follows: There is a complex conception of the common good—a harmonious, individual-developing sociability—and the system of justice in societies that abide by this common good requires impartial rules to apply this good. Impartiality is hence not neutrality, because the good itself cannot be neutral. Impartiality is a wise way of dispensing a (non-neutral) good. In addition, however, the good itself is partly constituted by the idea of impartiality. Were the good wholly constituted by impartiality, the argument would indeed begin to resemble Rawls's notion of fairness. But Hobhouse's impartiality emerges from a clear idea of ethical ends that are not contained in it, and its version of equality-cum-universality is a crucial *component* in the project of realising the common good. That component is that "all members of the community . . . simply as members have an equal claim

---

[30] J. A. Hobson, *Work and Wealth* (New York, 1914), p. 15.

upon the common good, while any difference in what is due to them or from them must itself be a difference required by the common good."[31]

Unlike Rawls's second, difference principle, Hobhouse's notion of difference was based on a substantive test to which rational actors who are *conscious and informed* members of a society could agree, and it was further based on the ontological assumption, buttressed by sociological evidence, that communities exist and that they are manifestations of human rationality. We are not invited to engage in a thought-experiment to determine a morally compelling position but to engage in a concrete extrapolation from already existing practices. We are not invited to conceive of a rational individual actor, for whom limited cooperation but not association or community is the sign of a just order,[32] but to conceive of an evolutionarily given rationally cooperating society. We are not invited to reduce the sphere of the political to that of respect for foundational processes or constitutional arrangements, but to extend it to an increasingly deliberate pursuit of policies designed to augment well-being. As the liberal Idealist philosopher D. G. Ritchie cogently put it, within the context of discussing justice, "With regard to equality, as with regard to freedom, people are very apt to fall a prey to abstraction, and in pursuit of the form to neglect the reality, preferring shadow to substance."[33] The new liberal substance was linked to concerted state action as well as to individual involvement. For Ritchie, on the one hand, state interference had to be considered from the viewpoint of its probable effect on the welfare of the community as a whole, for "all salutary State action must be such as will give individuals so far as possible the opportunity of realising their physical, intellectual, and moral capacities." On the other hand, the adage that man is a political animal meant that "if cut off from the life of active citizenship in a constitutional state, human nature fails to attain fully the best things of which it is capable."[34] Rawls's first principle also failed the new liberal test of justice, because "if no man may ever justly do what interferes with the equal liberty of any other man, this seems to me to bring us to a deadlock. . . . This 'equal liberty,' therefore, if in any subordinate sense it is recognized, is not an absolute and primary, but a derivative principle, dependent on some idea of common good or advantage."[35]

[31] Hobhouse, *Elements of Social Justice*, pp. 105, 108.

[32] J. Rawls, *Political Liberalism*, pp. 40–43. Because Rawls conceives of community only as a political society that affirms the same comprehensive doctrine (p. 146), he cannot incorporate into his argument any nuances of social structure that obtain between such an extreme totalitarian option and the minimal cooperation he endorses.

[33] D. G. Ritchie, *Studies in Political and Social Ethics* (London, 1902), pp. 36–37.

[34] Ritchie, *Studies*, pp. 57–58, 69.

[35] Ibid., pp. 58–60.

CONSTRAINTS ON COMMUNITY AND THE QUESTION OF AUTONOMY

We turn now to two kinds of questions: how did the new liberalism address problems of the relation of society to individuals, and how did it address problems of the relation of society to groups? The first issue was addressed by Hobhouse by means of his emphasis on personal development. Such development was only to be sought through an individual's rational choice, but rational choice also entailed contributing to the common good. A dual role of the state required the protection of personal rights as well as the attainment of common objects. Indeed, in a rationally engaged society, the protection of individual rights was not merely, as with many philosophical liberals, lexically prior to social welfare but an element of social welfare.[36] As Hobhouse famously put it in his classic *Liberalism*: "Mutual aid is no less important than mutual forbearance, the theory of collective action no less fundamental than the theory of personal freedom."[37] In employing these two mutually decontesting and interdependent terms, Hobhouse dissociated himself from a conception of autonomy as self-regarding action, a conception that slowly crept back into favour as the twentieth century drew to a close. Liberty meant inward growth and entailed external enabling conditions that, crucially, involved combined action: "every liberty rests on a corresponding act of control. The true opposition is that between the control that cramps the personal life and the spiritual order, and the control that is aimed at securing the external and material conditions of their free and unimpeded development."[38]

The second question is linked to the first, but it raises an issue of more specific concern to communitarian discourse, and it is through its exploration that another set of distinguishing features marking off current debate from the new liberal thinking becomes visible. In substance, it demonstrates that the present concern with individual autonomy was at best a problematic issue for the communitarian liberals on which we are focusing, and at worst an obfuscating category that cannot be superimposed on their analyses. Mulhall and Swift have rightly suggested that there exist current brands of liberalism, among them that of Raz, that limit the supremacy of autonomy within a field of liberal values.[39] Walzer is forced by the logic of his communitarian position to resort to an unsatisfactory term such as "relative autonomy" that, whether applied to distributive spheres or to individuals, illustrates the ill fit between the concept and its

---

[36] Hobhouse, *Elements of Social Justice*, pp. 37, 82, 85.

[37] Hobhouse, *Liberalism*, p. 124.

[38] Ibid., p. 167.

[39] S. Mulhall and A. Swift, *Liberals and Communitarians* (Oxford, 1992), pp. 290–94. See J. Raz, *The Morality of Freedom* (Oxford, 1986).

explanandum.[40] But these reservations have been the meat of liberal debate for most of this century in Britain, France, Germany, and Italy.[41] Nor is the issue a matter of choice between autonomy and heteronomy, as the dichotomy posited by these terms is inadequate in capturing the structure of discourse—and hence the conceptual equipment—at the disposal of communitarian liberals. Rather two dimensions of problematics emerge: is autonomy the primary end of individuals, rather than development or welfare; and among pluralist communitarians, is autonomy a concept that can express the structural relationships within human communities and the ontological understandings of human existence? First, the Hobhousian approach queries the methodology of assigning primacy to one human attribute, as is the wont of many political philosophers. Second, the extolling of autonomy assigns priority to the analysis of individuals over the analysis of groups. Community is then either perceived as inimical to autonomy, or as a means to individual autonomy. But Hobhouse's social anthropology and his acceptance of nonvoluntarist association pointed in a different direction. Autonomy was not a word Hobhouse used frequently. Even on a more generous interpretation of autonomy as self-fulfilment, or the reflective pursuit of individual projects, and not just the condition of being subject to one's own will, the concept is unhelpful in a theory that categorically states that "the development which each man can achieve is conditioned in kind and degree by the development of others."[42] Hobhouse even appealed to a suprahuman evolutionary process whose design was a developmental harmony of life, and this was "the aim not of the human mind in particular, but of Mind as such."[43] Autonomy was thus limited by purposive laws of social development and the emergence of a shared conscious social intelligence.

Ritchie, with far greater Kantian roots than other new liberals, did address the notion of autonomy, which he saw as individual self-government in accordance with the dictates of his reason; however, the source of that reason was the issue at stake. Ritchie understood it as the result of training and discipline that must at first be given us by others. Character and circumstances were prior determinants of our motives and volitions. As he noted: "How often have measures of social reform been opposed on the ground that they weakened individual responsibility—as if men's characters were perfectly isolated phenomena, and not affected at every moment by their antecedents and surroundings!"[44]

[40] M. Walzer, *Spheres of Justice* (Oxford, 1983), p. 10.

[41] For an excellent Italian instance of this perspective see Carlo Rosselli, *Liberal Socialism* (Princeton, 1994).

[42] Hobhouse, *The Rational Good*, p. 90

[43] Hobhouse, *Social Development*, p. 342.

[44] Ritchie, *Studies*, pp. 196–97.

THE FEDERAL OPTION

The twofold question of the relation of society to individuals and to groups was addressed by Hobson, employing his strong notion of community to develop the concept of federalism. In a central passage, Hobson declared that

> the unity of this socio-industrial life is not a unity of mere fusion in which the individual virtually disappears, but a federal unity in which the rights and interests of the individual shall be conserved for him by the federation. The federal government, however, conserves these individual rights, not, as the individualist maintains, because it exists for no other purpose than to do so. It conserves them because it also recognises that an area of individual liberty is conducive to the health of the collective life. Its federal nature rests on a recognition alike of individual and social ends, or, speaking more accurately, of social ends that are directly attained by social action and of those that are realised in individuals.[45]

Federalism, I submit, is a more appropriate term through which to address the specific features of new liberal ontology and ethics, both at individual and at group level, than the current reliance on conceptions of individual and group autonomy. Nevertheless, the latter still have to be addressed in any discussion of community. Ritchie had already criticised the notion of the "inviolable autonomy of nations" and it needs to be understood that in the parlance of the times autonomy was frequently interchangeable with national self-determination.[46] For Hobhouse, autonomy in the context of nationalities was not full independence, but being "a distinct constituent community."[47] Nations were based on history, sentiment, religion, race, or language and they were the viable macrosocial unit. Consequently, when a smaller nation was incorporated into a larger one, a centrifugal force emerged, leading to division and to sectionalism, a situation that the majoritarian principle could not address. Unfortunately Hobhouse offered no clear solution to the tension between the right of the smaller national community to self-determination and the common responsibility for cooperation between a national majority and a national minority within the same state. "To find the place for national rights within the unity of the state," he wrote, "to give scope to national differences without destroying the organisation of a life which has somehow to be lived in common, is therefore the problem."[48] At best, he could argue

---

[45] Hobson, *Work and Wealth*, p. 304.
[46] Ritchie, *Studies*, p. 175.
[47] Hobhouse, *Social Development*, p. 297.
[48] L. T. Hobhouse, *Social Evolution and Political Theory* (New York, 1911), p. 146.

that "the characteristic modern state . . . exhibits the most complete reconciliation yet achieved on the large scale of social cooperation with the
freedom and spontaneity of the component individual, localities, and nationalities." That was due to the specific link between the state and its
concomitant notion of group membership as citizenship, for "the principle of citizenship renders possible a form of union as vital, as organic, as
the clan and as wide as the empire, while it adds a measure of freedom to
the constituent parts and an elasticity to the whole which are peculiarly
its own."[49]

Of greater interest in view of current concerns of scholarship is the
internal conceptualisation of whole/group, and of group/group, relationships. Indisputably, the nation was the overarching social group for the
new liberals, and in that belief they merely inherited a nineteenth-century
assumption. What, then, was the status of groups within the national
framework? This is a question that has become central to the multicultural explorations of recent political theory. Those explorations still relate
to the problem of group recognition in terms of autonomy, either by leaving groups as much as possible to their own devices, or by utilising the
cultural group as a crucial contributor to individual autonomy. Part of
the problem is that contemporary theory has restricted its treatment of
groups to those moulding the cultural identity of their members. By contrast, the new liberals would have enumerated additional substantive
communal ends that extended from self-determination to the attainment
of welfare. Whereas for many current theorists the right to a distinct identity is a defining feature of the good life, for the new liberals this had to
be tempered by associated values such as cooperative human development. Even Kymlicka regards collective rights predominantly as those that
entitle the collective to their *cultural* heritage.[50]

This raises a second concern. Kymlicka is concerned not only with
choice in shaping the character of such a cultural community but, crucially, in a "context" of choice irrespective of the character of the community.[51] In his more recent work he has admittedly entertained weighty reservations about accommodating nonliberal minorities, arguing for a
moral appeal to groups that do not respect the internal rights of their
members to make and revise their choices. But, Kymlicka continues, "that
does not mean that liberals can impose their principles on groups that
do not share them."[52] Hence cultural communities are entitled to pursue
practices that in themselves may be conservatively held and unconsciously

[49] Ibid., pp. 147–48.
[50] Kymlicka, *Liberalism, Community, and Culture*, p. 138.
[51] Ibid., pp. 166, 168, 172.
[52] W. Kymlicka, *Multicultural Citizenship* (Oxford, 1995), pp. 163–65.

or unreflectively endorsed, inasmuch as those practices are central to constituting their members' identity. The boundaries of liberalism are far from clear-cut, however. Liberal states do impose some of their practices on their members, such as free speech or the right to vote (individual members may not wish to take up those practices, but the rights to such practices are secured to them irrespective of whether they regard them as legitimate). The thin liberalism Kymlicka has assimilated from Rawls, modified by Kymlicka's inclusion within it of individual autonomy,[53] cannot be easily insulated from the interconnected configurations of broader, yet still fundamental, liberal concepts.[54] The new liberals realized full well that, with all its tolerance and structural flexibility, liberalism was a competing Weltanschauung that required a wide range of moral positions, and those positions had to be translated into political action in order to survive the rivalry of ideological antagonists. Many current debates on community take the group on board simply in terms of the procedural granting of voice to the concerns of such a group, and only rarely, if at all, in terms of the substantive evaluation of the practices of the group. That is not an option that the new liberals would have encouraged, and the difference is, as ever, over the attributes and ends of the good life. Nor are the boundaries of coercion clear-cut. Kymlicka endorses speaking out against an illiberal practice. But that too may well be an exercise of considerable power.

There are two types of distinct nonrational ties that assist in constituting communities: an accumulated cultural heritage that moulds understandings of a socially inherited collective identity; and affective relationships that bond a group into a sense of mutual obligation and of common ends. The new liberals could not accept the first unreflectively for fear of uncritically condoning tradition and custom. As for the second, the new liberals recognised that the nonrational, in Hobson's case even the irrational, had a place in social life,[55] but they also conceived of social evolution as transforming those nonrational emotions and instincts into purposive and systemic conduct. Hobson spoke for all new liberals when he proffered self-determination as the coordination and cooperation of impulses and desires in conformity with a conscious plan.[56] Although both types suggested that groups could be based on nonvoluntary membership, in terms of entry and exit alike, the new liberals took the discussion further. While they believed the main nonvoluntary group to be the nation,

---

[53] Ibid., pp. 160–63.

[54] Freeden, *Ideologies and Political Theory*, p. 178ff.

[55] J. A. Hobson, "The Ethical Movement and the Natural Man," *Hibbert Journal* 20 (1922): 667–79; Hobson, "Notes on Law and Order," *Nation*, 24.10.1925, 14.11.1925.

[56] J. A. Hobson, *Problems of a New World* (London, 1921), p. 252.

grounded on both affective and instinctive ties, they also regarded the state as the rational agent of the nation-cum-community. In other words, the state was entrusted with the crucial function of enabling the transformation of a nation into a community, and the community ensured that the state was democratically answerable to it.[57] Unlike other groups, to and from which entry and exit were not only possible, but ethically and politically fundamental, the nation (seen as a natural grouping) and the community (seen as an inevitable evolutionary development) were thus elevated as an integrated entity to the status of ontological necessity.

What the new liberals share with recent theorising is the belief that groups are entitled to have their opportunities equalised in a society. They differ, however, in three major respects. First, over the nature of those opportunities; second, over the importance accorded to the internal purposive and democratic control of a group; and third, over the counter-claims of society, of the nation-cum-community, over the groups themselves. In this third dimension emerges another distinct contribution of the new liberals to conceptualizing community. When contemporary communitarians refer to cultural minorities, they focus on two aspects. First, they subscribe to a specific understanding of marginalised groups, one that concentrates mainly on the preservation of distinct community life-styles and practices, and tends to ignore alternative groupings in which members of a cultural group may be in an internally competitive, unequal relationship, say over questions of gender. Second, many contemporary communitarians underplay the multiple membership of individuals in cross-cutting groups, some of which promote practices of crucial importance to the goods their members require.[58] Some such groups are inimical to the concerns of nongroup members; others are not. Thus, in group as class, one defining feature could be the desire to maintain power and hierarchy, or to gain as large a share as possible of available economic goods. For the new liberals, one facet of group conduct was precisely the pernicious aspect of group sectionalism as a central concern of liberalism. The inequality of groups in terms of their economic interests and opportunities is, however, less pronounced in the particular ideology of egalitarianism contained in American political culture.

The other aspect of the new liberal attitude to groups was a recognition that some groups are significant in contributing to individual and social

---

[57] Hobhouse, *Liberalism*, pp. 226–34. On Hobson's mature summing up see J. A. Hobson, *Democracy and a Changing Civilization* (London, 1934).

[58] Walzer is an exception, arguing that tribalism can be transcended by multiple identities that divide passions. See M. Walzer, "The New Tribalism: Notes on a Difficult Problem," *Dissent* (Spring 1992): 164–71.

goods, but their mutual relationship—with a few notable exceptions[59]—
is not one of equals. While Hobhouse is disappointing in his lack of any
attempt to solve these problems, Hobson's notion of federalism was the
linchpin of his structural solution, in its endeavour to balance potentially
competing interests among groups. Hobson saw in each individual a
unique personality, a member of a class or group, and a member of the
wider community.[60] His democratic tendencies, notwithstanding his
strong conception of organicism, allotted instinctive wisdom to the people, even in highly civilised communities. Hobson believed that the social
attributes of human nature evoked a vital communion of thought and
feeling with race, society, even humanity.[61] Among groups, federalism allowed for both autonomy and union,[62] though in fact those two limited
concepts were replaced with a new one, more subtle and dynamic. Neither
individual nor social selves were completely separate. Federal arrangements were predicated on a belief in a broad area of mutual interest and
common sympathy, which also allowed for individual and group diversity
in all areas not inimical to that broad area. Federalism was equally emphatic in insisting that socioeconomic groupings require their own say,
and that such groupings impact upon the capacity for welfare, as distinct
from the capacity to choose one's identity and life plans. That set of beliefs
was so central to the liberal tradition that its anaemic philosophical counterpart must be seen as a somewhat different animal. In other words,
federalism eschews the introduction of a new laissez-faire legitimation of
the quasi-equal status and worth of different cultural groups under the
umbrella of group autonomy. Instead, it offers a mixture of integration
and separation that represents the manifold allegiances of individuals and
groups in society. Furthermore, it privileges a positive attitude to cooperation and puts a premium on the development of individual and social
attributes as a hallmark of a liberalism in which welfare, liberty, and sociability are mutually defining and constraining values, and in which all three
are conceived as goods to be pursued.

Contemporary philosophical liberalism is formulaic liberalism, all too
frequently sacrificing real-world complexity in the search for succinct
rules. The new liberals avoided this method, and one reason why they did
so was because they believed individuals to be in multiple, and asymmetri-
cal, relationships. The variety of human relationships pertained to the
concurrent association of individual to individual, individual to group,

---

[59] Hobhouse's views on the rights of national groups to their own self-determination are
one such instance.

[60] J. A. Hobson, *Towards Social Equality* (London, 1931), p. 5.

[61] Hobson, *Work and Wealth*, pp. 355–56.

[62] Hobson, *Problems of a New World*, p. 253.

and group to group. These nexuses were often, but not always, encapsulated in rights. Some of them served to promote liberty, some to promote welfare, and some to promote sociability, and the balance among these was in continuous flux, rationally monitored by responsible and critical individuals and groups. Revising one's ends was never the sole argument for liberal rights, nor was it posited in a zero-sum relationship with other liberal values that required rights protection. That was the liberal logic emerging from the interpretative position of the new liberals.

The new liberal case study reminds us that one of the features of liberalism is the dread of sectionalism, which is by definition the abandonment of the larger ethical purview. It attunes us to the fact that the mature liberal tradition has always sought to balance individual liberty and the requirements of community, not to support the one or the other. Indeed, the individualist-collectivist divide, that staple of late-nineteenth-century analysis, had long been jettisoned by scholars as a false categorisation, only to reappear recently under its current liberal-communitarian guise. The new liberalism reflected the sociological ontology of the times, cross-fertilised with developmental and welfare themes that have always been evident in the liberal tradition. It illustrates the polysemic range of the concept of community and the diverse ways in which it may be integrated with liberalism. It offers a more extensive notion of the political, with consequent benefits as well as pitfalls. It may also have been too optimistic about the benevolence of the state for our tastes, and too enamoured of the promise of social harmony. Conversely, if—paradoxically—late-twentieth-century approaches have something new to offer liberalism, it is the growing recognition that community has much to do with ties of emotion and sentiment, not merely with the consciousness of the purposive rational agent, be it individual or group.[63] This diachrony of horizons may, not least, enable us to put some of our own "self-evident" premises to the test in raising the question: What is liberalism?

---

[63] On this question, and its links with nationalism, see chap. 10, below.

CHAPTER THREE

The Concept of Poverty and Progressive Liberalism

> Up to the Eleventh of November 1918, the State was
> primarily an organisation for national defence or for
> aggression against other States. Since that date it has
> become primarily an organisation for the prevention or
> mitigation of poverty, by combating disease, ignorance,
> social disorder and unemployment, and for the care of
> such dependents as children, widows, aged persons, and
> others suffering from physical and mental disability.
> —Gilbert Slater, *Poverty and the State*

THOUGH THIS sweeping opinion, expressed in a book on poverty in Britain published in 1930, has not proved correct in the longer run, there was nevertheless more than a grain of truth in it.[1] The reasons for the elevation of poverty to a central concern of state and society lie in social and economic developments that began almost a century before 1918. But they were reinforced and further precipitated by new theoretical and ideological insights, especially in the generation before the First World War.

This chapter investigates the idea of poverty as developed by progressive liberals in Britain at the turn of the nineteenth and twentieth centuries as well as the transformations it underwent in the general process of formulating the thinking and policies at the root of the welfare state. This requires a focus not on what poverty was but on what it was thought to be, and how changing understandings of poverty shaped the reality that reflective employers of the term perceived and contributed to the formulation of welfare thinking. I shall therefore not concentrate in detail on the parallel issue concerning the methods of combating poverty, many of which were abetted by the legitimisation of state action that new liberal as well as moderate socialist thought endorsed and instigated.[2] In the period under examination a plethora of interpretations of poverty, old and new, combined to create a confusing and sometimes contested range of meanings. Out of these internal tensions there arose a complex and polysemic

---

[1] G. Slater, *Poverty and the State* (London, 1930), p. 443.
[2] I have discussed some of the relevant issues in M. Freeden, *The New Liberalism: An Ideology of Social Reform* (Oxford, 1978).

concept that played a singularly different role in the diverse ideological and historical contexts in which it was situated.

The greater comprehension of the nature and causes of poverty, far from resolving the debate over its form, revitalised and diversified the concept of poverty. This is all the more interesting in view of the prevalent assumption that poverty had been on the decrease in the latter half of the nineteenth century. Though that was asserted in absolute terms, and the notion of relative poverty was unknown, it was dawning on social reformers that poverty was not simply an observable occurrence but also a function of changing criteria. In particular the American reformer Henry George deserves mention for his influence on the thinking of British progressives in countering the rosy hypotheses of nineteenth-century capitalists. His pioneering approach challenged the prevalent assumption that modern civilisation was eradicating poverty. Instead he saw poverty as permanently associated with wealth making and progress, as long as the social injustices consequent upon land ownership and rent were not removed.[3] George's singular pursuit of the full taxation of land values resulted in too narrow an interpretation of the potential of his argument, for his message clearly focused on the wider ethical responsibility of societies for the phenomenon of poverty. It was left to later liberals and socialists to latch on to this by realising that a system that encouraged monopolies in general also produced poverty as a symptom of the exclusion of the many from the fruits of those monopolies.

Among the competing conceptualisations of poverty that vied with each other for recognition and legitimacy in the pre-1914 generation, four can be singled out. First, there still existed a residual association of poverty with criminality or antisocial behaviour; in that sense it was classified not so much as a condition than as a legal and administrative category. Second, poverty was defined in terms of the character shortcomings of specific individuals that, while not directly delinquent, deserved no encouragement from society. Third, poverty denoted a nonjudgmental characterisation of disadvantaged individuals located beneath a specified point on a quantitative scale of income or means at their disposal. Fourth, poverty referred to a spectrum of nonmonetary and nonmaterial indicators that removed certain individuals from a wide range of benefits a society had to offer. This last conceptualisation was invariably seen as the function of social arrangements that had become closely linked to the notion of poverty itself, a perspective that could optionally be attached to the third conceptualisation as well. Some of these positions obviously

[3] H. George, *Progress and Poverty* (London, 1931; 1st ed. 1879), pp. 9–13, 200–211, 385–92.

coexisted with others; most contained crucial subdivisions that require further exploration.

In addition, even disregarding the moral aspect of poverty to which the first two conceptualisations alluded, the identification of socioeconomic causes still left open the question of individual or social responsibility for poverty, depending on one's assumptions about the degree of human control over social and economic arrangements. For those who saw poverty as the inevitable by-product of a successful market economy, there was little to be done about the losers in the competitive venture, apart from apportioning them sympathy and a supererogatory measure of relief. As with the democratic political process, a zero-sum game was presumed to have been played in which not all could win, but the game was believed to be intrinsically fair. The condemnation of the losers, if at all, hinged not on their personal morality but on their relative inefficiency. Ineptitude was after all very a different defect from idleness and profligacy. Hence the Victorian age saw the emergence of new criteria of individual capacity that, while frequently run together with the more traditional issues of character, were drawn from the world of business and industrialisation. In its extreme version this viewpoint regarded the poor as superfluous, because nonproductive, members of society.[4] The malfunctioning individual, for whatever reason, was still the unavoidable by-product of an unalterable and proper social order.

From the 1880s changing perceptions of the causes of poverty rapidly transformed attitudes towards it. Instead of primarily indicating a moral weakness of individuals at the ethical and cultural margins of society, poverty began to be seen as the consequence of socioeconomic forces that necessitated the unmediated engagement of organised society in its treatment. The old distinction between the destitute and the poor—the former dealt with by the state, the latter mainly the province of disorganised private charity and philanthropy—was called into question, and the state was gradually persuaded to assume a broader sphere of responsibility. Leading social reformers began to strike a new note. Henrietta Barnett, who with her husband, Canon Samuel Barnett, ran the first and most famous settlement house, Toynbee Hall, wrote: "A national want must be met by a national effort. . . . while more than half the English people are unable to live their best life or reach their true standard of humanity, it is useless to congratulate ourselves on our national supremacy or class our nation as wealthy."[5]

---

[4] W.D.P. Bliss, ed., *The Encyclopedia of Social Reform* (New York and London, 1897), S. V. "poverty," p. 1074, especially the views of F. H. Giddings.

[5] H. O. Barnett, "The Poverty of the Poor," in S. A. and H. O. Barnett, *Practicable Socialism* (London, 1888), p. 20.

On one of the rare occasions when Parliament discussed poverty directly, in a debate on the "Poor in Large Towns" in 1889, it was pointed out that "if there is great and widespread poverty which requires relief, it is right and proper, and better for the country, that we should know of it, and, if possible, attempt some relief of it."[6] During a four-hour debate the chronic nature of much poverty was identified, thus removing the phenomenon from the realm of the vicissitudes of fortune and challenging its temporary nature. A Liberal motion was proposed that declared chronic poverty to be "a danger to the well-being of the State," and the responsibility for some aspects of poverty was shifted to the public sphere: "Civilized government fails unless it attends to the wants of the least influential of our fellow-creatures." But the moral-economic divide was by no means a mutually exclusive one. The seconder of the motion was categorically clear about a distinction between two types of poverty: "poverty which is the result of misconduct—the retribution which follows upon intemperance or indolence" and "preventable poverty which I and those who agree with me say bad laws have made and good laws can repair."[7]

Despite overwhelming opposition at the time, the artificiality of much poverty was recognised, as well as its contingent relationship to social arrangements that, being the product of social decisions, however unconscious or unplanned, were reversible. This may be appreciated as part of a broader detachment of late-Victorian liberal thought from the natural law theories that still held sway in many branches of political theory, whatever their current guise as precepts of political economy, human psychology, or, more traditionally, a divinely supported social order.[8] But nevertheless, as debate after debate demonstrates, it was almost impossible to make a statement on poverty without at least paying lip service to the theme of the undeserving poor.

This dual theme suggests that even among the great majority of progressive thinkers, an advanced appreciation of the general problem ran in parallel with disapproval of the conduct of the poor.[9] Throughout the prewar years, the concept of the deserving poor retained its appeal for the reform-minded. When debating the question of the aged deserving poor in 1899, Parliament typically conflated two separate issues, for whether or not one could bring poverty on one's own head through weaknesses

[6] H. Broadhurst, *Hansard*, Third Ser., vol. 334, 1440 (2.4.1889).

[7] R. T. Reid, *Hansard*, Third Ser., vol. 334, 1450 (2.4.1889).

[8] "What is going on under the operation of natural laws should not be interfered with," was the typical comment of one conservative MP in the poverty debate (S. Gedge, *Hansard*, ibid., 1463).

[9] As Ashford has observed, "the philosophical discussion of liberalism in Britain never lost its moralizing tone" (D. E. Ashford, *The Emergence of the Welfare States* [Oxford, 1986], p. 35).

of character, old age was hardly a morally culpable condition. Yet H. H. Asquith, future Liberal prime minister and later to become the chaperon of old-age pensions, agreed wholeheartedly with the limitation of pensions to those of good character, thus underlining the conception of pensions as a reward for useful service, or for decent social conduct, rather than as a recognition of the universal right not to suffer dehumanising hardship.[10] Similarly, Asquith's young colleague, the Liberal reformer and politician Herbert Samuel, announced in 1903 that "an attempt must be made to distinguish between deserving and undeserving persons, and that could only be done by the test of labour."[11] To the extent that unemployment was the immediate cause of poverty, workers of character would, it was argued, rise to the challenge to accept relief work—significantly modelled on the unattractive less-eligibility pattern of the 1834 poor law—as proof of their commitment to better themselves.

The run up to the 1908 Old Age Pensions Act repeatedly exemplified the moralistic undertone. "Conditions of some kind there undoubtedly must be—conditions as to character, conditions as to residence, and I should certainly say myself conditions as to means," announced Asquith as chancellor of the exchequer in 1906 to general approval in an early debate on pensions. He was supported in that view by the new liberal MP G. P. Gooch who, while insisting that pensions were "the most urgent and pressing of social reforms" demanded a "test of character."[12] R.A.B. Haldane, Liberal politician and intellectual, summed up the official Liberal approach in three categories. The "idle, parasitic" class "has to be dealt with by the quasi-penal policy"—old attitudes died hard. The second required curative policy, "the helpless, the sick, the insane, the children who are not looked after by their parents." The third were those "who have deserved well of their country . . . who through no fault of their own cannot maintain themselves."[13] The dichotomy between deserving and undeserving was simply accompanied by a humanitarian disposition towards those incapable of self-help and by a system of public rewards for those who had exhibited individual effort, however unsuccessfully. These official attitudes showed little innovation in reconceptualising poverty. It was by that time hardly a breakthrough to claim, in the words of the president of the Local Government Board, John Burns, that the time had come to go beyond "charity, pauperism and the relief of the destitute."[14] Albeit, a minority of opinion opposed attaching too

[10] H. H. Asquith, *Hansard*, Fourth Ser., vol. 70, 413 (24.4.1899).

[11] H. Samuel, *Hansard*, Fourth Ser., vol. 118, 315 (19.2.1903).

[12] H. H. Asquith, G. P. Gooch, *Hansard*, Fourth Ser., vol. 153, 1337, 1346–47 (14.3.1906).

[13] R.A.B. Haldane, *Hansard*, Fourth Ser., vol. 190, 664–65 (15.6.1908).

[14] J. Burns, *Hansard*, Fourth Ser., vol. 186, 68 (13.3.1908).

much importance to character because of the difficulty of devising a discriminatory test.[15] They were keen to establish pensions "in a manner that was wholly divorced from the Poor Law."[16]

In the event, the 1908 act incorporated not a stringent thrift test, but a more limited assessment, as David Lloyd George put it, "to exclude the loafer and the wastrel."[17] This represented a prominent shift in thinking about poverty. The criteria of business efficiency, initiative, and personal responsibility in financial affairs so central to the mid-Victorian ethos were played down, though not eliminated. Pensions provided the intellectual breakthrough that progressive reformers needed in order to argue the more general case for social solidarity and the reciprocity of socioeconomic relationships.[18] Paradoxically, the older conception of the no-gooder "free riding" on the back of society remained a spectre that haunted reformers, and the very successes of those reformers made some of them more eager to preserve the distinction between poverty and pauperism. As one writer saw it, it was precisely because it was now possible to "remedy the evils of poverty before they have ripened into the worse evils of pauperism" that "the more liberal treatment of honourable poverty and the more drastic severity with pauperism will . . . go hand in hand."[19] This logic was not followed through in pensions legislation, however. The disqualification of paupers was provisional (it would have been impossible to maintain administratively) and by 1911 an amendment to the act was passed that removed the disqualification for the recipients of poor relief.[20]

The immediate scene for a more sophisticated interest in poverty was set by its depiction in statistical terms, in particular from the 1890s onwards through the famous surveys of London and York conducted by Charles Booth and B. Seebohm Rowntree, respectively. Booth, though no progressive, was cited approvingly by those who knew of his pioneering survey. Rowntree, on the other hand, was associated with advanced liberal circles and continued to wield influence on questions of poverty for a further half-century. In part, theirs was an attempt to rescue poverty from its late-Victorian subjective, emotive, and literary representations and to set it on a scientific footing available to all politicians and social reformers irrespective of their beliefs and attitudes. The attempt failed, as all such attempts invariably must. Ideologies can always harness science

[15] J. Burns, *Hansard*, Fourth Ser., vol. 153, 1357 (14.3.1906); H. Cox (opposed to pensions), *Hansard*, Fourth Ser., vol. 169, 229 (13.2.1907).

[16] Sir F. Channing, *Hansard*, Fourth Ser., vol. 174, 478 (10.5.1907).

[17] D. Lloyd George, *Hansard*, Fourth Ser., vol. 190, 578 (15.6.1908).

[18] "Pensions and the Poor Law," *Nation*, 16.3.1907.

[19] "Poverty and Pauperism," *Nation*, 16.5.1908.

[20] Slater, *Poverty and the State*, p. 228.

to suit their particular perspectives and programmes, and so it was that yet again a plethora of attitudes could be attached to apparently uncontroversial facts.

The surveys of Booth and Rowntree, which found about 30 percent living beneath the poverty line, both rendered a great service to the comprehension of poverty and, correspondingly, a minor disservice. For the first time objective evidence was provided that demonstrated its immense spread and its detailed ingredients. Poverty was seen to be far more pervasive an occurrence than the destitution recognized by the technical status of pauperism. It was also portrayed in concrete terms that brought home the material and physical aspects of low income. Too facile a representation of the evidence, however, would also have encouraged the reduction of poverty to nothing more than a question of income or, rather, the lack of it. Rowntree's findings in particular, shocking as they were to a public conscience little aware up to that point of the actual conditions of the poor, seemed to indicate a unidimensionality of the issue. It appeared that in order to eradicate the problem of poverty all that was necessary was a slightly larger income for the poor third of the population of York.

There is relatively little indication of the ideological and theoretical aspects of the concept in Rowntree's report. But there are a number of indirect clues. His distinction between primary and secondary poverty is illuminating. Primary poverty related to insufficiency of earnings to maintain a minimum physical efficiency. Secondary poverty related to earnings that would have been sufficient for maintaining physical efficiency had not some portion been absorbed by useful or wasteful expenditure. The implications of this classification for the meaning of poverty are significant. Primary poverty would suggest that the remuneration of the individual was simply and totally inadequate, and that the fault lay first and foremost with the private employer, or with the illusory "freedom of contract" between employer and employee that had been the subject of so much criticism since T. H. Green wrote his famous pamphlet in 1881.[21] Secondary poverty saw the poor not just as passive victims of the decisions of others but as actively complicit in their own fate, for reasons good or bad. Drink was singled out as the main component of secondary poverty. Disappointingly, Rowntree failed to develop his notion of *useful* expenditure that would account for driving a family beneath the poverty line. He included expenditure on health, housing, and nutrition in his discussion of physical efficiency and therefore connected it to primary poverty. But one could have expected, for example, unforeseen spending on education, heating, or illness that would have been "useful" without being physically essential. What Rowntree was prepared to concede was that drinking and

---

[21] T. H. Green, *Liberal Legislation and Freedom of Contract* (London, 1881).

betting were themselves the consequence of adverse living conditions rather than character defects. He was also eager to see poverty not as an isolated issue but as part of the wider social problem, linked to "the relative duties and powers of the State and of the individual, and with legislation affecting the aggregation or the distribution of wealth."[22] To that extent, Rowntree reflected opinion as well as contributing to its change.

The 1890s witnessed the rise of sophisticated discussions of poverty that provided frameworks for the interpretations of both Booth and Rowntree, while the concept of poverty interacted with broader themes. Traditionally in the history of British political ideas a distinction has been drawn between individualism and collectivism, attached to a theory of state intervention as the central feature of ideological development. That framework—reducing complex phenomena to a unilinear sequence—is not the most auspicious for explaining the movement that occurred in welfare thinking. The changing mood concerning poverty was not just a reflection of the new role accorded to the state; that role was as much a consequence as a cause of a plurality of developments. The question of poverty is thus better served if seen as part of a number of different idea clusters: the popularity of organic theories of society is one, the emergence of the modern idea of citizenship is another, and the ascendancy of new perspectives on human nature and needs is a third.

On the whole the question of poverty was tackled indirectly, through specific preoccupation with its various symptoms—unemployment or idleness, drink, lack of housing, ill health, and low pay. The organic theory of society, however, drew these separate strands together, regarding them as both cause and consequence of poverty, while proclaiming poverty itself as a social problem in a deeper sense: not merely one that concerned other members of society but one that comprehended poverty as an intrinsic disorder of society, rather than of the individuals suffering it. Poverty was transferred from the realm of normal social life to that of an aberration of social organisation, and its elimination advanced beyond mere humanitarianism to incorporate the very survival of society.

It was in that vein that one of the foremost commentators on poverty, the statistician, politician, and writer Leo Chiozza Money, could claim that "a labourer, whether he worked mentally or physically, worked not only for his employer, but for the nation at large . . . . he was in a very real sense a contributor to the greatness and wealth of his country, and, therefore, it became the duty of the State to assert itself consciously on his behalf."[23] In his best-selling book *Riches and Poverty* Money had spelled out the message more clearly, arguing that the government of Brit-

[22] B. S. Rowntree, *Poverty: A Study of Town Life* (London, 1901), pp. 117–18, 175–80.
[23] L. Chiozza Money, *Hansard*, Fourth Ser., vol. 169, 242–43 (13.2.1907).

ain was poor, not only some of its most valuable subjects. To keep a government poor, with funds insufficient to satisfy the necessaries of the nation entrusted to it, meant to keep it weak, and thus to inflict on it an impoverishment of a different nature.[24] The organic analogy taught that if the part was diseased, the whole would be afflicted. Ultimately for reformers like Chiozza Money, "the only true riches of the nation, men and women, these are the people themselves."[25] Policies that undermined their flourishing were policies directly counter to the welfare of their society—a socially suicidal course of action. Poverty was hence seen not only to have deplorable social causes but damaging social effects.[26]

These themes began to infiltrate through to Parliament, not the least because so many radical social reformers exercised by questions of poverty—Chiozza Money, Rowntree, the politician and journalist C.F.G. Masterman, the Fabian and Liberal Percy Alden, the temperance reformer A. Sherwell—were MPs at the time of the reforming Liberal governments of 1906–14. Both Asquith and Lloyd George reflected the new mood in making it "the business of the State" to deal with problems of poverty. But it was not just a matter of saving the community "from the scandal of unmerited suffering or misfortune" that "reflect nothing but discredit upon the State which imposes them."[27] Samuel asserted that the problems arising from poverty were the largest and most urgent the nation had to deal with, and declared, in organic fashion, that such issues were questions of national concern because if they are neglected, "the whole nation is the poorer." He put the issue in the context of the liberal self-developmental aspiration to the best life, to include not only material comfort but health and knowledge, all of which poverty prejudiced.[28]

To a considerable degree, Liberal MPs presented these growing apprehensions in a manner by which it might be easier to convince the better-off, that is, by dressing them up as a financial proposition: "as far as the State is concerned nothing is so costly as poverty," or, more blatantly with respect to the minimum wage, "it is only enlightened capitalism to see that they fit the working man of this country to be efficient for the purpose of a working man, and therefore for their own interest, by every means that modern science can command."[29] Indeed, the liberal weekly *The*

---

[24] L. Chiozza Money, *Riches and Poverty* (London, 1905), pp. 319–22.

[25] Ibid., p. 329.

[26] See J. Harris, *Unemployment and Politics. A Study in English Social Policy, 1886–1914* (Oxford, 1972), p. 147.

[27] D. Lloyd George, *Hansard*, Fourth Ser., vol. 190, 585–86 (15.6.1908); H. H. Asquith, *Hansard*, Fifth Ser., vol. 16, 841–42, (8.4.1910).

[28] H. Samuel, *Liberalism: Its Principles and Proposals* (London, 1902), pp. 8–11; Samuel, *Hansard*, Fifth Ser., vol. 63, 1579 (22.6.1914).

[29] S. C. Buxton, *Hansard*, Fifth Ser., vol. 50, 514 (13.3.1913); C. A. M'Curdy, ibid., 482.

Speaker had already written unabashedly: "It is cheaper for society—waiving the question of humanity, which is perhaps out of place in politics . . . deliberately to set itself to stop the ravages of apathy, charity and despair, than to trust to the clumsiness of 'natural adjustment.' "[30] Though the vestiges of perceiving poverty as a manifestation of personal inefficiency were retained, that inefficiency was now regarded as dangerous to *society* and as curable by it, rather than viewing society as a self-serving aggregate of individuals who could simply turn their backs on self-destructive but otherwise harmless, because useless, members.

But even advanced progressives regarded poverty primarily as a malfunctioning of the *economy*, as a question of insufficient *means* at the disposal of particular groups. Thus Chiozza Money, while displaying organic and communitarian tendencies, deemed poverty to be the consequence of the maldistribution of goods. He sought to prove that "while we have acquired enormous wealth, and enjoy a magnificent national income, that wealth and that income are not distributed as to give a sufficiency of material things to all our population."[31] He thus represented the third conceptualisation of poverty at its most advanced: the elimination of poverty was a function of a redistribution that would bring financial gain to all.[32] His community was one of wealth-producers as well as wealth-consumers, from which the poor were excluded not because of what they were or what their status was, but because they could not afford the material benefits the system offered.

An instructive episode in the development of concerted thinking on poverty was the publication in 1909 of the much-awaited Report of the Royal Commission on the Poor Laws. Much has been written on the Report and on the divergences between, and overlapping of, the Majority and Minority Reports.[33] Here I focus on some advanced liberal responses in order to assess the Report's impact on the conceptualisation of poverty. Like many of its kind—the 1942 Beveridge Report springs to mind—the 1909 Reports were more of a culmination of social thinking than a revolutionary starting point. The Reports seemed to confirm the shift of emphasis to the causes of poverty; in addition, the Minority Report, written mainly by Beatrice and Sidney Webb, also put paid to the vestiges of the existing distinction between the relief of destitution and the specialised treatment of the manifestations of the much broader problem of poverty. Its much heralded "break-up of the poor law" appealed to the principle

[30] "The Coming of Distress," *Speaker*, 22.10.1904.

[31] Chiozza Money, *Riches and Poverty*, p. 5.

[32] Chiozza Money echoed Hobson's underconsumptionist economic theories, but did not follow Hobson into the fourth conceptualisation of poverty, as we shall see.

[33] See, e.g., A. McBriar, *An Edwardian Mixed Doubles: The Bosanquets versus the Webbs. A Study in British Social Policy, 1890–1929* (Oxford, 1987).

of classification that had been frequently aired in parliamentary debate, and squarely located the responsibility for addressing poverty in the lap of communal agencies. The Minority Report's excessive fondness for expert and detached treatment came in for criticism both from those who favoured self-help and from those who feared the undermining of the spirit of community by an autocratic registrar of public assistance.[34]

Nevertheless, most new liberals supported the Minority Report with varying degrees of vigour. L. T. Hobhouse in particular greeted it, in a leader in the *Manchester Guardian*, as "pregnant with . . . the hope of a great and beneficent change in the relation of the State towards poverty." With the typical caution of the liberals of the period he reminded his readers that "the individual has obligations as well as rights," but he also insisted that action to alleviate the plight of the poor should always take precedence over apportioning blame.[35] In a later comment, Hobhouse commended the Minority Report for replacing relief with public prevention, and in so doing hinted at the growing role of planning in communal strategies to improve the quality of life. The key reversal of mentality was in regard to public assistance "as a good rather than an evil, of which men should be encouraged to avail themselves rather than dissuaded from resorting to it." Hobhouse emphasised the significance of the evolution of opinion from "the conception of relief as a necessity to be kept within the narrowest possible limits by imposing the test of destitution, to the conception of public assistance as a normal incident of life, from which society and the individual may alike be the gainers."[36] Assistance was transformed from the hallmark of individual failure to a defining feature of human interaction, entrenched in the concepts of reciprocal rights and duties. Poverty could now be tackled in radical ways because some of the most efficient methods for its elimination had been transferred from the realm of ideological impossibility to that of ideological desirability. Hobhouse's colleague J. A. Hobson described the Report as "the most depressing document of our time," giving "some idea of the failure of modern society." He, too, inclined towards the Minority Report, but was concerned to ensure against the undue bureaucratisation of its proposals.[37] It must be said, however, that just as the Reports failed to have a major administrative impact, they did not—contrary to Beatrice Webb's

---

[34] See J. E. Raphael, "The Minority Report of the Poor Law Commission," in M. Freeden, ed., *Minutes of the Rainbow Circle, 1894–1924* (London, 1989), p. 190. The Rainbow Circle (on which see chaps. 4 and 8 below) was disappointingly untheoretical on this issue.

[35] L. T. Hobhouse, "The Poor Law Commission's Reports," *Manchester Guardian*, 20.2.1909.

[36] L. T. Hobhouse, *Social Evolution and Political Theory* (New York, 1911), pp. 172–73.

[37] J. A. Hobson, "Considering the Poor," *South Place Magazine* 14 (1909): 100.

aspirations—radically change the nature of the debate on poverty or the notion of poverty itself.

A development of considerable importance was the introduction of the notion of citizenship into public discussion. The association of poverty and citizenship suggested above all that the poor were debarred from certain benefits of social membership that, irrespective of their physical plight, resulted in impoverishment both to them and to their society. As with the concept of citizenship itself, more than one layer of meaning was involved. On the more elementary level, it was a question of the full formal status and recognition of individuals who were in some way equal partners in the communitarian enterprise. The status of pauper had of course involved the loss of the franchise—the formal mark of a citizen. That penalty was not only regarded as wholly inappropriate for the poor in general, but formal rights of citizenship were expanding beyond the legal sphere, and their denial entailed losses too great to be justified on the basis of economic misfortune. Initial arguments insisted that it was a matter of justice that "the State should make a provision for its citizens as a right and therefore free of the taint of pauperism."[38] Samuel registered the wider implications, speaking about the employed poor: "In the constant endeavour to obtain the means of livelihood they find their lives absorbed and lost. They have no opportunity for self-education or recreation, for enjoying family life or undertaking the duties of citizenship. This is not merely an individual loss to them; it must be regarded as a national evil."[39] In more forceful terms, the Labour MP George Lansbury reminded the House that the poor were citizens who "have the inherent rights of humanity."[40] And Hobhouse attempted to raise Rowntree's poverty line to the level of "the ethical demand embodied in the conception of the 'living wage,' " as a "birthright of every citizen of a free state" to be brought "within the grasp of the mass of the people of the United Kingdom."[41]

Other reformers were conscious of these matters but embarrassed to raise them in public for fear of being misinterpreted as unduly socialistic— a term that was increasingly used by conservatives to damn even the most timorous advances in social thinking. It is therefore both curious and significant that much of the debate on poverty was furthered through pleading the relatively uncontroversial case for children's welfare. When matters of principle were met head on, a deflection of argument on to the

---

[38] Sir F. Channing, *Hansard*, Fourth Ser., vol. 174, 480 (10.5.1907).

[39] H. Samuel, *Hansard*, Fourth Ser., vol. 186, 695 (18.3.1908).

[40] G. Lansbury, *Hansard*, Fifth Ser., vol. 21, 640 (10.2.1911). Lansbury was a member of the Royal Commission on the Poor Laws and signed the Minority Report.

[41] L. T. Hobhouse, *Liberalism* (London, 1911), pp. 163–64.

socially and morally innocent provided the means through which the concept of poverty could be deftly transformed with respect to adults as well. Because children's characters were considered to be as yet incompletely formed,[42] the question of social culpability so central to the debate on poverty did not arise. Consequently, arguments about the state's responsibility towards its citizens received a more uninhibited airing when children were discussed, simultaneously providing new perspectives on the issue of citizenship. By arguing that "the children are our future men and women, and much of our prosperity or otherwise will depend upon the amount of succour we give them in their childhood," a discreet bond was forged between society and individual, in which the welfare of *all* members of society was considered to be a matter of public interest. By commenting on children's "capacity for being of service to their country" a rudimentary expectation of contribution towards community ends was implied.[43] In return, a beginning was made towards asserting reciprocal rights and duties which were to become the nexus of citizenship.

With regard to children more than any other subject, progressive thinkers no longer felt the requirement to express poverty in terms of individual misfortune or to relegate it to the domain of private charity, and they were open about the direct benefits accruing to the community. "Every stunted child was a charge on the nation's resources; every well-developed child was a valuable addition to the nation's assets . . . every child born into the nation imposed on the nation a responsibility" —these were the words of a Labour MP voicing the opinions of many progressives.[44] For all but the most obtuse, these arguments had implications for the matured child—the adult—as well. It was "not only our duty but our business to see that they have a reasonable chance of becoming satisfactory citizens."[45]

Naturally, the definition of a satisfactory citizen was a contentious one. For some, it meant mainly the ultimate ability for self-reliance directed at supporting the existing social order. For the more progressively minded it was predicated on the claims of individuals to a full share in social goods, for which a minimum income was a prerequisite.[46] But however important this latter notion was to the elucidation of poverty, the question of citizenship could be, and was, extended further, and with it the understanding that poverty could no longer be reduced to the absence of material means alone, and its eradication could not be secured simply by spreading money around. In its widest sense the notion of citizenship in-

---

[42] R. Bray, "The Children of the Town," in C.F.G. Masterman, ed., *The Heart of the Empire* (London, 1901), p. 111–63.

[43] H. Broadhurst, *Hansard*, Third Ser., vol. 334, 1443–44 (2.4.1889).

[44] J. W. Taylor, *Hansard*, Fourth Ser., vol. 152, 1427–28 (2.3.1906).

[45] Sir R. Price, *Hansard*, Fifth Ser., vol. 16, 784 (8.4.1910).

[46] "The Claim for a Share in Life," *Nation*, 28.9.1912.

corporated not just the consumption of social goods but active participation in communal life, as well as a network of mutual rights and obligations that included direct contributions to communal purposes and direct assistance from the community towards human flourishing.[47]

C. F. G. Masterman was engaged for much of his life in bringing the condition of the poor to the attention of a wider public. A product of the Settlement Movement, which placed university graduates in residential quarters among the poor to learn and to assist, Masterman focused on an important shift in the nature of poverty. It had previously characterised specific social black spots, which were both geographically and substantively pools of vice, crime, and abject suffering. Now it was recognised as an indigent condition that affected vast numbers of the population. Indeed, as the first type of poverty was destined to disappear under the assault of the forces of civilisation, there arose as a product of that civilisation "a phenomenon and a problem unique in the history of the world."[48] Perceptively, Masterman identified the crucial feature of poverty as a segregation of one class of humanity from the rest. It pertained to a condition of exclusion from the fruits of a humane society or, in terms used above, a denial of the rights of citizenship that transcended material deprivation. Poverty was an impenetrable ghetto, a bisection of the community that sapped its strength and creativity, a continual source of human waste.

Apart from the specific social ills that most reformers identified as part of the poverty syndrome, Masterman enumerated "certain results of the modern life—the class segregation, the severance from nature, the abolition of a background—which denote a more deep-seated disease."[49] That background, he asserted, provided a unifying common bond despite the discordance of the competitive struggle. Poverty detached individuals from their normal habitat—physical, social and moral. The richer conception of human nature referred to earlier was taking shape. Masterman described the common bond as a "deep, imperative, need" of the masses, adding that "no material comfort, increased intellectual alertness, or wider capacity of attainment, will occupy the place of this one fundamental need."[50]

As part of emerging welfare thought, the community was assigned the role of meeting those human needs that individuals could not satisfy on their own. But as understandings of what it meant to be human changed, so did the comprehension of the needs without whose fulfilment people

---

[47] See M. Freeden, "Liberal Communitarianism and Basic Income," in P. Van Parijs, ed., *Arguing for Basic Income* (London, 1991), pp. 185–91.

[48] C.F.G. Masterman, "Realities at Home," in Masterman, ed., *The Heart of the Empire*, p. 11.

[49] Ibid., p. 20.

[50] Ibid., p. 30.

would be dehumanised. Poverty in the material sense was only the symptom and the rudimentary defect under which the disadvantaged laboured. It was vaguely realised that society could not function adequately without eliminating poverty in a broader sense, thus securing its own well-being. Rejecting with other progressives the old individualistic ethos, as well as the assumption that the poor would simply benefit through the increased riches of their masters, Masterman concluded: "We now know only too well that from an aggregation of individual selfishness no healthy, consistent, harmonious social fabric can be woven. . . . No commercial success, climatic advantage, or universal domination can ever resist the dry rot of isolated effort after material satisfaction, tearing individuals and classes apart, and breaking up the organism into an aggregation of isolated atoms."[51] In his acclaimed and eloquent book *The Condition of England*, Masterman called attention to "a poverty which is removed, for the most part, from actual lack of physical necessities." Echoing radical continental thinking he described it as "industrialism." A fraction of the poor, he noted, endeavoured through trade union membership "to climb into citizenship . . . with the individual development that comes from self-ordered life and some suggestion of freedom."[52]

The direction taken by the fourth conceptualisation of poverty is becoming evident. From the viewpoint of the social organism, the segregation of the poor was akin to the loss of a vital limb and the individual dehumanisation that it induced was paralleled by a qualitative as well as quantitative depletion of community. As Hobhouse argued, poverty highlighted the sectionalism that set group against group, encouraging the wrong kind of social virtues. It resulted in the inequality of power; without that equality the fair treatment of individuals was impossible. And it deprived people of the wherewithal to fully develop their character and nature in the manner to which a rational and freely choosing person would be entitled.[53]

In addition, many new liberals adopted a stronger organicist notion of community that considered it to be not only the prime locus of human sociability, or the necessary setting for individual development, but a rights-bearing entity with needs and purposes of its own that complemented those of the individuals comprising it.[54] That view of community combined with the comprehensive theory of citizenship to create a compelling view of the qualitative conception of poverty. Hobson had advanced slowly from the third conceptualisation of poverty—reflecting ma-

[51] Ibid., p. 50.

[52] C.F.G. Masterman, *The Condition of England* (London, 1909), pp. 105, 163.

[53] L. T. Hobhouse, *The Labour Movement*, 1st ed. (London, 1893), p. 17; *The Labour Movement*, 3d ed. (London, 1912), pp. 14, 16.

[54] See M. Freeden, *Rights* (Milton Keynes, 1991), pp. 67–76.

terial maldistribution—to one commensurate with his strong liberal view of community as constituting a partnership between individual and social needs. Within that framework he criticised private charity. In an attack on the Charity Organisation Society (C.O.S.), that guardian of the Victorian family through organised voluntary aid, Hobson dismissed charity as "a feeble sort of conscience money, an irregular and inadequate return of fragments of unearned income to those who have earned it, and who are disabled from ordering their lives in decency and reasonable care because it has passed from their legal possession in those processes of economic bargain where the poor are taken at a disadvantage."[55] This was "giving back in doles a portion of the profits of monopoly"[56]—a munificently hypocritical return to the poor of what was theirs to begin with.

Hobson saw the merit of the C.O.S. in attempting to retard the common process of commuting charity for payments of money, that is, in resisting the association of poverty purely with lack of financial means. He commended it for its intention to reintroduce the spirit into the form of charity, by realising that poverty needed to be contained through systematic efforts towards rehumanising its victims. But the C.O.S. had failed due to its monadist view of society as composed of individuals and separate families. Poverty could only be assailed if one recognised "the interdependence and interaction of individual character and social character as expressed in social environment."[57] That was part and parcel of the phenomenon of poverty itself—the denial of that interrelationship and the integral membership of all in the community. Only the state could offer that holistic perspective, which is why Hobson called for the "nationalisation of charity" on the understanding—in line with his reservations about the Minority Report—that the state-regulated battle on poverty be subject to strict public-spirited democratic control.[58]

Ultimately the debate was also dependent on the conceptions of human nature available to different kinds of reformers. For the C.O.S. the recipients of its services were impoverished because they were devoid of personal responsibility, incentive, efficiency, family life, decency—the moral fibre that made up character. For advanced liberals these characteristics were either of exaggerated significance or, if important, removed from their proper context. They were merely a part of a range of human features balanced in a rational harmony that was also socially influenced and shaped. Such views were echoed in Parliament. As the Liberal industrialist

[55] J. A. Hobson, "The Social Philosophy of Charity Organisation," in Hobson, *The Crisis of Liberalism* (London, 1909), p. 198.

[56] Ibid., p. 203.

[57] Ibid., p. 207.

[58] J. A. Hobson, "Charity as an Instrument of Social Reform," *South Place Magazine*, August 1909, 161–63.

W. H. Lever observed, "with regard to thrift he was not quite sure that that was the largest virtue that could be asked of citizenship. He believed there were many virtues far more useful to cultivate than that of thrift."[59]

Linked to these developments were changing perceptions of human needs. As Hobson put it in his first major contention with the issue, "By striving to educate, intellectually, morally, sanitarily, the poor, we have made them half-conscious of many needs they never recognised before."[60] Those needs were not merely physical or moral, but came to include emotional and psychological needs that pertained to individuals in a social context. Such innovative ideas about human needs were recent developments in middle-class social thinking, newly shifting views about the conditions for human flourishing.[61] Behind them was a view of human nature that was gaining ground, a nature endowed with social instincts and a propensity to attain cooperative and collective ends, and in which the more traditional individualist features of human nature were firmly kept in check by a self-critical collective consciousness directed at enhancing individual freedoms.[62] With that came a portrayal of poverty as deprivation from the opportunity to fulfil an optimal range of human needs that affected individual and community equally.

If there was a moral cause of poverty, asserted Hobson, it was to be found not "in the corrupt nature of the poor" but "in the moral cowardice and selfishness of the superior person." In the final analysis poverty reflected a deficiency in "the moral force of the community" and its elimination would follow the application of that force to the reform of economic structure.[63] That new socially anchored morality, combined with the growing ability of societies to provide material comfort for all, contrived to remove poverty from its old status as a necessary, to that of a surmountable, evil. But despite Hobson's own great interest in problems of distribution, he was indirectly critical of those who, like Chiozza Money, believed poverty to be a corollary of the inadequate distribution of the wealth of the nation. The exact equalisation of incomes, a suggestion that only George Bernard Shaw took seriously, could drag all down to poverty and, more importantly, would miss the point, which for Hobson was that "the main cause of poverty is inequality of opportunity." What some socialists did not realise was that stimulus was needed to engage the productive energies of man and that "this stimulus in its turn depends chiefly

---

[59] W. H. Lever, *Hansard*, Fourth Ser., vol. 174, 472 (10.5.1907).

[60] J. A. Hobson, *Problems of Poverty*, 3d ed. (London, 1896), p. 28.

[61] M. Freeden, "Rights, Needs and Community: The Emergence of British Welfare Thought," in A. Ware and R. Goodin, eds., *Needs and Welfare* (London, 1990), especially pp. 65–68.

[62] See chap. 6, below.

[63] Hobson, "The Social Philosophy of Charity Organisation," p. 217.

upon the opportunity open to every member of the community to do his best work." In sum, poverty was the absence of equal access to the requisites for the development of one's human potential.[64]

As the *Nation* explained, turning the old competitive ideology of capitalism on its head, "Individuals are not born with equal personal endowments, but it is the first business of civilised society to see that they are provided with equal opportunities, to make the best use of such capacities they possess for their own advantage and for the commonweal."[65] Likewise Hobson, linking again the question of poverty with liberal ideals, warned that state action—however desirable—would not in itself cure poverty, but would rather "enable poverty to cure itself by securing liberty for all to use their powers to the best advantage for their own gain and for the common good." That epitomised the new liberal approach to poverty, "the organic remedy." Poverty was predominantly the absence of the full individual development that the generation of Millian liberal theorists saw as the purpose of rational individual conduct, and that a later liberal generation also regarded as essential to communal flourishing; indeed, a requisite that a welfare-seeking community would wish to encourage and initiate. That would be achieved by opening up to its constituent parts a maximalist interpretation of equality of opportunity through public ownership or control of land, transport, credit and insurance, education, public law, and the control of monopolies.[66]

By 1914 a spectrum of conceptualisations of poverty was at the disposal of social reformers. While many conservatives still refused to abandon the label of criminality with which poverty had been tainted, progressives were faced with a different range of options through which to interpret poverty, drawing mainly from what we have termed the third and fourth conceptualisations. From those perspectives poverty represented a denial both of humanity and of sociability; an assault both on individual and on community; and an undermining of the possibility of optimising human capacities and recognising the full range of human needs. New theories of citizenship and community transported the concept of poverty into a different dimension: away from the issues of material misery and insufficient spending-power and into the realm of the negation of human status, participation, self-control, and opportunity. That progressive debate over poverty, although a century old, is still of considerable value to social democrats and liberals who wish to construct a persuasive case against such fundamental dehumanisation.

[64] J. A. Hobson, "Poverty: Its Causes and Cures," in Hobson, *The Crisis of Liberalism*, pp. 160, 164–66.

[65] "The Social Policy of Liberalism," *Nation*, 27.11.1909.

[66] Hobson, *The Crisis of Liberalism*, pp. 171–72. See also Freeden, *The New Liberalism*, pp. 149–50.

CHAPTER FOUR

Layers of Legitimacy: Consent, Dissent, and Power in Left-Liberal Languages

THE CONCEPT of legitimacy is part of the belief system of a political entity. There are no empirical indicators for when a state of legitimacy has been reached; nor are there practices that, when observed or described, lead us to assert unequivocally: this is legitimate. There is nothing in a street demonstration against cutbacks in state pensions that, had I just parachuted onto this planet, will signal to me whether marching down a road, waving banners, and shouting aggressive slogans is a legitimate act, unless I am pre-equipped with a map instructing me on whether populist and chaotic expressions of will are normal and regular, possibly even desirable; or whether they are pathological and dangerous forms of conduct that need to be eradicated. Marxists may claim that these are a necessary and legitimate challenge to an illegitimate state; liberals may maintain that these are acceptable, if somewhat exaggerated, expressions of healthy dissent without which a state would atrophy; fascists might present them as conduits of physical energy that have to sweep away the decay revealed in democratic institutions; while conservatives may condemn them as abnormal and destabilising assaults on the legitimate constitutional processes of decision making.

To establish legitimacy is, first, an act of judgment and an act of interpretation. An institutional arrangement is judged according to some set of rules, and particular practices are interpreted according to some scale of values or preferences. Legitimacy exists in the eye of the beholder. But there is far more to it than that. We need also to take on board that, second, legitimacy is not a single unified phenomenon, nor is it vested in one political object. Rather, legitimacy is layered and can be associated with the three-tier, expanding, political structures that ascend from government, through regime/constitution/state, to nation. It can be conferred on one tier and not on the others. More likely, it will be apportioned unequally among the three tiers, creating internal legitimacy tensions, and raising the issue of the sufficient or insufficient spillover of legitimacy from one sphere to the others.

Third, legitimacy can be analysed on the basis of sources and genealogy (a revered constitution, or tribal convention); processes (rituals or legal procedures); status and ascriptions (for example, a religious leader or king); ends/actions (for example, the protection of natural rights). There are of course overlaps and trade-offs among all these, but the point is that legitimacy is distributed differentially among political structures, conduct, and discourses. And fourth, rather than merely delineating a set of rules (= legality), legitimacy is a broader concept. It identifies a loosely demarcated field in which support is produced and political satisfaction and approval—themselves intangible phenomena ill-suited to objective measurement—are attained.

Even the best dictionaries trail behind the professional understandings bestowed by specific disciplines on their vocabulary. Among the definitions offered for the term "legitimate" by the Oxford English Dictionary is the following: "Normal, regular, conformable to a recognized standard type." The OED also enters under "legitimate": "Comformable to, sanctioned, or authorized by, law or principle; lawful; justifiable, proper." I have no major quarrel with these except to say that much of this is too high-minded. If we were to go to the very heart of legitimacy and identify its ineliminable component it would have to be, I believe, the acceptability of a political entity or arrangement on the basis of explicit or implicit understandings prevailing in a society. The bestowers of that acceptability need to be the members of that society or those directly affected by its arrangements, though external judges of such acceptability are not ruled out. Law and principle are optional extras here but fail to contain the richness and elusiveness of legitimacy.

Like all political concepts, moreover, legitimacy does not stand alone but is permeated by a series of adjacent, logically implied, and interlocking concepts such as authority (the rightful use of power) and political obligation (justified obedience to a political entity), and the various practices associated with those. And from within the ambit of each of these concepts, certain culturally privileged conceptions obtain priority. Constant alterations occur in whatever arrangements attract legitimacy, and these are crucially linked to prevailing competitions over ideas concerning the nature and role of the state and the conceptions of citizenship attached to those ideas.

Because of all these legitimacy is a key ideological feature. It correlates a set of practices with a set of approved maps of preferred social meanings. It also attempts—through the very notion of constructed normality it wishes to convey—to insulate the aura of legitimacy against contestation. Normality tends to invisibility—and invisibility is the preferred garb of an ideology until someone recalls the emperor's new clothes. Post-Marxists might, I suspect, refer not to Hans Christian Andersen but to H.G. Wells's classic story *The Invisible Man*. Rather than insisting that "clothes maketh the man" they might want to point out that the clothes may be all there is.

In British political thought in the half-century preceding 1914 there is surprisingly little direct engagement with the term "legitimacy." But the major debates all fall within the domain of legitimacy. Specifically, they revolve around the correct manner in which a state should act vis-à-vis its citizens, and around the institutional arrangements that should attract their general approval. In evidence, though, are both polarisations and reformulations. There was, of course, a prominent default conservative position, against which progressives had to battle. When the freethinker W.E.H. Lecky—an old liberal of an increasingly conservative disposition—wrote his noted *Democracy and Liberty* in 1896 he observed in some distress: "The most remarkable political characteristic of the latter half of the nineteenth century has unquestionably been the complete displacement of the centre of power in free governments, and the accompanying changes in the prevailing theories on which representative government should be based."[1] Lecky was concerned that what made governments legitimate was no longer merely their success in preserving order and security, or in acting on the basis of a valid contract between rulers and ruled, or even their protection of fundamental natural rights, of which property, he believed, still was one. All these had concentrated on the able and decisive discharge of authority. Even the giving of continuous voice to diverse social and political groups was now suspect, because those groups no longer coincided with the stable classes that had constituted British society. Rather, argued Lecky, the rise of what we would now call mass democracy based the state on ignorance and endangered the love of liberty. The corruption, instability, and—mainly—discontinuity these brought in their wake were clearly delegitimating forces.[2] Alluding to the French Empire after 1852, Lecky tellingly maintained that the desire for stability could be based on the fear of democracy's consequences, a fear that could itself elicit "genuine consent" for order over liberty. Hence, in a parliamentary system such as Britain's, "according to all rational conceptions of constitutional government, it should be the object of the legislator to strengthen the influence of intelligence, loyalty and property in the representation, and in every change to improve, or not to injure, the character of Government."[3]

Let us unpack these concepts for a moment: intelligence referred to the quality of decision making and understanding of public affairs on which legitimate government could rely, located firmly in the capable few. Loyalty was the preference for a disposition that favoured governmental and national projects, conjoined with the unquestioning acceptance of govern-

---

[1] W.E.H. Lecky, *Democracy and Liberty*, 2 vols. (London, 1896), p. 1.
[2] Ibid., pp. 214–15.
[3] Ibid., pp. 217–18.

mental political decisions. And property related to the correspondence of material interests between the government and the people, as well as to the preservation of a wide sphere in which the private liberty to transact property was placed beyond the legitimate domain of the state. That was the formula that ensured legitimacy both of the state—the depository of "real interests"[4]—and of the government that acted to realize those interests. Obligation to the government was undifferentiated from obligation to the state. Active and increasing interference on the part of the state, to the contrary, undermined trust; and reduced individual independence produced an increase in "national responsibility."[5] Curiously, such augmented responsibility would not enhance the prestige of the state but decrease its standing. Crucially, though, in a *malfunctioning* polity it was not the government that ran the risk of delegitimation but the state whose representative the government was.

It may be helpful to go back in time a bit, in order to appreciate the subtle changes that were taking place in understandings of legitimacy in what may broadly be called the "progressive" camp. J. S. Mill's lucid voice embodies one such position. It embraced the idea of representative government as a sine qua non, but incorporated much of the elitism the British political tradition has always associated with government, both in terms of status and in terms of capacities. Mill adapted utilitarian arguments to propose good and ideal forms of government and consequently saw the test of governmental legitimacy in "the degree in which it tends to increase the sum of good qualities in the governed, collectively and individually."[6] The immediate corollary was the need for allowing a direct input from society into government of "the individual intellect and virtue of its wisest members," and securing "the acquired knowledge and practised intelligence of a specially trained and experienced Few," for "a government is to be judged by its action upon men and by its action upon things."[7] Mill was traditional in his ring-fencing of the role of the government as a repository of good sense, and in ensuring that occupiers of governmental office were sharply distinguished by their skills from those they governed. Unlike Lecky, however, Mill wished to recruit those skills freely and not lock them into a class structure, and to that end the actual participation of citizens in government, local or national, was imperative. Moreover, he was radical in redefining the functions of government as enabling the orderly progress and self-development of individuals as well as the general welfare of the community.[8]

[4] Ibid., p. 218.
[5] Ibid., p. 278.
[6] J. S. Mill, *Considerations on Representative Government* (London, 1910), p. 193.
[7] Ibid., pp. 195, 241.
[8] Ibid., p. 243.

What, then, about room for dissent? In contrast to the second half of the twentieth-century, in which, understandably in view of the totalitarian tyrannies, as well as the rediscovery of cultural minorities, a resurgence occurred in the literature concerning the right to resist and concerning civil disobedience, dissent is notably underemphasised in most of the period under discussion. Dissent is clearly a form of political power, and its identification as countervailing power paralleled the recognition that governments exercised power, and that liberals in particular have traditionally been uneasy about the wielding of governmental power. Liberals frequently warned against "the corrupting influence of undivided power" but, as with Mill, they recognized the necessity of governmental and constitutional power, "adequate to preserve order and to allow of progress in the people,"[9] and they assumed that the taming of political power would be attainable simply through appropriate institutional arrangements involving accountability and democratic elections.

Dissent was, of course, the order of the day in relation to unrepresentative governments, let alone corrupt governments. But these were believed to be located in an early phase of an evolutionary curve, at the end of which beckoned the civilised state, equipped with a government that would elicit general support. The role of minorities was only partly recognised; more importantly, the possibility of dissent was not heavily built into institutional pluralism because of the latent homogeneity of interest and purpose presumed to exist in British society. Mill was, after all, one of the advocates of a theory of rational human harmony that—when fertilised with a theory of cooperative human evolution and notions of *social* utility—had a powerful impact on fin-de-siècle thinking at the turn of the twentieth century. His musings on minorities do not formalise dissent. Minorities are numerical, not cultural; they are often geographically dispersed, when they should connect a nationality—in sum, they are clusters that embrace no group features. A numerical minority was typically a temporary aggregate from which its members sought to escape, rather than an entity, usually believed to be permanent, in which they took pride. For Mill, national minorities, too, were best served by blending with more advanced national groupings or by acquiring a separate state of their own.[10] The liberal fear of sectionalism and of class, while according the right to dissent generously to individuals, reinforced the delegitimation of group dissent. Even when upholding that right for individuals, it should be said, civil disobedience was rendered superfluous by a model that placed total faith in free speech and open channels of debate, supported by proportional representation. Persuasion, rather than coercion, was the

[9] Ibid., pp. 242, 325.
[10] Ibid., pp. 363–66.

guiding method. The one minority accorded superior respect was that of "instructed minds,"[11] but even then British intellectuals rarely recognised themselves as an intelligentsia, continental-style. The legitimate state, to put it forcefully, was the state incorporating intelligent government, tempered by democratic participation. In Mill's words, "a democratic people would in this way be provided with what in any other way it would almost certainly miss—leaders of a higher grade of intellect and character than itself. Modern democracy would have its occasional Pericles."[12]

It was precisely the capacity of the modern state to adapt to change, rather than its craving for continuity, that generated a new consensus and constructed a new legitimacy, even if the language of politics needed to move slowly. There emerged a gradual acknowledgment of the changing function of the state as the broker of, reactor to, and even initiator of reform, rather than a responder to isolated *grievances*—as they had formerly been described—for private injustices, or to deviation from accepted legal norms. The state was now increasingly recognised as the prime instrument for catering to group demands and to social *needs*. Hence, the *status* and *stasis* of the government as the principal basis of legitimacy were diluted in favour of a continuous assessment of its *actions*. Whereas the conventional emphasis, even among reformers, continued to identify the fair representation of all members of society as a *necessary* condition for legitimacy—which led, among others, to debates about the virtues of the referendum, advocated by J. A. Hobson as "a countermove to the despotism of the industrial and political bosses"[13]—representation was no longer a *sufficient* condition. In the light of the British obsession with form and heritage, a new normality had to be carefully fabricated.

One example of the cautiously changing language of legitimacy may be found in the writings of Ramsay MacDonald. Against the unadventurous formulations of Lecky and Mill, the new vocabulary was innovative though far from revolutionary, as befits the moderate socialism that emerged in Britain, respectful of the state and of its political institutions. On one level, MacDonald was very protective of the "dignity and authority" of parliamentary government, for example when the Opposition employed delaying tactics to prevent the passing of a bill. "The House of Commons is being degraded," he wrote in 1910, "and a degraded House

---

[11] Ibid., p. 266.

[12] Ibid., p. 269.

[13] J. A. Hobson, "The Referendum," in M. Freeden, ed., *Minutes of the Rainbow Circle, 1894–1924* (London, 1989), p. 128 [5.10.1904]. See also J. A. Hobson, *The Crisis of Liberalism* (London, 1909), p. 15, and J. Meadowcroft and M. W. Taylor, "Liberalism and the Referendum in British Political Thought, 1890–1914," *Twentieth Century British History*, vol. 1 (1990), pp. 35–57.

of Commons really means a degraded democratic authority."[14] A year later, he ridiculed the sacred cow of British political practice, referring to "that most fatal of all Parliamentary theories, that it is the duty of an Opposition to oppose."[15]

The respect for the British Constitution was paramount in the following, rather startling, words from a socialist leader:

> When we are dealing with the illogical, but all the more natural, habits and methods of Parliamentary government that have grown up through centuries . . . we have to remember that it is utterly impossible to protect the organisation thus created by amended rules or by mechanical devices of any kind. The fabric of the organisation has been built of the stuff of which honour, good sense, reverence, respect, consist.[16]

That appeal to a natural political culture in which legitimacy was ingrained through deference to tested political practices would have pleased any conservative, and would have irritated Mill. On the other hand, Mill would have praised MacDonald's apparent mirroring of his own position that a specialised political nucleus, the "professional politician," differentiated from the body politic as a whole, would supply the "skilled intelligences" the "art and science of government" required.[17] Such ideological overlap was not unusual, though its sources were different—the elitism of civilised culture envisaged by liberals meshed with the socialist expectation that a science of society would produce an elitism of technical expertise.

Nevertheless, there was another, much more intriguing, aspect to MacDonald's theory of the legitimate state. An unexpected incarnation of Rousseau's general will made a sudden appearance. Why this device re-emerged in the early years of the twentieth century, after having been derided in the British empiricist tradition for its strange continental features, is itself a curious matter. But its vital importance lies in the shift of arguments for legitimacy away from constitutional issues alone towards the provision of human well-being as the acid test of the conceptual triad of legitimacy, authority, and obligation. The general will could only achieve that because it was successfully grafted onto well-being as a feature of *social*, not individual, utility. At the end of this long road the welfare state comes into view, its notion of welfare combining with democratic accountability as the two characteristics of the legitimate polity.[18]

---

[14] J. Ramsay MacDonald, *Socialism and Government*, vol. 1 (London, 1910), pp. 115–16.

[15] J. Ramsay MacDonald, "The British Parliament in Relation to Proposals for the Future. . . ." in A. Parsons, ed., *Second Chambers in Practice* (London, 1911), p. 129.

[16] Ibid., p. 118.

[17] Ibid., pp. 119, 124.

[18] See M. Freeden, "The Coming of the Welfare State," in T. Ball and R. Bellamy, eds., *The Cambridge History of Twentieth-Century Political Thought* (Cambridge, 2003), pp. 7–44.

At the heart of MacDonald's theory of legitimacy was a deep faith in the existence of a national, and hence indivisible, will. If older theories of legitimacy referred to *sovereignty* as indivisible, by which was meant the ultimate location of unchallengeable authority in a state in order to overcome and stifle internal conflict, the progressive mind was turning to the *elimination* of conflict and dissent through postulating an organic theory of society. Social unity replaced legal unity as the distinguishing feature of advanced human organisation. In MacDonald's desire to limit the opposition and to abolish the second chamber was an evident distaste for pluralism and dissent uncommon even among his new liberal colleagues.

In referring to legitimacy in the period under examination, the position of the House of Lords patently requires a mention. On one level the controversy surrounding it constituted the most salient case of attempted institutional delegitimation of the times. Yet the lack of democratic accountability of the House of Lords was so obvious to progressives that in a significant sense it was not central to their *theories*, as distinct from its centrality for their political *agitation*. The removal of an anachronistic hindrance would merely pave the way for releasing the suppressed forces that social and political theory had conclusively identified. As an aspect of the problem of legitimacy the issue of the House of Lords was, strictly speaking, merely a particular case of the broader relationship between legitimacy and representation. As Hobson had warned, "There can be no more foolish error than to represent the veto of the House of Lords as the only, or even the chief barrier to the free realisation of the will of the people."[19]

Concealed behind the obvious appeal to constitutionalism was this second layer of expectations aimed at the state.[20] MacDonald again:

> The part which the electors directly play in legislation is equivalent to the part which the general life of an organism plays in the modification of any special function of itself. The whole body has a life, the organ contributes its part to that life and accommodates itself to that work. A State has to accommodate itself to the ideals and beliefs regarding economics, international influence, justice, and the final purposes of the Society to which it belongs.[21]

Significantly, an organic theory could not envisage a tension between the actions of a well-appointed state and its government, thus eliminating the standard case for civil disobedience when a government failed to realize the fundamental purposes of the state. MacDonald came to the same view

---

[19] Hobson, *The Crisis of Liberalism*, pp. 7–8.

[20] On MacDonald's view of the state see J. Meadowcroft, *Conceptualizing the State: Innovation and Dispute in British Political Thought, 1880–1914* (Oxford, 1995).

[21] MacDonald, *Socialism and Government*, vol. 2, p. 3.

adopted by conservatives when collapsing the space between government and state, but for very different reasons. Whereas for conservatives, as Max Weber had understood, the maintenance of traditional rule simply obviated the need for raising the issue of legitimacy in the first place, Mac-Donald used a different path of argument. After all, "the State, after a democratic suffrage has been established, is no longer an authority external to the individual . . . democratic government is an expression of the will of the people who have to obey the law—not perhaps the will of every individual, but the communal will, voicing the need of all classes in relation to the community."[22] A community could not disobey its own rational voice, for "self and government are but aspects of the same individuality."[23]

Crucially, also, it was far more difficult to delineate the rules of civil disobedience when these were triggered by a failure to provide social utility. Civil disobedience was, conventionally, a decision related to individual conscience, when a government had breached a clear law or principle. It was mediated through conceptions of private morality, even if it adopted a public and collective format. It could not easily be reformulated as a socially instigated withdrawal of approval for failure to further the interests of the community. It also seemed, in turn, that legitimacy could no longer be conceptualised as problematic by social- or general-will theorists, because they discarded it as a determinate characteristic of the relations between individual and state. Nevertheless, it is precisely because legitimacy was now sustained by social approval rather than legal obedience that progressives still referred to it.

Hobson had toyed with even stronger versions of a general will. For him, too, legitimacy was the result of eliminating the gap between individual and state:

> This failure to sympathise with the government or to recognise its actions as his actions, the tendency of the man in the street to be against government, are due to certain solid facts in the structure of politics which prevent the will of the people, the general will, from exercising real control. Between the ordinary citizen and actual government stands a false party system, financed and operated by little cliques of wealthy, leisured, ambitious, often unscrupulous, men.[24]

Hobson began by rejecting the older contract theory, according to which the social contract implied "equality of reason" and "expected benefits on the part of the contracting parties," while translating such benefits into individual rights. Instead, he echoed John Ruskin in accepting that "the actual inequalities of human nature carry with them certain rights of au-

---

[22] J. Ramsay MacDonald, *Socialism and Society* (London, 1905), p. 71.

[23] MacDonald, *Socialism and Government*, vol. 2, p. 155.

[24] J. A. Hobson, "Political Ethics of Socialism," *South Place Magazine* 13 (1908): 129.

thority and duties of obedience. Reverence naturally, necessarily, follows any recognition of superior powers." For Hobson, however, the test of legitimacy was a question of identifying an unconventional seat of authority. Rather than locating it in an enlightened upper class, as Ruskin had done, or in an educated elite, as Mill had done, Hobson found those superior powers to lie in society itself, as a self-governing, democratic, organic nation. Social inequalities would pale into insignificance in relation to the fundamental superiority of an organic perspective over that of any individual member.[25]

In a companion article, Hobson went on to develop "the doctrine of the general will . . . which Rousseau, among moderns, was the first clearly to enunciate." It may well be that the renaissance of the general will was nourished within the debates of the Rainbow Circle—that progressive discussion group of which both MacDonald and J. A. Hobson were active members. A year before writing both articles, Hobson had attended a Circle talk on Rousseau by the cofounder of the Social Democratic Federation, Herbert Burrows, at which Burrows insisted that "the 'general will' and the principle of 'give and take' must be at the root of the true social organism of the future."[26] Hobson asserted in turn that "the idea of Society as a political organism insists that the general will and wisdom of the Society, as embodied in the State, shall determine the best social use of all the social property taken by taxation."[27] In early-twentieth-century writings such as these, Hobson came down on the side of emphasising the rights of the social organism as against an egalitarian individualism, rejecting Mill's preference for plural voting for the educated, but accepting their disproportionate role in governmental decision making. "Political power," he insisted, "ought to be distributed in proportion to the ability to use it for the public good." Even then, significantly departing from MacDonald's monolithic view of society, Hobson recognised the ancient "right to resist" as a safeguard against governmental injustice: "the right to petition against grievance on the part of the organs and their cells is accompanied by an ultimate 'veto,' or the right of rebellion, which is the basis of popular government." The justification for this was not, however, through the conventional language of individual rights. Rather, "it is advantageous to the organism that these rights of suggestion, protest, veto and revolt should be accorded to its members."[28]

[25] J. A. Hobson, "Ruskin and Democracy," *Contemporary Review* 81 (1902): 107–8, 110, 112.

[26] H. Burrows, "Rousseau," in M. Freeden, ed., *Minutes of the Rainbow Circle, 1894–1924*, p. 86 [27.3.1901].

[27] J. A. Hobson, "The Re-Statement of Democracy," *Contemporary Review* 81 (1902): 265–66.

[28] Ibid., pp. 267, 269.

Once again, the governing class were to be the experts who determined the organic policy; once again, the requirement was to control that group through fostering a wide, "self-protective intelligence" in the nation at large. As with Mill, Hobson feared bureaucracy and lack of education more than he feared bad government, which, presumably, would be more directly accountable to the voters. This was not always the case among liberals, though. Herbert Samuel had remarked already in 1896: "The question of the democratic franchise is . . . mixed up with that of who is the wise citizen." And he directly identified the issue that still worried some reformers: "A universal suffrage may still militate against the welfare of individuals in other directions."[29] And Ramsay Muir, one of the future organisers and propagandists of the Liberal party, observed in 1910: "Just when the Englishman is becoming most passionately alarmed about the danger of bureaucracy, he is also becoming in practice more and more dependent on bureaucracy." Yet, he concluded, "it is obvious that the business of government has become inconceivably more complex, elaborate and minute than it used to be . . . it has become so vast and so multifarious that it can only be carried out by an enormous and carefully graded hierarchy of officials, each expert in his own field."[30]

These nuances aside, legitimacy was invested in the state acting as the responsible agent of society. The identification of state with social interests transferred the test of legitimacy from representation to the discharge of crucial social functions, and defused the traditional antagonism between government and individual through redefining the core political relationship as that occurring between a mutually supportive state and society. From another perspective, in recognising society as the locus of moral values, the Idealists H.J.W. Hetherington and J. H. Muirhead suggested an imaginative distinction between ultimate ethics and institutional proximity: "If our highest obligation is to a Society that transcends the State, our nearest is to the State itself." But like most progressive thinkers they assumed that, in the long run, the state would assist in realising the human ideals embodied in the community.[31]

All this implied that a dual transformation attached the legitimate state to a new social unit—society—and assessed the acceptability of state activity in terms of its morally necessary role in furthering social welfare. The ideology of modern welfarism was beginning to take shape. This process was abetted by a systematic liberal shift: the forbidding importance of political power was no longer exaggerated as a menace that re-

---

[29] H. Samuel, "The Democratic Franchise," in M. Freeden, ed., *Minutes of the Rainbow Circle, 1894–1924*, p. 38 [7.10.1896].

[30] R. Muir, *Peers and Bureaucrats* (London, 1910), pp. 4, 7, 11.

[31] H.J.W. Hetherington and J. H. Muirhead, *Social Purpose* (London, 1918), p. 256.

quired the sheltering of individuals from wayward usurpers, tyrants, or bullies, but was modulated in a standpoint that accorded unity of purpose to a beneficent, responsive, and enlightened state. Power was depathologised but also deproblematised. Hobson expressed this succinctly: "Power is not an evil in itself, nor is the desire to exercise power. . . . Force applied selfishly by individuals or sections is bad. Force applied socially by organized society is good."[32]

Paradoxically, the very institutions liberals had feared in the past, and whose excesses had hastened the rise of liberal thinking in the first place—the state and its government—were now hailed as the agencies through which a flawed society could be reconstituted and redirected along liberal principles. The conventional notions of the state as wielder of force, as locus of sovereignty, as symbol and source of authority, were not forgotten, but they were marginalized at the expense of seeing the state as enabler, provider, agent of social virtue, and honest broker. Accordingly, constitutional mechanics were no longer deemed adequate to counter the problems of concentrated power. Rather, this required instilling a new civic spirit of mutual concern in which individual rights and communal welfare would be balanced.

The experience of the First World War modified such views considerably—not in the relinquishing of the social aims of the state so much as in shattering the confidence of progressive thinkers in the close fit between such social interests and governmental action. The preservation of individual liberty consequently resurfaced as a standard by which to measure good government, precisely because the right to dissent regained some of the urgency it once carried.[33] That urgency reflected the disillusionment with the kind of consensual society that new liberals and progressive socialists had confidently predicted. They had done so on a wave of continental social theories: some primarily German, promising individual self-realisation in an ethical (*Sittlich*) state; others predominantly French, reassuringly underpinning social knowledge with scientific "facts."

Even prior to 1914, liberal thinkers such as L. T. Hobhouse were contemplating the relationship between liberty and compulsion in the new theories of social welfare and the interventionist state. Let us recall that in the *preutilitarian* liberal state a central criterion of legitimacy was the amount of free action that the state, as locus of political power, reserves for the individual. While both mutual aid and mutual forbearance were the twin ends of social life, Hobhouse recognized that the latter was the more difficult to secure. It covered not only privacy, but also personal

---

[32] J. A. Hobson, *Democracy After the War* (London, 1917), p. 23.
[33] See M. Freeden, *Liberalism Divided: A Study in British Political Thought, 1914–1939* (Oxford, 1986), pp. 18–44.

idiosyncrasies and development, in line with the progressive growth model of human nature that had become salient in the wake of the Enlightenment. Hobhouse was keen to pursue the difference between state and society that Idealist thought had elided, and to that end—unlike other progressive theorists—he addressed the question of legitimacy directly. First, the state occupied the sphere of definite institutions, laws, and rules and, second, it was a compulsory association. Within these constraints the state was expected to address the moral and spiritual interests of its members. For, "it follows further that the legitimate functions of the state must depend upon the whole circumstances of the society which is under consideration." Such circumstances referred to a community's composition. For instance, a culturally homogeneous society required less compulsion in maintaining basic order and cohesion. It could therefore permit itself to introduce compulsion for more specific and advanced purposes, such as furthering social cooperation.[34]

Here a tension emerged within the progressive camp. The revolution that occurred was, Hobhouse believed, in ceasing to regard law as something imposed on the people by a superior, parental authority. Popular government introduced the combined efforts of a mass of people, a "collective sense of responsibility" based on popular reason, earnestness, and self-sacrifice—a view not quite in tune with the greater elitism of Mill, MacDonald, or Hobson. The corollary of Hobhouse's argument was a stronger emphasis on liberty and individual rights but—employing the language of the future welfare state—a genuine right was only one that also served as a condition of social welfare. State legitimacy, ultimately, was a question of securing "the best conditions for the common life" when only compulsion could do the job.[35] Unlike many other progressives, displaying a liberal unease with the concentration and exercise of power, Hobhouse had a fresher sociological understanding of their inevitability. Legitimate power was power employed to underpin community, when community would not otherwise be forthcoming. But community at all times entailed a respect for the socially orientated free choices of individuals. State regulation—of private contracts, for example—was justified as extending the sphere of individual liberty.[36] T. H. Green's appreciation of the pernicious role of economic power underlying a bogus freedom of contract, paralleled also in Hobson's analysis of imperialism as a maldistribution of power, had made its mark. Yet both for Green and for Hobson, this extended field of power could simply be eliminated by employing virtuous social practices.

---

[34] L. T. Hobhouse, *Social Evolution and Political Theory* (New York, 1911), pp. 186–89.
[35] Ibid., pp. 198–99.
[36] Ibid., p. 201–2.

A key feature of the liberal vision had always been the rational abolition of social conflict. In the mid-nineteenth century the ideology of free trade had offered a rationale for such aspirations, promoted through the widening circle of civilisation, as liberals would spread their message of harmony across the globe. That expectation, however, clashed with another feature of the liberal vision, namely, the encouragement of pluralism as diversity and eccentricity. On closer examination, such pluralism was itself only possible within a relatively homogeneous cultural community, as it relied heavily on the absorption of fundamental ideological codes through which the ends of both society and state would correspond. Political obligation to the nation—often silently equated with society—was never in doubt, but neither was there, as I have argued, a likely gap between obligation to a state and its government. Democratic organicism, after all, had promised to bridge that gap.

The conservatives, too, had their vision, one in which respect for state authority would bring in its wake a stability in which civil society could go about its business unmolested by any attempt at planning or coordinating individual lives and the activities of voluntary groups. Even the left-liberal vision had initially allowed for civil disobedience only against corrupt forms of government. Left-liberals engaged, together with their moderate socialist equivalents, in a quasi-Marxist exercise of willing power away from human relationships and thus rendering the question of legitimacy superfluous in the long run. The experience of the war, however, brought that vision down to earth through rediscovering the very human imperfectibility that conservatives had always proclaimed. Nevertheless, the criteria of legitimacy were reformulated inasmuch as the state assumed the responsibility of smoothing the paths of the natural social forces that human development and social evolution had identified. Ethics and science were made to coincide, as they had so often done in the course of the nineteenth century, when the legitimate state became the rational agent of change as well as the traditional guardian of individual rights; specifically, when it became the embodiment of collective control over the benevolent currents through which civilisation flowed.

By 1914, some of the inadequacies of organicism and of rational liberal harmony had been realised. Those inadequacies, now ran the new pluralist argument, encompassed both a blindness to the inevitable diffusion of power in society, and an unwillingness to conceive of society as containing *three* units of analysis: society itself, individuals, and groups. Consensus and dissent were thus placed in a more complex interrelationship. A. D. Lindsay gave theoretical expression to the resurgence of pluralism and to the need to recognise that a legitimate state had to gain acceptance from groups as well as individuals. A multiplicity of organisations other than the state was typical of modern societies, he maintained, and forms of corporate will had to be added to the notion of the general will. Diversity of belief was accompanied by a plethora of independent associations and—of particular significance—of loyalties and the liberty to express them. State legitimacy would presumably have to satisfy such groups as well, but it would be diminished insofar as it attempted to intrude upon areas in which those associations performed their functions more adequately than could the state. Sovereignty as ultimate authoritative power was therefore far from being vested absolutely in the state.[37] As Hetherington and Muirhead argued, "when a conflict arises between the claims of the State and those of other associations, the State may not assume, as a matter of right, its own priority."[38]

These analyses, however, had their limits. Hetherington and Muirhead recognised that increased obligation to the state could result from the particularly vital social purposes it discharged, and that a government would derive authority from the training of educated citizens.[39] Nor did a greater stress on group heterogeneity entail a significant *cultural* pluralism. Lindsay, too, regarded a common culture and sense of nationality as a prerequisite of good government, and a single state as based on a common standard. The upper tier of political obligation towards a nation was never under challenge.[40]

To conclude, in terms of political language, the vocabulary of social contract had gone out of fashion, while progressives regarded Weber's traditional rulership with great ambivalence. Legal processes were still treated with gravity in a country that prided itself upon the prudent nature of its procedures and rules, but the preservation of legality itself was no longer the cure-all for a well-run polity unless it was subject to broad, participatory, democratic input, and unless it was supportive of fundamental, welfare-enhancing, social processes. The political institutions of society, hitherto imagined as existing on a separate external plane, were relocated into its midst. The quest for the authority of ability was extended beyond the ambit of individuals to include also the acknowledgment of social and evolutionary intelligence. The question of the justified approval of the state, its institutions and activities, reflected the plasticity and flux of the objects of legitimacy. Legal, political, ideological, and social criteria offered different layers of legitimacy, occasionally reinforcing, occasionally competing with each other. At a period of dramatic conceptual and social change, and of a reassessment of the nature of the state,

---

[37] A. D. Lindsay, "The State in Recent Political Theory," *Political Quarterly* 1 (1914): 128–45.

[38] Hetherington and Muirhead, *Social Purpose*, p. 228.

[39] Ibid., pp. 208, 228.

[40] On this issue see also chap. 10, below.

the reliance on informal tests of legitimacy, tentative and not yet firmly established, became the hallmark of the era. It may be exaggerated to claim that legitimacy had relocated to an emotional base, but certainly the treble reference to substantive standards of social justice, to the granting of a voice to rising social groups (including, importantly, women), and to the provision of welfare measures was in part a recognition of the utilitarian appeal to broadly based need-satisfaction rather than to the intellect of constitutional lawyers.

Much of this was as yet tacit. The language of legitimacy provided concepts that were still too constricted for the dynamic emerging practices of social reform, and the complex consensual relationship between individual, society, and state had to be interpreted through alternative vocabularies of organicism, welfare, social utility, and social function. Whether this conjured up a new quasi-conservative equilibrium is a matter that critics of the welfare state argue about to this very day.

CHAPTER FIVE

J. A. Hobson as a Political Theorist

J. A. HOBSON was one of the half-dozen most influential political thinkers in late-nineteenth—early-twentieth-century Britain, a fact that even the partial revival of his fortunes has infrequently brought to light. The main reason for this oversight has two complementary facets: Hobson's contribution lay chiefly in his formulation of a liberal version of British welfare thought, an ideological genre that until recently was accorded insufficient recognition; and, conversely, recourse to conventional modes of political theorising, utilising existing traditions, or referring to the constructs of leading individuals, was not paramount in his work. It is symptomatic that in the various reading lists Hobson appended to his more political writings, he cites mainly the works of his progressive contemporaries, for he was a leading member of a group that refashioned both the substance and the methods of argument employed in applying political analysis to contemporary affairs. L. T. Hobhouse, H. J. Laski, C. Delisle Burns, G. Wallas, and H. N. Brailsford are more likely than Locke, Mill, or Green to appear as authorities to which Hobson deferred, and they would often return the compliment.

But this was no mere mutual admiration society; it reflected a dual shift in the understanding of the formation of political thought and of the practical level of relevance on which it was believed to be functioning. The "greats," the men of genius whose personal input forged the nature of generations of political thinking, were no longer in evidence, and their past exemplars were perceived to talk in an abstract and generalised language that served little immediate purpose. The spread of education and the rise of new means of disseminating and popularising views, especially the press and the mass-circulation book, allowed the development of a via media in political thought between the rarefied reaches of professional philosophy and the utterances of the common people. It highlighted the fact that political systems were best appreciated as responding to the ideas of what, had the term not been so alien to British tongues, might be termed an "intelligentsia."

It is significant that Hobson, whose self-description as an economic heretic related not the least to his principled scepticism and personal bitterness with respect to academic economics, permitted those views to colour his opinion of philosophy as well. In a piece on William James's pragmatism, the philosopher was praised for opposing "the jargon of false prophets in Oxford or elsewhere who will not accept what they consider a degraded view of the philosophic function." Hobson was attracted to James, despite serious reservations about the subjectivity of his pragmatism, because James believed it was "possible to unstiffen the academic notions about ultimate truth and reality."[1] Yet again, the world of formal scholarship loomed as a stuffy and threatening obstacle in the path of the creative and experimental thinking Hobson considered himself to be undertaking. And, not for the first time, Hobson sought the middle way between the doctrinaire and absolute oneness of some philosophical positions—a specific reference to the Idealism he had encountered and rejected at Oxford—and a "loose, man-made multiverse."[2] Not the least valuable aspect of his method was his assertion that an "ought" was a second-order "is"—an ideal worthy on its own of being a subject of scientific inquiry, an assertion that opened up ideological and moral utterances to scholarly examination.[3]

Nevertheless, it is of some value to appraise directly Hobson's performance as a political theorist in the conventional sense. This can involve examining his assessments of, or more usually allusions to, some of the political thinkers who belong to the great apostolic tradition—assessments serving as a rule as reference points to Hobson's own political ideas. It would also involve evaluating Hobson's employment of key political concepts, among which I have chosen to single out rights, liberty, and equality.

Hobson approached the central political thinkers of the Western tradition quite understandably not as a political philosopher but as a historian of ideas. As a firm espouser of evolutionary progress he evaluated them either as contributing towards, or retarding, the socially oriented rational humanism he believed was reaching its maturation. Sometimes they merely served as vulgarised tags to be hung on well-known positions. Thus the political principles of Hobbes and Machiavelli were described as "imposing the narrow self-interest of each State as its supreme law,"[4] in contradistinction to the contemporary emergence of an international morality. Other theorists received closer attention. In a revealing centenary piece on Tom Paine, illustrating yet again Hobson's continuous quest for the middle ground, Paine was criticised for his excessive rationalism: "his overconfidence in the efficacy of abstract reasoning upon the rights of men, and his disregard of the sentiments and traditions which *mainly* govern human

---

[1] J. A. Hobson, *A Modern Outlook* (London, 1910), pp. 42, 46.

[2] Ibid., p. 50.

[3] J. A. Hobson, *Free-Thought in the Social Sciences* (London, 1926), p. 223.

[4] J. A. Hobson, *The Crisis of Liberalism* (London, 1909), p. 249. See also idem, *Free-Thought in the Social Sciences*, p. 199.

conduct."[5] Lest this remark be misunderstood as a possible conservative undercurrent in Hobson's critique, it should be placed within Hobson's holistic appreciation of human ability and his increasing awareness of the role that biological forces and psychological and emotional attributes played in normal human behaviour.[6] Indeed, Hobbes was elsewhere denounced by Hobson as a "moral anarchist" for asserting that reason must always be the servant of the passions, when human beings were capable of exercising directive control over their vital and necessary drives.[7] On the other hand, Paine was praised precisely for forsaking the "cold utilitarian conception of individual rights" and for the warmth and passion he injected into his "rich human gospel of a commonwealth."[8] Moreover, Paine had performed the important historical function of introducing a revolutionary note of antiauthoritarianism into British political debate.[9]

The major political thinker most frequently mentioned by Hobson was J. S. Mill. I will concentrate here on Hobson's comments on Mill's political principles as distinct from Mill's economic teachings. Here, too, we have a centenary piece as evidence, written by Hobson in 1906. His appreciation is hardly original, but that is not the point. Hobson's interpretation of Mill, however vicarious, is but a means to understanding the issues that concerned Hobson. Two of them are conspicuous: the degree to which individual thought reflects the "spirit of the age" (Mill's own phrase, of course), and the emphasis on the communitarian aspect of human life. In line with his evolutionism, Hobson saw both Mill's early Benthamism and economic individualism, and his later conversion to a form of moderate socialism, as products of the different moods of social inquiry that Mill's life had spanned. The "rigid theoretical individualist," with a Spencerian view of the minimalist state gave way to the "political individualist," still mistrusting officialdom, and finally to the denouncer of Benthamite philosophic radicalism and laissez-faire. Mill's conversion to socialism was not misinterpreted by Hobson. He rightly realised that Mill went no further than adopt a type of cooperation and issue a plea for social (and economic) reconstruction. Hobson had already quoted in the past from Mill's *Essays on Socialism* bemoaning the lack of any idea of distributive justice in present society.[10] Mill's famous distinction between self-regarding and other-regarding actions, just as famously dismissed by many of Mill's contemporaries, was for Hobson an instance of

---

[5] Hobson, *A Modern Outlook*, p. 93 (my italics).

[6] See M. Freeden, *Liberalism Divided: A Study in British Political Thought, 1914–1939* (Oxford, 1986), chap. 7.

[7] J. A. Hobson, *Wealth and Life* (London, 1929), p. 17.

[8] Hobson, *A Modern Outlook*, p. 94.

[9] J. A. Hobson, *Democracy* (London, 1934), p. 7.

[10] J. A. Hobson, *The Social Problem* (London, 1901), p. 16.

Mill's restricted conception of man's social nature and the consequently narrow role he accorded the state.[11] In his later work Hobson reviewed the issue more carefully and independently, offering an alternative criterion for intervention in individual actions: "The only absolute rule of social interference is the consideration whether such interferences conduce upon the whole, and in the long run, to enfeeble or to strengthen the will and capacity of the subjects of such interferences to realise themselves in ways serviceable to society."[12]

This passage must not be read as asserting the supremacy of society over the individual, for Hobson specifically tied it to "the value set upon the unique in personality," and to the right to make mistakes not too costly to others.[13] Indeed, Hobson was inspired by Mill's pluralism and love of liberty, in particular the value Mill bestowed on experimentation. These fit into Hobson's own biological and psychological theories, in which eccentric outbursts of social disorder—caprices, impulses, superfluous vital energy—could endow society with the creativity and originality necessary to its development.[14] The respective stress on either order or adventure bore differing social costs, and would influence the degree of state and social intervention. The role of expertise, which Hobson is sometimes accused of carrying too far, was in fact assessed by him in typical Millian tones: "It is the problem of a reliable, disinterested, and progressive expertism on the one side, and an intelligent assimilative public on the other"—"the active intelligence of the consumer" of standards of behaviour.[15] A science of consumption was nothing but the corollary of democratic control over knowledge and power.

It is also instructive that, when discussing the role of disinterested free thought, Hobson replaced Mill's moral perspective with a psychological one. Mill's rational belief in the persistency of truth when confronted with falsehood was dismissed by Hobson in favour of the hypothesis that "seeing facts and thinking straight are more attractive to the mind than seeing falsehoods and thinking crooked." Good arguments satisfied both the sense of creative power and—a point made far too infrequently—appealed to the aesthetic feelings.[16]

In assessing Mill's contribution to contemporary thinking, Hobson predictably focused both on the holism of Mill's mature system and on its

[11] J.A. Hobson, "John Stuart Mill," *Speaker*, 26.5.1906.

[12] Hobson, *Wealth and Life*, pp. 332–33.

[13] Ibid., p. 333. See also J. Allett, *New Liberalism: The Political Economy of J. A. Hobson* (Toronto, 1981), p. 187.

[14] J. A. Hobson, "Character and Society," in P. L. Parker, ed., *Character and Life* (London, 1912), pp. 94–96.

[15] Hobson, *Wealth and Life*, pp. 334–35.

[16] Hobson, *Free-Thought in the Social Sciences*, pp. 279–80.

failure to bridge the gaps caused by the increasing specialisation of the disciplines. Though Mill "destroyed the hedonistic calculus" at the basis of Benthamite utilitarianism, "unfortunately it survived almost intact in the economic science where it was sustained by an illusory interpretation of distinctively economic conduct."[17] Mill was nevertheless cited by Hobson for his "humane liberalism," for his early adumbration of a theory of social progress, and for his break with the economics of self-interest. This kind of careful pruning in search of support was essential to the intellectual status of Hobson's theories, denied as they were a formal podium of academic respectability.

The other major theorist to whom Hobson often referred was Marx. As a rule Hobson did not differ from his countrymen in overstressing Marx as the diffuser of a one-sided and crude value theory of labour, advanced as dispassionate "scientific" analysis,[18] as well as the progenitor of a revolutionary materialist theory of history, proffering "a doctrine of the absorption of all industry by the State"[19]—the latter a common misunderstanding of Marxist argument. In 1902 Hobson gave a talk on Marx to the Rainbow Circle, the debating society in which he was a central figure. This offered a far more benevolent, if equally limited, view that identified Marx as the main creator of democratic socialism, "a popular policy of progress with intellectual foundations, a systematic shape, and practical ends." All these were words with positive connotations in Hobson's vocabulary, especially the notion of an orderly, democratically evolving, and just society. The rational, evolutionary message that lay behind the revolutionary theory elicited Hobson's sympathy. Hobson's reservations about Marxian economics and about Marx's presumed predilection for violence did not detract from his appreciation of Marx's gospel of proletarian self-help and Marx's virulent arraignment of a pernicious private capitalism.[20]

The best statement of Hobson's political ideas can be found in *The Social Problem*, the most sophisticated and original of his books on social and political issues. In this work Hobson adumbrated his communitarian theories and presented a version of utilitarianism that has been central to British welfare thought, though remaining almost unrecognised by contemporary philosophical critics of utilitarianism. As Hobson put it in an important statement referring to the work of T. H. Green:

The premature abandonment of the utilitarian setting by many thinkers, through pique arising from the narrow and degrading interpretation given to

---

[17] Hobson, *Wealth and Life*, p. 109.
[18] Hobson, *Free-Thought in the Social Sciences*, chapter 5.
[19] Hobson, *The Crisis of Liberalism*, p. 137.
[20] M. Freeden, ed., *Minutes of the Rainbow Circle, 1894–1924* (London, 1989), p. 99.

the term, has not been justified . . . even philosophers, like the late Professor Green, who are stoutest in repudiating Utilitarianism, invariably return to that terminology to express their final judgment on a concrete moral issue. . . . The particular vices of some special form of utilitarianism, the insistence that desirability was entirely to be measured by quantity and never by quality, the stress upon physical enjoyment, and the short range of measurement, which were somewhat incorrectly attributed to Bentham's system, are not inherent in utilitarianism, and need not deter us from using its convenient language.[21]

In sum, Hobson was not prepared, as are so many scholars, to condemn utilitarianism simply because its extreme version was linked to a measurable calculus of pleasures and pains, or because it appeared to overrule other ethical and humanitarian claims on individual action. The search for the best social arrangements *compatible with* individual flourishing was the first responsibility of a rational community, and it was undeniably a utilitarian perspective bereft of its earlier shortcomings. Instead of the unconstrained version, opposed by philosophers for threatening the equal respect that should be accorded to each person and for cherishing collective above individual welfare,[22] Hobson favoured a constrained version that wishes to maximise or optimise only a liberal-humanitarian conception of human nature.

The outcome was a Hobsonian synthesis crafted out of the reinterpretation of utility as welfare, an organic conception of society, and a developmental view of human nature. Hobson's originality and importance as a political theorist rest on this particular concoction.[23] But that synthesis was also assisted by an examination and re-evaluation of some political concepts in a manner that underpinned Hobson's radical ideas. His most innovative treatment was reserved for the notion of rights, and here we also have the opportunity of linking his opinions on classical political thinkers with his conceptual analysis.

The predominant mode of rights theory in late-Victorian Britain was still firmly attached to natural rights doctrine. That doctrine was characterised, among others, by the following features. It entertained a nondevelopmental notion of rights—a fixed list impervious to space or time. It postulated a presocial conception of the origins of rights, and regarded societies and states as institutions whose purpose was to guarantee them. It held to an absolutist weighting of rights as trumps that override other interests or considerations.[24] Finally, it offered a highly individualistic in-

---

[21] Hobson, *The Social Problem*, pp. 4–5.

[22] See, e.g., R. Frey, ed., *Utility and Rights* (Oxford, 1985).

[23] I have elaborated on this view in *The New Liberalism* (Oxford, 1978), and in *Liberalism Divided*.

[24] R. Dworkin's suggestive phrase in *Taking Rights Seriously* (London, 1977), p. xi.

terpretation of the functions of rights, as protectors of personal capacities against infringements by other people and, in particular, by governments. It is scarcely surprising to find Hobson criticising Locke, Rousseau, and Paine for propagating such views. It is just as interesting to note that current rights theories reproduce some of these perspectives, and that Hobson is no less radical in comparison with late-twentieth-century rights discourse than he was a century ago with respect to past thinkers and to his contemporaries.

The initial critique of Locke gave way to an appreciative but somewhat tendentious interpretation of his contribution to a theory of limited rights. Hobson saw Locke's strengths not only in his labour theory of value, which paved the way for a rudimentary economic science; Locke was now singled out not so much for his famous theory of private property as for his limitation of the use of property by the requirements of personal need or enjoyment, and by the property rights of others. In particular Hobson was quick to stress a point close to the hearts of his contemporary radicals: "There can be no 'natural right,' in Locke's sense, to superior natural opportunities. Monopoly and rent are ruled out *ab initio*."[25] The fault lay hence not in Locke but in the failure of modern societies to evolve along the path that Locke had begun to pave. It lay also in later thinkers, Rousseau in particular, who used a method that ran contrary to scientific anthropological evidence when postulating the state of nature, rather than resting content with the poetic and imaginative vision implicit in his sense of social right.[26]

Be that as it may, the doctrine of natural rights was still one to contend with. Its ideological biases are evident even in its refined modern versions. The main thrust of such versions has been a dual one: first, they base the claim for human rights on what is unique in human nature—the God-given abilities to live rationally and morally, later secularised as an intrinsic measure of human dignity that each person bore, grounded on his or her capacity for choice and autonomy. Second, they emphasise the concept of an atomistic person, a self-contained bundle of capacities who has to be protected from harm inflicted by fellow human beings. Hobson queried these assumptions, and did so in a way unsurpassed by later theorists. Why this specific achievement remains virtually unknown is yet another mystery about the percolation of his noneconomic ideas and the particular patterns of influence that historians of ideas succeed or fail in tracing.[27]

[25] Hobson, *Wealth and Life*, pp. 99, 142–43.

[26] J. A. Hobson, "Rights of Property," *Free Review*, November 1893, 130–31.

[27] For a general analysis of this problem, see M. Freeden, "The Stranger at the Feast: Ideology and Public Policy in Twentieth Century Britain," *Twentieth Century British History*, vol. 1, (1990).

Instead of accepting the concern of rights theory with the securing of human moral features, Hobson used his ideas on vital human capacity to fashion a novel meaning of "natural" not, as was usually the case, in the sense of "innate" as an abstract postulate, but as relating to the empirically demonstrable powers and capabilities without which human bodies and minds would not function. As will be explained in the following chapter, the natural right to property derived both from the requirement to satisfy physical and psychological needs, the ignoring of which would dehumanise their subjects, and from the requirement to elicit from individuals conduct essential to the adequate performance of societies. It covered both welfare needs and incentives to produce and behave in socially as well as individually beneficial ways.

Hobson's contribution to rights theory is of special interest because he expanded and crystallised the innovative views that the Idealist philosopher D. G. Ritchie had concurrently been openly airing. If the essence of rights had been to demarcate the divide between public and private spheres and to ensure that the state held back from its authoritarian tendency to control the lives of its citizens, Hobson inverted the function of rights by employing them as a device to integrate collective and individual action, to consolidate the mutually dependent relationship between individual development and social progress, and to utilise the state as an enabling agency without which human rights, however obtained, were meaningless. To use later phrases, Hobson emphasised "welfare rights" at the expense of "forbearance rights."

Hobson was insistent that a right was a social concept that could not pertain to individuals per se: "If an individual is living a solitary, self-sufficient life out of society, the attribution of these natural rights is an empty form; the word 'right' has here no content or significance." Crucially, individual rights had no natural or absolute validity, for "society, and not the individual, must clearly claim, in the social interest" what such rights were. Turning the absoluteness of the notion of a right on its head, Hobson asserted that "social utility must be paramount and absolute in marking the limits of such 'rights.' "[28] This is of course precisely what critics of utilitarianism dread and, taken in isolation, Hobson's statement is a clumsy one. Though his argument that the rights to life, liberty, and property are neither absolute nor wholly individual—because a right without a power that affects others is impossible (an extension of Mill's logic)—is a reasonable one, Hobson's early writings on rights are ambiguous from a liberal viewpoint, and they exhibit his early difficulties in remaining within liberal boundaries. While conceding that the right to life was not a useless phrase, he then added, in a fashion with which Sidney

[28] Hobson, *The Social Problem*, pp. 88–89.

Webb or the young William Beveridge would have sympathised, that "it is the supreme duty of society to secure the life of all serviceable members, together with an implication that the life of every member shall be deemed serviceable, unless known to be otherwise." The rider left much to be desired: what was the basis of such knowledge, and who were the knowledgeable? Nevertheless, bobbing and weaving, Hobson again followed this by spelling out "a clear individual right to property in all 'necessaries of life,' " a doctrine he thought tended "to undermine radically existing notions of . . . rights." He even criticised Ritchie, albeit without justification, for moving towards the abandonment of all individual rights.[29]

Instead of basing rights on entitlements, Hobson identified needs as their principal rationale, a perspective still central to welfare thought. He refused, however, to do away entirely with traditional views of property—though linked not to hereditary birthright, but to reward for effort, a manifestation of human conduct essential to productivity. No less interesting was Hobson's readiness to employ the concept of rights where his contemporaries had recourse only to the notion of duties. It was for example commonplace at the turn of the century to discuss duties towards children without making the logical connection to children's rights.[30] Hobson challenged this approach with respect to animals, maintaining that "what the nature of a duty is for which no one has a right to claim fulfilment, I cannot myself conceive."[31] Rights and obligations were for him indisputably correlative, an issue that still elicits much disagreement among rights-theorists.

Hobson's organic holism led him to a freshness of analysis that may be contrasted with a salient modern, and frequently stunted, approach to rights shared by many philosophers. Current approaches are grounded on a view of human nature as uniquely rational and moral, and seek consequently to safeguard those attributes, and those attributes alone, by means of rights. This conception of human nature is not so much incorrect as reductionist, regarding the features conducive to the capacities for choice, autonomy, and agency as making human beings what they distinctively are.[32] Hobson would have none of this. Because he held that human features were interconnected on their various levels—physical, psychological, and emotional—he extended the meaning of "property" rights to accommodate and protect a totalist, needs-oriented understanding of human nature. Initially this meant "the satisfaction of those physical, in-

---

[29] Ibid., pp. 90, 94.

[30] See M. Freeden, "Rights, Needs and Community: The Emergence of British Welfare Thought," in A. Ware and R. Goodin, eds., *Needs and Welfare* (London, 1990), pp. 54–72.

[31] Hobson, *The Crisis of Liberalism*, p. 250.

[32] I have dealt with this issue more broadly in M. Freeden, "Human Rights and Welfare: A Communitarian View," *Ethics* vol. 100 (1990): 489–502.

tellectual, and moral wants which serve to maintain and raise individual efficiency for social service"—a position too subservient to the social perspective.[33]

In later years, equipped with a clearer and broader recognition of the psychological make-up of people, Hobson refined his position to include giving "to each what each is capable of utilising for a full human life. Capacity of use or enjoyment, not 'needs' in its narrow significance of physical or even spiritual necessities of life, must be our humanist interpretation."[34] Hobson, however, had no solution for the "limitless needs" problem. In providing neither ceiling nor standards of discrimination for the rights that could be claimed to promote human welfare, the concept of rights was potentially weakened precisely because it could perform its basic function—the prioritising and protection of human and social attributes considered essential to well-being—only with great difficulty.

Finally, on a dual social level of analysis, Hobson identified private property as an indispensable support both for personality and for community,[35] and he pushed liberal argument to its outer limits by suggesting that the community was entitled to claim separate property rights of its own in order to further specifically social ends. In his seminal 1893 article, "Rights of Property," Hobson distinguished a claim of society to property that "rests upon precisely the same basis of nature and rights as the claim of an individual," namely, ownership over one's productions.[36] To this argument he later added the distinct social needs and features society exhibited that required rights-protection.[37]

To sum up the topic of rights: Hobson countered the stasis of natural rights with evolutionary laws of development and hence with nonabsolute rights that underwent modification. To the individual as unit of analysis, he added society—both as a distinct entity and as providing ends that fashioned human character and need, all of which required rights-protection. To the morally significant attributes of choice and autonomy he added *all* features without which human life would be impoverished if not endangered outright. And to the function of rights as impediments to the intrinsic human capacity for harming others, he opposed rights as claims to elicit beneficial conduct from others, claims to reciprocate with duties arising out of the nature of the social relationship.

Hobson's views on liberty and equality predictably interconnect with his treatment of rights. Though he reiterated Green's overused distinction

---

[33] Hobson, *The Social Problem*, p. 162.

[34] Hobson, *Wealth and Life*, p. 230.

[35] Ibid., p. 164.

[36] Hobson, "Rights of Property," p. 145.

[37] Hobson, *The Social Problem*, pp. 149–50.

between negative and positive liberty, Hobson took Green's ideas a few important steps further. To begin with, it is helpful to recall that Hobson's prewar economic arguments were conducted against the backdrop of the free-trade debate. Any notion of liberty had to take account of the ideological dimensions implicit in that debate, and Hobson duly attempted to do so. He identified two freedoms at the heart of free trade: freedom of production and freedom of exchange. The former was an individualist, private, even egoistic freedom, because it was based on the accepted right of "of every man to do the kind of work which he thinks will yield him the best return." The latter was dressed up as a negative right: "the right to sell . . . produce and to buy the produce of others without legal or other unnecessary hindrance."[38] In fact, Hobson deftly extracted a communitarian rationale from this latter freedom. Instead of regarding exchange merely as a means of obtaining private economic ends, the act of exchange itself became a desirable end. Complete liberty of intercourse not only secured "a more effective division of labour, a larger general production of wealth, and a bigger share for each participant,"[39] but encouraged the promotion of a vast community of international interests. A genuine free trade would further an economic internationalism and "render the advantages in natural resources and in labour which any country might possess available to the whole world."[40] Internally, too, the abolition of "trade individualism" by means of various restrictive practices that set unions and capitalists against each other would give way to a "pooling of interests of employers and employed."[41] Clearly, too, Hobsonian free trade was only free within the framework of rational social control and coordination. As he elsewhere argued, effective economic liberty involved challenging monopolies and therefore "large permanent measures of public control."[42]

Here we arrive at the nub of Hobson's conception of liberty. "Liberty conceived in vacuo," he wrote, "the right of not being interfered with by someone else, has no substance, no value."[43] Hobson's analytical technique was both praiseworthy and faulty. His dismissal of liberty as having no intrinsic value, being instead a means to the achievement of other values, is most plausible. It has never been clear in libertarian argument what individuals are supposed to *do* with their highly prized liberty, regarded as an end. Liberty, like other political terms, is an essentially contested

---

[38] J.A. Hobson, "Protection as a Working-Class Policy," in H. W. Massingham, ed., *Labour and Protection* (London, 1903), p. 39.

[39] Ibid., p. 47.

[40] Hobson, *Democracy*, p. 22.

[41] J. A. Hobson, "War or Peace in Industry?" *The Reformer*, 15.2.1898.

[42] Hobson, *The Crisis of Liberalism*, p. 4.

[43] Hobson, "Rights of Property," p. 132.

concept, one on which no theoretical agreement is possible. Particular senses of mainstream political concepts are in practice grouped together to form decontested clusters—logically arbitrary but culturally significant, and without which no political action is possible—and Hobson certainly illustrated how concepts, rather than standing alone, only gained substance through defining each other. On the other hand, Hobson himself was unable, perhaps unwilling, to rise above the dependence of his political concepts on his ideological preferences, especially on the versions of human nature they were employed to further. To that extent, his conceptual analysis was always parti pris. Rather than playing the role of a disinterested theorist,[44] a role he criticised in later writings, he was an ideologist who made no attempt to disguise his preferences.

When discussing liberty Hobson opted for intermeshing it with equality. Especially in his earlier writings, Hobson expounded liberty as a means to attaining the goods attendant upon social membership or, as we might want to call it, citizenship. Freedom denoted "equal opportunity . . . of such access to all material and moral means of personal development and work" as would contribute both to individual and to social welfare. To that were added spiritual and intellectual opportunities through education.[45] In a well-known article Hobson elaborated on equality of opportunity as concerning access to natural resources, to industrial power, to state credit facilities, to public justice, knowledge and culture, and geographical mobility.[46]

The connection between liberty and equality is not logically entailed, however. Liberty can alternatively be interwoven with individual self-determination, choice, or rationality. Conversely, the requirement of equality may be seen as impeding free choice and action. If Hobson acknowledged those options, it was only to dismiss them both as ethically inferior and scientifically groundless. Proceeding instead from the distinction between absence of restraint and presence of opportunity, he signalled his own position by calling for a "more evolutionary idea of liberty."[47] His insistence that concepts did not have permanent meanings was a tripartite statement. It placed them firmly within a historical context; it allowed for the social construction of their meaning; and it repudiated the innate sense of words. Instead, Hobson sought to set liberty within an idea environment, currently emerging in Britain, from which a new import to the concept could be derived. This he achieved by associating liberty with a specific variant of equality—equality of opportunity.

[44] Hobson, *Free-Thought in the Social Sciences*, chaps. 1–3.
[45] Hobson, *The Crisis of Liberalism*, pp. 93–94.
[46] J. A. Hobson, "The Extension of Liberalism," *English Review* 3 (1909): 673–86. See also chap. 3, above.
[47] Hobson, *The Crisis of Liberalism*, p. 93.

Equality of opportunity is of course just as vacuous a term as liberty, and its meaning will depend on whether it is injected with a minimal or maximal interpretation. It may be restricted to the absence of legal or formal barriers to individual action—a position adopted by libertarians. Obviously, if one holds to a view of human nature as self-developing or fully capable of rational choice, and of life chances as dependent on one's own ability, this is a fair version of equality. When Hobson unsurprisingly chose his much fuller interpretation, he nonetheless desisted from adopting wholly the Rousseauist-Hegelian understanding of liberty as the acting out of a universal notion of rationality: a self unencumbered by transient, egoistic, private, and unreflective wants and desires.

The key to Hobson's concept of liberty lies in the idea of development. Because human nature was, among others, the expression and reflection of a process, any interference with that process—that is, with the growth and maturation of human abilities—was itself a cardinal suppression of such abilities. But was the process not a necessitarian one to which liberty did not apply? In two senses this was not the case: first, even an inevitable process could supply individuals with the beneficial attributes without which meaningful choices could not be made; second—as Hobson's colleague Hobhouse had emphasised—where human beings were concerned evolution itself brought forth a rational mind that assumed control over its future course. This was what Hobson meant when rephrasing the fuller and more positive liberty to which liberalism had to devote itself in the following question: "What are the equal opportunities which every Englishman requires to-day in order to secure real liberty of self-development?"[48]

In analysing liberty, there is no need to make a choice between its "negative" and "positive" aspects. Any humanistic notion of liberty will include both options. The acknowledgment of individuals as gregarious and dependent on others for their realisation does not rule out circumscribed but clearly available areas of *self*-development. If the crux of the matter is a capacity to control one's own life,[49] there can be no objection to intervention in an individual's life when such intervention is specifically tailored to increase his or her capacity to make the rational choices endemic in such control. Hence the loss of liberty as the absence of deliberate external constraints could enhance liberty as the biological, psychological, and intellectual working out of one's own potential, though some liberty as external nonconstraint had inevitably to be indefeasible. Hobson was never very good at spelling this out, but he undoubtedly aimed at such a resolution of the issue.

[48] Ibid., p. 97.
[49] See J. Raz, *The Morality of Freedom* (Oxford, 1986), p. 409.

If it had occasionally appeared that Hobson was regarding personal development as the minor theme, and communal welfare as the major, the First World War induced him to restructure that internal balance. In a discussion on the loss of liberty suffered in Britain, he reformulated Mill's concern for free speech for a social viewpoint: "It is often said that thought is always free, because our thoughts are our own, and no one can deprive us of them; but this is not strictly true. A man's thinking is severely restricted if the ideas of his fellow-men are made inaccessible to him." But just as importantly, Hobson returned to stress the personal aspects of liberty: "private judgment and personal responsibility lie at the root of representative government. . . . we hold the state exists mainly to develop the personality of the individual, and that this development involves a real freedom of choice on the part of the citizen."[50] In general, Hobson saw personal liberty as the culmination of a welfare society, attainable once common needs had been catered to.[51] In his later work, he repeatedly dropped his earlier insistence on the social utility of individual choices and allowed for freedom of action as long as the free play of individuals was unharmful, even if no discernible social advantage was immediately evident.

In the 1930s Hobson still bewailed the fact that liberty counted for more than equality in Britain. The equality Hobson opted for was, however, of a specific kind. By then he had become increasingly uneasy with the notion of equality of opportunity.[52] He replaced that term with social equality, and he took care to unravel it from other types of equality that pushed in the direction of uniformity. He also hinted at a possible detachment of equality from the earlier and too strong link with liberty and attempted to place it in an idea-environment that included fraternity, comradeship, cooperation, and community.[53] Equality of opportunity now became for Hobson merely one of the desirable components of the concept, and it had to be accompanied by the breakdown of class barriers and the reattribution of social status, an issue of "class-psychology" more than of economic distribution or access to goods.[54] Yet again as a theoretician Hobson signalled his awareness of the range of meanings attached to equality, and of its dependence on being linked up with different adjacent concepts, but in his employment of political terms he preferred his role as ideological player to that of analytical observer.

[50] J. A. Hobson, "The Liberties of Englishmen" [Lecture delivered on 16.1.1916], *South Place Monthly List* (1915–16): 3–5.

[51] See, e.g., J. A. Hobson, *The Modern State* (London, 1932), p. 21.

[52] Freeden, *Liberalism Divided*, p. 246.

[53] Hobson, *Democracy*, pp. 14, 83–84.

[54] J. A. Hobson, *Towards Social Equality* [Hobhouse Memorial Lecture] (London, 1931), p. 17.

Hobson had an impact on political thought in three areas: first, he broadened the spheres from which rational political thinking could be culled and helped to break down the monopoly on the spread and development of political ideas exercised by a few leading and isolated individuals. This he accomplished through perusing unconventional sources, and consequently legitimising the utilisation of new forms and means of political expression: of groups, of individuals placed at strategic points in the distribution of ideas, and of professions whose political thought was only incidental to their activity. Second, he exposed the multidimensionality of the political concepts he explored, revealing their intricate internal structure and their plasticity within an extensive spectrum of conceptual environments. But in the final analysis, it is in a third area, as an ideologically sophisticated but committed thinker, that Hobson must be deemed to have made his chief mark. He contributed not only to the understanding and redefinition of key political concepts, but also to the role they play in political discourse. He bequeathed more than we care to admit to the way we handle important areas of liberal welfare thought; whether or not we approve of his ideas, his influence there is uncontestable. But his appeal for a disinterestedness based on the scientifically determinable nature of human beings, however worthy, masked his own predilections and the limitations of any ideological enterprise. It is inevitably on the viability and persuasiveness of those predilections that he must ultimately be judged.

CHAPTER SIX

Hobson's Evolving Conceptions of Human Nature

IT IS A TRUISM to suggest that every social and political theory is rooted in a conception of human nature. Hobson was no exception to that rule, but his interpretation of human nature was novel and wide-ranging. It did not merely refer to an abstract model, artificially—even cunningly—employed to explain or justify this or that social practice. Rather, it was grounded in concrete, commonsense, empirical observations; it encompassed a broad openness to different aspects of human behaviour; and it attempted to incorporate insights from new developments in philosophy, psychology, sociology, and physiology as well as relate to older moral conventions. Most significantly, on closer inspection it served to underpin many of the better-known theories that Hobson had developed in his critiques of economics and imperialism and in his reconstruction of liberal ideology. As with so much of his work, his scattered writings on human nature exhibit both a derivative and often sketchy approach to highly complex problems, but also an ability to cut through existing traditions in order to arrive at clear and bold statements of a highly innovative character.

Throughout his writings, but especially in his early works, Hobson's thought has two recurring characteristics: extensive reading and retention of new information for the purpose of shoring up his arguments, and carelessness, if not stingy reluctance, to attribute these sources. Hobson's avid assimilatory powers enabled him to synthesise the latest writing in a whole range of disciplines concerning man and society. He was aware of the trends in philosophical and psychological thinking, and able to attach them to an evolutionary perspective that had profound impact on his arguments. Concurrently the radical circles he moved in infused his views with strong social and collectivist, if not socialist, predilections. Uniquely and in a genuinely pioneering sense, though without the meticulous and scholarly basis that was necessary to achieve academic recognition, Hobson wove those different strands together to produce his first major non-economic work, *The Social Problem*, undoubtedly one of the most important and original of his books. The product of Hobson's lecturing and journalistic activities in the 1890s, originally published in thirty-six parts in 1898,[1] it contains his most suggestive early treatment of human nature, and reflects the impressive development of his thinking over a decade in

---

[1] In *Ethical World*, between 26.3.1898 and 26.11.1898.

a number of areas, especially in crystallising his thoughts concerning the interconnections among the human and social sciences.

Hobson's early views on human nature were a compound structure culled from a number of sources and deftly employed to reinforce one another. New philosophical and psychological theories suggested the importance of mind as a propeller of human conduct, but also the close link between physiology and psychology. On another level Hobson developed a markedly communitarian conception of human nature, sustained by the works of Idealists such as J. S. Mackenzie, and nourished by Hobson's growing ideological antipathy towards the Individualist treatment of persons as independent entities, whose social organisation was entirely predicated on voluntary contracts. And from a third point d'appui Hobson was increasingly attracted by evolutionary theories that identified a process of growing rational and conscious control of man over his actions and his environment.

Ultimately, Hobson's highly personal version of organicism must be seen as his outstanding and innovative contribution to all the above themes. By means of the notion of the interconnectedness of scientific knowledge at a period when the social and moral sciences were embarking on intense specialisation, it supplied him with a principled justification for what might otherwise have been seen as a dilettantish raiding of various disciplines. Though many theorists and practitioners endowed their professional field with more acute and academic contributions, Hobson was one of the very few modern British thinkers of his generation to underscore the integral connections between social philosophy, psychology, economics, and the natural sciences, employing not the past abstractions of utilitarians or "dismal scientists," but what he believed were sensible empirical observations buttressed by the most recent scholarly truths. At the same time his organicism enabled him to engage in a bridge-building enterprise that disposed of entrenched dichotomies between mind and body, individual and society or even reason and unreason. On this quasi-amateurish level he succeeded in integrating insights of empirical psychologists with those held by Idealists and evolutionary philosophers, thus anticipating the more technical discourses of academics such as Hobhouse and McDougall, and, in a modest way, performing a function not dissimilar to Mill's, by introducing (almost anonymously) some of the ideas prevalent on the Continent to the British reading public.

Hobson's views of human nature embodied three guiding ideas that served to direct his more general social, political, and economic analyses. First, in line with his strong insistence on the organic nature of human beings, he affirmed the interlinkage between the physiological and psychological components of their behaviour. Second, he denied current notions of dominant innate human greed and selfishness, emphasizing instead the natural gregariousness and sociability of individuals. Third, he subscribed to prevalent ideas about the unfolding and development of wholesome human capacities, specifically in the form of the expenditure of vital energies beyond what was necessary for survival. These principles recur repeatedly throughout his work, though at different times they attached themselves to various particular issues, problems, and theories that preoccupied him.

Looking back from *The Social Problem* over the previous decade, Hobson's encounter with J. S. Mackenzie's *An Introduction to Social Philosophy* was obviously one of his most profound formative experiences, one that set him along a path he was to adhere to for the rest of his life. An examination of Mackenzie's book shows emphatically how seminal it was to the development of Hobson's thought, though his early ideas can by no means be reduced to that work alone. Hobson must have been flattered to find in it some of the first references to his own pathbreaking, but at the time highly controversial, underconsumptionist venture with A. F. Mummery, *The Physiology of Industry*. Mackenzie had been impressed by the refusal of Mummery and Hobson to identify wealth with material possessions and by their stress on consumption, even if they had not, in the former's opinion, distinguished sufficiently between different kinds of consumption.[2] Mackenzie had already attained distinction as a Scottish Idealist, and in his "truly remarkable" book attempted to integrate Idealist teachings with some of the latest writings of social reformers, mainly on the progressive side of the political spectrum.[3] Mackenzie's admonishment that "some of the laws of Economics . . . lend themselves so readily to a purely abstract treatment that there is still a danger of their relations to human well-being becoming neglected altogether" together with his view of economics as both science and art became central themes in Hobson's later writings.[4] Mackenzie's observations on Ruskin, singling out the latter's notion of "illth," and his ethical approach to practical economics may well have provided the original impetus for Hobson's later book on Ruskin.[5]

In Mackenzie's holism Hobson found the inspiration for his own later organicism that attempted to do away with boundaries between ethics, politics, and economics. Mackenzie saw in the organic perspective an explanation for "most of the great questions in which human nature is con-

[2] Cf. J. S. Mackenzie, *An Introduction to Social Philosophy* (Glasgow, 1890), pp. 302, 322.

[3] Review by Hobson of Mackenzie, *An Introduction to Social Philosophy*, in *International Journal of Ethics* 2 (1890–91): 389.

[4] Mackenzie, *An Introduction to Social Philosophy*, pp. 49, 56.

[5] Ibid., pp. 58, 303. Mackenzie's footnotes drew Hobson's attention to P. Geddes' study of Ruskin as an economist (*John Ruskin, Economist* [Edinburgh, 1884]).

cerned."[6] In particular, Hobson distilled from Mackenzie's organicism his rejection of monadism, and its replacement by a view that "regards the rights of the individual as inseparable from his obligations to society, and his obligations as equally inseparable from his rights,—each being but a different aspect of the demands of his nature from him as a being who cannot but be social."[7] The important balance between the individual and the social aspect of man that Hobson grappled with throughout his life was, however, clearly adumbrated in Mackenzie's book: "an organic view of society would be one which regarded the relation of the individual to society as an intrinsic one; one which recognised that the individual has an independent life of his own, and yet which saw that that independent life is nothing other than his social life."[8] For Mackenzie, as consequently for Hobson, "if man is to become rational, he must make for himself a rational environment. This rational environment he finds for himself in society . . . . It is only through the development of the whole race that any one man can develop"[9]—a formulation diametrically inverted with respect to the famous ending of Mill's *On Liberty*.[10]

It was in that sense, indeed, that a mild ethical socialism could appeal both to Mackenzie and to Hobson.[11] Already then becoming aware of the multiple connotations of the term "organic," Hobson accepted it in the sense both of human growth and of the intertwined link between such individual growth and social progress. For, as Mackenzie put it, the organic point of view meant on the one hand that "man is a developing being, rising from sense to thought" and that "the idea of development . . . is coming to be applied more and more to everything that is fundamental in human affairs,"[12] and, on the other hand, that there existed "a system in which the parts have a certain relative independence, but an independence which is conditioned throughout by its relation to the system—an independence, in short, which is not freedom *from* the system, but freedom *in and through* it."[13] Here were the germs of much that can be found in Hobson's own organicist concept of human nature. Yet at that stage, prior to Hobson's closer acquaintance with current psychological theories, his thinking still eschewed the fuller physical implications of the organic analogy, and he praised Mackenzie for being "careful

---

[6] Ibid., p. 131.
[7] Hobson, review of Mackenzie (quoting from Mackenzie, p. 135).
[8] Mackenzie, *An Introduction to Social Philosophy*, p. 136.
[9] Ibid., p. 180.
[10] J. S. Mill, *On Liberty* (London, 1910), p. 170.
[11] Mackenzie, *An Introduction to Social Philosophy*, p. 285.
[12] Ibid., p. 178.
[13] Ibid., pp. 128, 130.

to protect himself from errors likely to arise from the exclusively physiological associations of the term he employs."[14]

Hobson, however, was never attracted to Idealism as a central perspective, and he quickly returned to more material evidence concerning psychology and physiology. Indeed, though he referred in his autobiography to the influence of his townsman Herbert Spencer and his *The Study of Sociology* on his early thought, Mackenzie did not even rate a mention.[15] Spencer was employing and developing psychological theories of the type advanced by Alexander Bain, who had asserted that the division between mind and body was without basis, and Bain's interest in the physiological mechanisms underlying behaviour led to an emphasis on the dynamism and activity of the human organism, propelled by inner drives.[16] Spencer had reviewed Bain's *The Emotions and the Will*, praising him for being the first to appreciate the importance of the participation of bodily organs in mental changes.[17] He had also perused Bain's *Mind and Body*, in which the latter had examined "the intimate connexion between Mind and Body . . . furnished by the effects of bodily changes on mental states, and of mental changes on bodily states."[18] In *The Study of Sociology* Spencer reasserted the close links between feelings and action as a basis for a theory of mind,[19] thus contributing to a tradition of thought that both Hobson and his friend and contemporary Hobhouse took up. Throughout, Spencer was keen to emphasise the primacy of noncognitive feeling, of emotion, as a cause of conduct; in other words, to identify a particular influence of mind on bodily actions.[20] Concurrently, however, a reading of Spencer would have directed Hobson to search for the affect upon the mind of physical human characteristics (examined by Spencer in questionable detail with respect to differences between men and women).[21] It is understandable, therefore, to find Hobson writing about human nature in language closely reminiscent of that school of thought, though one

[14] Hobson, review of Mackenzie.

[15] J. A. Hobson, *Confessions of an Economic Heretic* (London, 1938), p. 23.

[16] See A. Bain, *The Emotions and the Will* (London, 1859), R. Thomson, *The Pelican History of Psychology* (Harmondsworth, 1968), pp. 28–30, and J. C. Flugel, *A Hundred Years of Psychology* (2d ed., London, 1951), pp. 80–84.

[17] H. Spencer, "Bain on the Emotions and the Will," in *Essays: Scientific, Political, and Speculative*, Second Ser. (London, 1863), p. 122.

[18] A. Bain, *Mind and Body: The Theories of their Relation* (London, 1873), p. 8 and passim.

[19] H. Spencer, *The Study of Sociology* (London, 1907 ed.), p. 354.

[20] Although in the wider sense Spencer regarded human nature as inherited and only marginally changeable. Spencer's psychological theories are far more complex than indicated here, and I refer here only to those aspects reflected in Hobson's writings.

[21] Ibid., pp. 368–77.

must also recall that Hobson had the interests of an economist at heart. Those concerns might explain his preference for reversing Spencer's relative emphases, and for moving away from Mackenzie's, by underlining the affect of the body on the mind. Thus he now observed: "The loose notion that, because 'the soul' has the direction or determination of [moral and social purposes], they somehow escape the limitation of the body, has no warrant."[22]

In particular, Hobson was influenced by Spencer's frequent forays into the physiological needs of the human body. Spencer had expounded on the common traits of human nature, observing that human beings "have all needs for food, and have corresponding desires. To all of them exertion is a physiological expense; must bring a certain return in nutriment, if it is not to be detrimental." To that Spencer added an evolutionary perspective that traced the development of "vital power" in men, for whom "individual evolution continues until the physiological cost of self-maintenance very nearly balances what nutrition supplies" whereas "in women, an arrest of individual evolution takes place while there is yet a considerable margin of nutrition: otherwise there could be no offspring."[23]

Hobson echoed much of this in an early piece written in 1893, and reproduced in part in *The Social Problem*. As Hobson had put it then: "On the plane of physical exertion and material consumption the law that action and reaction must be equal and opposite demands that every output of vigour in production shall be repaired and balanced by corresponding consumption."[24] By the end of the century he had attempted a reconciliation of the Idealist social philosophy of growth with empirical and material evidence from the burgeoning sciences of individual and society. Furthermore, Hobson interwove these sociophysical analyses with his radical economics as well. His organic appreciation of the human condition and its physical roots was linked to the act of consumption and thus added considerable depth to the underconsumptionist theories he was expounding in parallel throughout the 1890s. Like Spencer, he drew attention to the prime dependence of human beings upon an intake of food converted into muscular and nervous energy, "which may be given out in forms of physical or mental work." Here, indeed, was to be found the clue that linked up these Spencerian insights with Hobson's economic concerns: "Physiology assigns certain laws of individual property in tracing necessary relations between the output of vital energy in work and the replacement of that energy through nutrition. Every kind of human effort given out in the production of material or nonmaterial wealth must

---

[22] J. A. Hobson, *The Social Problem* (London, 1901), p. 268.
[23] Spencer, *The Study of Sociology*, pp. 51, 369.
[24] J. A. Hobson, "Rights of Property," *Free Review*, November 1893, 130–49.

be attended by a consumption of material forms, adjusted both in quantity and in character to the expenditure of force."[25]

Hobson's qualitative notions of wealth and consumption, adapted from Ruskin, were now bolstered by an empirical analysis on Spencerian lines that regarded the science of hygiene as one of the bases of wholesome human life. Furthermore, Hobson went on to convert Spencer's observations about the "margin of nutrition" produced by women into a more general precursor of his notion of surplus value, applied to all individuals: "Man is the owner of a recurrent fund of superfluous vital energy, over and above what is needed to procure the necessaries of physical life, and he is willing to use this energy for pleasurable activities of self-expression."[26] Conversely, "every act of consumption which requires no previous act of production, is a natural, and, in the long run, an inevitable check upon future effort";[27] hence the idle rich suffered the ultimate indictment of nature. What later became Hobson's famous concept of unearned surplus, or improperty, was initially condemned here for the physical atrophy and destructiveness it brought in its wake. "The convex congested paunch of the torpid plutocrat who consumes without the effort of producing, implies the concave anaemic body of the inefficient starvling as its equal and opposite"[28]—a structure of argumentation that Marx would have found quite familiar. Clearly, Hobson was forming a general view of human nature in which the link between the physical and the mental was overriding, and in which bodily needs were to be regarded not as embarrassing or irrelevant, but as a wholesome foundation of optimal human performance.[29]

Current psychology was, however, affording Hobson a further range of insights, this time derived from the French social psychologist Gustave Le Bon. As with his first mentor, Spencer, Hobson adopted Le Bon's scholarly insights while rejecting their highly Individualist and conservative packaging. In *The Psychological Laws of the Evolution of Peoples* (published in 1894) Le Bon had maintained, in unmistakably élitist and racist tones, that "the very great anatomic differences which distinguish the various human races are accompanied by psychological differences no less considerable."[30] In reviewing the English translation of the book, Hobson turned this to his own advantage; indeed, Le Bon had a major impact on his writings between 1899 and 1901. The message Hobson distilled from

[25] Hobson, *The Social Problem*, pp. 265, 98. Cf. Hobson, "Rights of Property," p. 135.

[26] Hobson, *The Social Problem*, p. 108.

[27] Hobson, "Rights of Property," p. 137.

[28] Ibid., p. 139.

[29] For a statement expressing Hobson's appreciation of Spencer's holistic opus, see J. A. Hobson, "Herbert Spencer," *South Place Magazine* 9 (1904): 49–55.

[30] A. Widener, ed., *Gustave Le Bon: The Man and his Works* (Indianapolis, 1979), p. 50.

Le Bon was a denial of the theory of "common humanity" and its corollary that progress was unilinear, one nation therefore being able to civilise another. Moreover, Le Bon's assertion that the pace of moral progress was determined by average people was, for Hobson, a highly serviceable protest against the undue optimism of some reformers.[31] Hobson consequently departed in *The Social Problem* from a uniform conception of human nature by making similar allowances for the "wide variants of natural environment and of race . . . [that] oblige us to conceive civilisation as 'multiform.'" Conceding that those differences could be either physical or psychical, Hobson was prepared to contemplate a notion of national character by explicitly endorsing Le Bon's assertion that "common race character" consists of "certain few fixed sentiments or ideas which are virtually permanent . . . [and which] mould the destiny of nations, and are the real ultimate determinants of the work which they can do in the world."[32] Hobson, however, who rarely abandoned his fierce critical independence even when drawing upon the scholarship of others, parted company with Le Bon by insisting that no civilisation was better than another, merely different.[33]

Le Bon had, however, a more persevering effect on Hobson. In the earliest expression of a theme that was to reoccur frequently in his work, Hobson employed him to alight upon human irrationality as a motive force in politics. The enduring nature of war, he speculated, could be explained by fighting, nomadic, and acquisitive instincts that, while subdued in the individual, may abide in the race.[34] Hobson elaborated on this theme in his *The Psychology of Jingoism*, where he used Le Bon's conclusions with devastating effect against the mass hysteria of the Boer War. Hobson referred to "a recent French writer" who had attributed to a crowd "a character and conduct which is lower, intellectually and morally, than the character and conduct of its average member." This irrational, volatile and savage mob-passion Hobson now detected in the populist British reaction to the war in South Africa,[35] though it is interesting to note that he had originally developed this insight during his South African visit, with reference to *that* nation's inhabitants.[36] Characteristically, Hobson was inclined to read far more into Le Bon than the latter was willing to suggest, namely, that the behaviour of the crowd revealed the more

[31] The book was translated as *The Psychology of Peoples* and reviewed by Hobson in *Ethical World*, 18.2.1899.

[32] Although in Hobson's earlier review he had rebuked Le Bon for overstating the degree of permanence and impermeability of a race.

[33] Hobson, *The Social Problem*, pp. 275–76.

[34] J. A. Hobson, "The Reason of a Nation," *Ethical World*, 1.4.1899.

[35] J. A. Hobson, *The Psychology of Jingoism* (London, 1901), pp. 17–20.

[36] J. A. Hobson, "The Psychology of the War Spirit," *Ethical World*, 9.12.1899.

general attribute of a group mind, of which crowd behaviour was merely a corruption.[37]

In fact, Hobson had already alluded to Le Bon in 1898, three years before *The Psychology of Jingoism* was published, in support of this second important facet of human nature he had come to emphasize—man's sociability and communitarian essence. Building on Le Bon's better-known *The Psychology of the Crowd*, published in 1895 and translated into English a year later, Hobson noted then that "the modern science of psychology brings a cloud of witnesses to prove the direct organic interaction of mind and mind: the familiar experience of everyone exhibits thoughts, emotions, character, as elaborate social products." He now described that organicist insight derived from works such as Mackenzie's as "this commonplace of most social philosophies," and sought rather to base it on a scientific footing. That was apparently supplied by Le Bon, who had demonstrated that the feelings and conduct of a crowd were not that of its constitutive parts: "Do we not know that the contagion of emotion will give a moral life, a character, even to a casual throng of citizens, inspiring beliefs and impelling actions which do not reflect the mere activity of the separate minds?"[38]

In all this one must not forget the immense impact of evolutionary thought on progressives during the late nineteenth century.[39] Man was evolving higher, more rational, more conscious and more sociable modes of organisation and behaviour. A naturalistic evolutionism now included man as part of nature, yet capable through emerging consciousness and self-control of channelling his behaviour towards ethical and communitarian ends. "For what is nature but reason working itself out in the universe?" queried Hobson.[40] He subjected the question to close examination in his analysis of property rights. In "Rights of Property" Hobson had broadened his treatment of human nature while dissecting the notion of natural rights—foreshadowing in part the noted work of the Idealist D. G. Ritchie.[41] Rejecting the separatist and detached notion of natural rights, Hobson proposed an original inversion of their meaning—namely, ratio-

---

[37] As Hobson observed: "Nor need we accept [Le Bon's] view that the standard of feeling and reason of the crowd is always lower than that of its individuals; there is some evidence to indicate that it may sometimes be higher—at any rate, so far as feelings are concerned." (Ibid., p. 20) For his immediate purposes, however,—the examination of the war-spirit—Hobson preferred the unadulterated Le Bon.

[38] J. A. Hobson, "Rich Man's Anarchism," *The Humanitarian* 12 (1898): 391–93. I am indebted to Michael Taylor for drawing my attention to this article.

[39] See M. Freeden, *The New Liberalism: An Ideology of Social Reform* (Oxford, 1978), chap. 3.

[40] Hobson, *The Social Problem*, p. 96.

[41] See D. G. Ritchie, *Natural Rights* (London, 1894).

nal and ordered functions of human activity. Utilising a conception of human nature that regarded its essence as involving activity, work, and life, he drew the logical conclusion: "that which is required to maintain the productive energy of workers is their natural property."[42] In other words, a specific physiological feature of human nature became a major identifier of human needs and determinant of social arrangements. Immediately, though, Hobson added a psychological given of human nature that necessitated further social arrangements. The "natural" expenditure of physical energy was not an instinctive or biologically determined aspect of human nature; mind had to instruct body to expend energy. This, too, was natural, but in the wider and holistic sense that was part of the organic linkage between body and mind that Hobson had come to accept. "The human will is a part of human nature, and the 'property' required as a sufficient motive to operate upon this will is as 'natural' as that required to furnish the physical energy used up in production."[43] This insistence on the need for stimulating the effort of production was later to become a major component of Hobson's ideological position, distinguishing him from purist socialists in his insistence on the importance of incentives in any practical socioeconomic policy.[44] There was, however, a third feature of human nature that also deserved its due in social organisation. Man was a social entity in a very real sense, so that his physiological and mental productivity was itself formed only through social assistance, cultural and economic. The safeguarding of some form of social property was hence essential to nourish the social nature of the individual, namely, that aspect that led individuals to identify themselves more closely with the welfare of others.[45]

Drawing the various strands together as the new century dawned, Hobson had become well-equipped to make the fuller statement on human nature that emerges from the pages of *The Social Problem*. He elaborated the need to replenish energy as the conservative aspect of human nature and the psychological desire to induce effort as the progressive aspect, putting forward new wants. The latter was a natural component of the progress both of individual and of social character.[46] Especially enhanced was Hobson's treatment of work as a focus of material, mental, and ethical perspectives. Work was raised to the level of a definer of human essence in virtually socialist language. "True work" was "lovable as a means of wholesome and agreeable self-expression." But it was also the means

---

[42] Hobson, "Rights of Property," p. 135.
[43] Ibid.
[44] Hobson, *The Social Problem*, p. 104.
[45] Hobson, "Rights of Property," p. 142–49.
[46] Hobson, *The Social Problem*, p. 105.

of satisfaction for a society, for "social relations . . . are inseparable from the individual nature."[47] Later Hobson was to elaborate, maintaining "that man is naturally active, that he likes to discover and apply power of body and mind to constructive work, arranging his natural environment, partly for the sheer pleasure of doing things, partly for the satisfaction of enjoying what he has done or made."[48] At the same time, Hobson—as was his wont—remained unclear on the question of whether society was an amalgam of socially oriented individuals, or an entity making claims in parallel with individual needs (albeit not separately and not in conflict with them). He could in the same paragraph refer to "the conditions of health and progress for a complex organism" and stress that the relation between individual and society was merely one of "harmonizing the different sides of [the individual's] nature."[49] In other writings he was to vacillate even more markedly.[50]

The Edwardian years brought with them new theories that Hobson was quick to incorporate. William McDougall may not currently be remembered as an important psychologist, but in the early twentieth century he was widely published, read, and quoted. By now it was inevitable that he would add grist to Hobson's mill. For McDougall was dressing in professional garb many of the ideas that Hobson had been cobbling together by means of his syntheses and the further inspiration derived from Hobhouse. McDougall had been trained at England's first exclusively psychological laboratory,[51] and in 1908 published his influential and much-reprinted *Social Psychology*. For intellectual historians, the interest of this work must lie not in its novelty as in its reflection of the psychological-philosophical tradition that sought to explain human conduct in terms of instincts and drives working their way up to the level of conscious, rational behaviour.[52] What McDougall later graced, or burdened, with the term "hormic psychology" was more simply this central concern of his contemporaries and their immediate predecessors. Hobson was clearly pleased to discover in McDougall's work scientific backing for his philosophical intuitions. It rendered unnecessary his previous recourses to analogies from the animal kingdom, as when referring to Maeterlinck's *The*

[47] Ibid., pp. 110, 218, 222.

[48] J. A. Hobson, *Wealth and Life* (London, 1929), p. 224.

[49] Hobson, *The Social Problem*, pp. 222–23.

[50] Cf. Freeden, *The New Liberalism*, pp. 104–9.

[51] N. Rose, *The Psychological Complex: Psychology, Politics and Society in England, 1869–1939* (London, 1985), p. 116.

[52] Graham Wallas's acclaimed *Human Nature in Politics*, published in the same year (London, 1908), emerges in this light as a book curiously detached from the debate on psychology, mentioning Le Bon and Spencer only in passing, and virtually ignoring the strains of thought identified in this chapter.

Life of a Bee for evidence of common psychic purpose within a social group,[53] even though a quotation from Henri Fabre's recent work on the social instincts of wasps is found in proximity with reliance on McDougall.[54] McDougall listed a range of primary human instincts to which emotions were attached. They included among others flight, repulsion, curiosity, and pugnacity, with their emotional counterparts of fear, disgust, wonder, and anger. But they also included a parental, a reproductive, and, crucially, a gregarious instinct.[55] The latter, interestingly, was described on its elemental level in terms reminiscent of Le Bon, as herd or horde behaviour "liable to a morbid hypertrophy under which . . . emotions and impulses are revealed with exaggerated intensity," and in particular membership of crowds that "exert a greater fascination and afford a more complete satisfaction to the gregarious instinct than the mere aimless aggregations of the streets."[56] But it was in that instinct also that McDougall found the explanation for the development of active sympathy of human being for human being.

Hobson referred to McDougall's theories in *Work and Wealth*, published in 1914, where he replicated McDougall's survey of instincts. Hobson was, however, eager to argue that reason could coordinate the instincts, raising the "instinctive movements of the popular mind" to the level of a conscious and controllable "general will."[57] Many of Hobson's notions on this subject followed Hobhouse's, who had himself combined philosophical and psychological work to account for the development of instinct into conscious rational behaviour. Hobhouse subscribed to the notion of orthogenic, or progressively organised, evolution, which was solidly based on his pioneering studies in animal psychology and behaviourism. A direct sequence of development could be traced from a number of sources: hereditary mechanisms, permanent needs (root interests), and instincts. These guided the impulses, which in the course of experience were sustained first by feeling, and then emerged as intelligence operating through an articulated and controlled consciousness. The social interests and impulses, which could develop into sympathy for others, were singled out for special consideration. Hence human needs pertained not only to the body but to the mind. This rational growth process of mind was correlated with social development and was the crux of the evolutionary process.[58] Many, though not all, of Hobhouse's theories on the subject were

---

[53] Cf. J. A. Hobson, "The Re-Statement of Democracy," *Contemporary Review* 81 (1902): 264.

[54] J. A. Hobson, *Work and Wealth* (London, 1914), pp. 352, 356.

[55] W. McDougall, *Social Psychology* (23d ed., London, 1960), pp. 39–76.

[56] Ibid., pp. 73–74.

[57] Hobson, *Work and Wealth*, pp. 356–58.

[58] Cf. J. A. Hobson and M. Ginsberg, *L. T. Hobhouse* (London, 1931), pp. 149–56.

formulated before McDougall's books had been published and appeared in the first edition of his *Mind in Evolution*.[59]

Hobson's *Work and Wealth*, one of his most complex and careful books, teased out more detail and added new observations to enrich the earlier adumbrations. In particular, Hobson—unlike his friend Hobhouse—asserted not only that the antithesis between instinct and reason was illogical, but that reason itself was far more directly based on "blind" instinctive drives of gregariousness and curiosity. This assumption was predicated on Hobson's organic whole-parts distinction, which allowed for the organic whole to have interests and purposes not accessible to the units, except as the latter develop communion of thought and feeling with fellowmen and humanity at large. For "prior to the dawn of 'reason' in organic evolution, the instincts carry and apply a wisdom and direction of their own."[60] Behind this lay a tension that only evolution itself could resolve. Men and women were not only individually endowed with social instincts and inclinations, but were capable of realising collective ends qua members of a social group. Hence, human beings were social in the lesser sense of mutual interdependence and in the greater sense of essentially constituting components of a social whole.[61] The problem was one of finding a balance between these two natural states. On the physical plane this could become one between the needs of the individual and the species; on the nonphysical, between self-regarding and humanistic-ethical activities and purposes. Occasionally the species was overinsistent in its demands; occasionally the individual attempted to break away from the natural ties that made others of concern to him. Crucially, as we have seen, the biological-psychological needs of the individual were already defined in terms of their social propensities; crucially, also, the "self-regarding impulses are made socially profitable by allowing them free expression" in creative, artistic, and adventurous directions, for "the well-ordered society will utilise the energies of egoism," if not permit them to predominate.[62] On one important dimension the "dawn of reason is the dawn of selfishness," as individual life broke away from the thrall of the instinctive sacrifices that living creatures make for the survival of family and race, and a sense of personality emerged. The very essence of human evolution lay, however, in its ability to enter a third stage—a rationalisa-

---

[59] Hobhouse recorded there a special debt to the American sociologist Lester Ward, but many of his ideas also derived directly from the frame of reference Spencer had contributed to—e.g., man as energy-expending and impulse-generating—even if Hobhouse's reaction was partially critical. It was only in the second edition in 1915 that Hobhouse mentioned the work of McDougall.

[60] Hobson, *Work and Wealth*, p. 357.

[61] Ibid., pp. 14–16.

[62] Ibid., pp. 291–93.

tion on a higher sphere of a socialised consciousness that enabled the "social race-life" to "reassert its sway."[63]

Hobson was now eager, in quasi-dialectical fashion, to stress both the unity and diversity of human nature. Ultimately, these facets could be reconciled and harmonised (using one of Hobhouse's favourite terms) through the organic conception of society. Though both unity and diversity were ineluctable, they could be either beneficial or harmful. Individuals effectively had the choice to develop the different potential characteristics within them, for "there is reason to believe that human nature is exceedingly rich in all sorts of variations from the normal, and that very many of these variations have valuable uses." Yet some were of debatable worth; others categorically harmful. The businessman, for example, was endowed with the ability to innovate, to make rapid judgments, and with courage, but the human cost was moral callousness and recklessness.[64] Elsewhere, Hobson observed that the actual manifestations of human nature could tend to vices or excesses injurious to others and opposed to sensible standards of value.[65] Here Hobson's fervent commitment to issues of economic distribution had a role to play. Maldistribution had damaging effects both on the rich and the poor: in the former encouraging those human features that are parasitic and unproductive; in the latter destroying the capacities for creativity and enjoyment.[66] The development of useful human characteristics was in the hands of human agency, but of the collective kind: the deliberate, organised intervention of a social environment—itself an aspect of intelligent rational nature—could play a part in forming individual human behaviour. As Hobson argued: "It is often urged that man is by nature so strongly endowed with selfish and combative feelings, so feebly with social and coöperative, that he will not work efficiently . . . . he must be allowed free scope to . . . exercise his fighting instincts, to triumph over his competitors . . . or else he will withhold the finest and most useful modes of his economic energy." As against these assumptions, Hobson held out the possibility that the redistribution of material life chances could "sow the seeds of civic feeling and of social solidarity among large sections of our population."[67]

The direction of human development was also given clearer shape. Hobson continued to expound on the centrality of creative work to his conception of human nature, but he now emphasised two facets. First, human beings needed to exercise a range of productive faculties, and they

---

[63] Ibid., pp. 22–26.
[64] Ibid., pp. 50, 55–56.
[65] Hobson, *Wealth and Life*, p. 60.
[66] Cf. also J. A. Hobson, *The Problem of the Unemployed* (London, 1896).
[67] Hobson, *Work and Wealth*, pp. 283–84.

needed variety in their activities. Second, Hobson linked this with an out-spokenly liberationist perspective that assumed an innate "latent creative energy" whose emergence had to be facilitated.[68] Human powers were thus multiform, active, and progressive. Their full expression had to be enabled through wholesome social arrangements. This elaboration was accompanied by another theme that became salient as Hobson grew older. It concerned a softening of the intellectualist bias of liberal thought.[69] Instead, Hobson underlined the importance of play, spontaneity, and plea-sure. He proceeded to point out in evolutionary terms the role of faults, sports, or mutations, which "in human conduct, individual or social, . . . seem to play a larger part, chiefly by reason of the operation of the so-called 'freedom' of the human will." That will was decisive in scattering mutations over the realm of human behaviour and was hence a source of continuous evolutionary innovation.[70]

The growing interest in the role of motherhood, in population and eu-genics questions, and in women's emancipation before 1914 prompted Hobson to turn his attention to a rare consideration of the role and nature of women, but in a disappointingly thin manner. Despite his basically humane and liberal approach to the subject, what stands out is Hobson's assumption of the dual nature of male and female, in his assertion of "the right and duty of women to form womanly standards of judgment and conduct for themselves instead of receiving them from men, as a necessary condition for a more enlightened society." The consequence was a variant of the "separate-but-equal" doctrine. Hobson interestingly extended his analysis of imperialism to apply to the relations between the sexes: "The actual physical and economic domination exerted by man has made woman after his own image, and by imposing his ideal has thwarted hers." Indeed, Hobson drew a direct analogy between this condition and the relation between master and subject races.[71] The stress was on that of equal but different components of the human species.

What, then, was female nature? By physique and disposition, women were more stationary than men. In addition, standards of behaviour im-posed by males had "impaired the character of their intellectual life," and had created a dependence that disturbed "the just balance of human forces in the development of social forms." In thus reintroducing the no-tion of harmony from another angle, Hobson argued that the emancipa-tion of women would augment the divergence of sex types. It would re-lease many people from the pressures to marry and would consequently

---

[68] Ibid., pp. 62, 289.
[69] Cf. G. Gaus, *The Modern Liberal Theory of Man* (London, 1983), p. 28.
[70] Hobson, *Work and Wealth*, pp. 240–41, 336.
[71] J. A. Hobson, *A Modern Outlook* (London, 1910), pp. 121–25.

increase the likelihood that "womanly women" and "manly men" would survive.[72] In particular, Hobson—armed with his strong prewar eugenic sympathies[73]—upheld the convention of regarding women as specialists in parentage and in "the arts of an ideal home." "Eugenics will defend a . . . sex discrimination, which will be no offence against equality, but a defence of the great creative work of women in the world." Feminine creativity lay fundamentally neither in individual self-assertion nor in the intellectual life, but in maternity.

There was, however, some confusion here. Hobson was identifying as natural what he had just claimed to be imposed by a male culture. Maternal feelings and a subordination of self to the well-being and progress of the race were the natural—even though not sole—vocation of women.[74] The further implication was that "male" characteristics were both more individualistic and less emotional. Women exercised the evolutionarily crucial, but socially undeveloped, function of the altruistic sustenance of the social race-life. Men exercised the innovative, experimental, and mutational functions. As Hobson elsewhere observed, the "male modes of manipulating the environment" were in the form of explorative, constructive, and decorative work, as well as expressions of the "hunting and fighting instincts."[75]

After the war, Hobson's thinking on human nature entered its final phase. Though he did not abandon most of his earlier views, he increasingly turned for support and inspiration to the still nascent science of psychology. Above all, Freudian psychology—to which Hobson fleetingly referred—shifted him away from the old body-mind relationship towards a reassessment of the interaction between rational and nonrational behaviour. This was no longer the province of either Bain or Le Bon,[76] but an examination of the "animalistic" foundations of mental as well as physical conduct. In search of the "natural man," Hobson expanded on his previous emphasis on the importance of play, of irregularity, in expressing the "sporting and artistic instincts" that he considered to be the sources of natural human creativity. Already in 1915, Hobson had alluded "to the psychology of Freud, which is based upon the fact that we all have in ourselves certain elements kept under by modern civilisation." These dormant and potentially ruinous forces could find innocent outlets and

---

[72] Ibid., pp. 110, 114–17.

[73] See chap. 7 below.

[74] Hobson, *A Modern Outlook*, pp. 130–32.

[75] Hobson, *Work and Wealth*, pp. 25, 149.

[76] Freud himself had endorsed Le Bon's view of the group mind. Cf. S. Freud, "Le Bon's Description of the Group Mind," in *The Standard Edition of the Complete Psychological Works of Sigmund Freud*, ed. J. Strachey, vol. 18, pp. 72–81.

constitute "an adequate answer to the Puritanism which insists that every kind of art which is not dedicated to the cause of virtue is evil conduct."[77]

Hence Hobson's more subtle understanding of psychology steered him away from the starker reactions with which he had confronted the Boer War. Although the First World War had shaken his belief in human rationality, it had not eroded it.[78] To the contrary, it found Hobson far better equipped to accept a modicum of human irrationality that was not inimical to the ultimate wholesome and rational development of personality. He now challenged the differentiation between "higher" spiritual and ethical activities and "lower" physical and biological ones as underplaying the significance of "animal needs and creature comforts." Sublimation, which he misunderstood as a deliberate act prescribed by practitioners of the "new psychology," was a questionable process. It was often better to allow natural urges free rein rather than channel them in "civilised" directions that—as Hobson had learned from his own historical investigations—could be far more destructive. Indeed, these instincts had a positive import: "There is no ground for holding that any adequate satisfaction of them is attainable by methods of sublimation, therefore you are bound to find a proper place for them in your conception of a *good* society."[79] Stepping back from the harmony-postulating prewar new liberalism, Hobson ruminated on the possible inevitability of physical conflict, and on the shaky basis of the intellectualism that history, philosophy, and economics—his own included—had been pursuing. Here was a new instance of the fallacy of dualism, for a long while already the butt of Hobsonian attacks. One had to accept the view that "all, even of the most sublimated and refined of our sentiments and processes of thinking, are in origin and nature products of this animal humanity of ours." True, man had a "second nature," the product of his natural sociability as well as of his own rationality. But, as Hobson cannily remarked, modern psychology, in exposing the rationalisation of institutions, theories, and motives, was offering "an immense new field for the operations of what Meredith termed 'the comic spirit.' "[80]

Hobson's understanding of human nature always differed in fundamental respects from those socialist or anarchist versions that claimed it to be entirely communitarian and altruistic. His insistence on the importance of incentives in socioeconomic organisation addressed itself to his

---

[77] J. A. Hobson, "Raffles," *South Place Monthly List*, May 1915, 9.

[78] Cf. M. Freeden, *Liberalism Divided: A Study in British Political Thought, 1914–1939* (Oxford, 1986), p. 44.

[79] J. A. Hobson, "The Ethical Movement and the Natural Man," *Hibbert Journal* 20 (1922): 671–74, 675 (my italics). Cf. also J. Allett, *New Liberalism: The Political Economy of J. A. Hobson* (Toronto, 1981), pp. 214–15.

[80] Hobson, "The Ethical Movement and the Natural Man," pp. 676–78.

full recognition of the role of individual instincts and wills in serving private ends. With all his reservations about the business mentality, which had so frequently sustained military-imperialist cliques, Hobson accepted the necessity of temperamental qualities that included initiative, calculation, judgment, risk taking—all "active powers of intellect and character." There was a biological foundation to the type of activity engaged in by the entrepreneur: people were not geared to regular, continued, and specialized activity but to "short, irregular and varied efforts."[81] Hobson frequently displayed an ungrudging admiration for individuals, men of genius or at least talent and originality who harnessed "the spirit of discovery and adventure."[82] Ultimately, Hobson would have preferred to engage the motive of public-spiritedness, though this was only feasible in areas of national importance. Other spheres would be wisely left to "a certain type of masterful business man able to put immense personal energy, initiative, and skill into his business on condition that he runs it for his own gainful end."[83]

In the interwar years, with their harsher economic and ideological climate, the recognition both of egoistic motives and of social instincts became more pronounced in Hobson's brand of liberalism. His earlier employment of the organic analogy allowed for a private realm that, because and as long as it did not prejudice communal ends and accepted instead final communal control, was conducive to social interests. This now received greater emphasis: "It is idle to expect that, either in the individual or the nation, the self-seeking and acquisitive impulses can quickly, wholly, or even generally be displaced by sentiments and aspirations for the welfare of the whole. But neither can it be maintained that human nature in individuals, or groups, is immutable and intractable."[84] Hence, though both egoistic and communal leanings were natural, so was human growth. And the latter assumed a pluralistic potential of human nature that could be developed in socially desirable fashion: "Substantial changes in our environment or in our social institutions can apply different stimuli to 'human nature' and evoke different psychical responses . . . it seems reasonably possible to modify the conscious stress of personal gain-seeking and to educate a clearer sense of social solidarity and service."[85] Nor would such manipulation, or direction, be contrary to human nature; on the individual level, it would simply support the social drives; on the social, it would invoke the rationality of a group mind. This

---

[81] J. A. Hobson, *Incentives in the New Industrial Order* (London, 1922), pp. 29, 31–32.

[82] Ibid., p. 70.

[83] Ibid., pp. 87–92.

[84] J. A. Hobson, *Free-Thought in the Social Sciences* (London, 1926), p. 261.

[85] Hobson, *Wealth and Life*, p. 234.

fused into Hobson's identification of the various layers contained within a person. There was "in each individual a unique personality, a member of a class or group, and a member of the wider community."[86]

What of the similarities or differences among people? Hobson was happy to maintain that "in body and mind we are, say 95 per cent, alike,"[87] and that consequently a great similarity of needs, desires, and interests existed; yet differences of body, mind, and character were valuable precisely because they denoted differences. Some socialists could push these notions to extremes, however, denying innate differences and promoting "an excessive 'environmentalism' to meet the claims put forward for the superior productivity of men of ability as a justification for their high rewards. The democratic doctrine that 'men are by nature equal' finds useful support in the biological doctrine of reversion to a mean, and in appraising nurture above nature."[88] The influence of eugenics, which in early years had sometimes driven Hobson to overstep the boundaries of liberalism, was retained in combination with his sensitivity to the physiological and innate determinants of behaviour. They served as a brake on his ethical predilections, predilections that for most progressives signalled an environmentally sustained universal development of the human race.

Hobson's views on human nature are of more than passing interest. As intellectual history, they afford a vista of a changing climate of ideas, illustrating how some of the nineteenth-century fashions of thought—on the inevitability of development, on the interaction of body and mind, on human rationality, and on the relationship of the individual to society—were carried forward and adapted for the educated reading public. These modifications took place in the light of new scientific findings and the rise or transformation of professional disciplines. Hobson belonged to a generation increasingly beset by the difficulties of combining ethics and science: more accurately, of reading their ethical and humanitarian preferences into the mass of new scientific evidence available to students of society, and then harnessing that tamed and "socialized" science back into the service of humanity. Hobson's prevailing image of a world unified in the four different senses of his organicism—vital, interdependent, communitarian, and continuous—was being undermined by the fragmentation and specialisation of knowledge as well as by social and political events that weakened those confident worldviews.

Nevertheless, Hobson continued in his attempt to diffuse a message whose ideological content had changed but little, and his multiform ideas

[86] J. A. Hobson, *Towards Social Equality* (Oxford, 1931), p. 5.
[87] Ibid., p. 25.
[88] Hobson, *Wealth and Life*, p.52; *Free-Thought in the Social Sciences*, p. 250.

on human nature helped to buttress both his belief in the wide bases of the social sciences and in the political programmes he persistently endorsed. Psychology afforded insights into human nature that could partly replace the important functions of questioning, exposition, and criticism that philosophy had provided in the past, to "liberate, cleanse, and nourish with fresh vigour the damaged or endangered theories of economics and politics."[89]

On one level, then, new findings about human behaviour could shake up the complacency of existing systems of knowledge. On another, they could equip those systems with new methodologies, so that "Politics and Economics and other social arts present themselves as groups of problems of the interaction and co-operation of minds in the conscious handling of physical environment."[90] Beyond that, and central to the Hobsonian enterprise, modern psychology and sociology upheld an ethical liberalism dedicated to the pursuit of human welfare, and doing so in the complex sense of "resolving all political and economic systems into terms of collective and personal feeling, thinking, willing."[91] A recognition of all those levels of human activity bore a clear ideological message to the older and cruder liberalism of the past: "Absolute individualism, complete equalitarianism, mechanical rationality, the ruling principles of the [old] liberal politics as of the [old] liberal economics, have been justly discredited by the close study of human nature in its individual and collective behaviour . . . and have rendered necessary a complete recasting of the theory and art of government."[92]

[89] Hobson, *Free-Thought in the Social Sciences*, p. 276.
[90] Ibid., p. 264.
[91] Ibid.
[92] Ibid., pp. 268–69.

PART TWO

Ideology Redivivus

Ideologies are ubiquitous forms of political thinking. Let's put this more forcefully: the access we have to the actual political thought of a society is always through its ideologies, that is, through the configurations and clusters of interdependent political concepts and ideas that circulate in that society at different levels of articulation. It is not attained through individual concepts or through individual thinkers, because neither language nor societies host these elements in isolation. The raw material of political thought at the disposal of any society is immense, and the meanings and semantic structures of political language are necessarily indeterminate. That indeterminism entails a fundamental pluralism of meaning that is partly captured by Gallie's notion of essential contestability.[1] Political concepts are contestable both because of the value judgments they express, concerning which no preferred position can be allocated indisputable and incontestable status, as Gallie claimed, but also because the intension of any political concept contains more components than any particular instance can hold at a given time.[2] Ideologies act as constraints on the infinite range of political meanings that a society produces, constraints that are not only logical but cultural (for logic is still an arbitrary carrier of meaning). Ideologies thus inject an aura of determinacy into political language through decontesting the essentially contestable—in other words, through linking together particular interpretations of each constituent concept that have been selected and prioritised out of an indeterminate range of meanings they may signify. The outcome is a distinct conceptual morphology that is absolutely vital to the making of decisions, and decisions are, after all, the prime political act.

Conceptual decontestation occurs at different levels of political discourse and can create holistic groupings of ideas within a large spectrum. For example, a particular combination of conceptions of time, of the priority of groups, of the value and fact of human equality will form a

---

[1] W. G. Gallie, "Essentially Contested Concepts," *Proceedings of the Aristotelian Society*, 56 (1955–56): 167–98.

[2] For a more detailed exposition of this argument see M. Freeden, *Ideologies and Political Theory: A Conceptual Approach* (Oxford, 1996), chap. 2. On the polysemy of words see P. Ricoeur, *Interpretation Theory: Discourse and the Surplus of Meaning* (Fort Worth, 1976).

field that sits well within the realm of what have conventionally been identified as socialist ideologies. But extract the priority of groups from that field and attach it instead to a xenophobic dislike of aliens and to a political exclusiveness, and the new cluster is located within what we term the field of nationalism. Some of these ideological groupings may be reasonably disparate; others may overlap. Some may ignore other ideological discourses, but many will compete over the diverse specific meanings potentially available in the same semantic field in the typical bid of an ideology for control over political language. Ideological morphology is plastic and malleable through time, space, and the contingency of events. Its default position is, as we have seen, pluralist. That is why ideologies, and their study, always come up against the problem of boundaries. Ideological boundaries are simply limits placed on the unavoidable fluidity of political meaning, but those boundaries are necessary to impose a Gestalt on our worldviews and to enable political choices to be made. Some boundary issues relate to stretching the conventional core of an ideology into new terrain; others relate to the initial fact that even the most doctrinaire of ideologies still constitutes a potentially ephemeral internal coalition of ideas—its indeterminacy and pluralism cannot be overridden for too long.

The theory of ideology that I have endeavoured to develop over the past two decades stems from an interest in the ubiquitous existence of ideology itself as a central manifestation of political thought, and from the parallel dissatisfaction with previously dominant modes of approach to the topic. To this very day the popularised Marxist view of ideology as the masking of truth with dissimulations that are substantively insignificant as research areas—and ideology-critique as the exposure of that cover-up—is still prominent in works on political theory.[3] It is as if the radical rethinking of ideology, especially over the past two decades, had never taken place. We are still enormously in Clifford Geertz's debt for launching the view of ideology as a symbolic mapping device without which members of a society are disoriented.[4] Conceptual historians have done their level best to persuade scholars of ideology that concept and context are interlocked, that history like political theory is subject to continuous hermeneutic rereadings as horizons of interpretation change, and that conflict over the "proper" meanings of concepts is a central facet of sociopolitical life. Sophisticated theories of historical intentionality and

[3] For one recent example, see I. Shapiro, *The Moral Foundation of Politics* (New Haven, 2003).

[4] C. Geertz, "Ideology as a Cultural System," in Geertz, *The Interpretation of Cultures: Selected Essays* (New York, 2000).

contextuality, such as Quentin Skinner's,[5] have invigorated our abilities to decode texts and to assess the meaning of meaning, applying the "linguistic turn" to the study of society. We have equally to acknowledge the important contribution of post-Marxist thinkers such as Ernesto Laclau and Chantal Mouffe, who have revived the idea of an ideology as a hegemonic articulatory discourse and who have emphasised the role of floating and empty signifiers in the construction of temporary social "realities,"[6] a path taken further by Slavoj Žižek through his cultural explorations inspired by Lacanian psychoanalysis.[7] Paul Ricouer, in turn, has enlightened us about ideology, not the least by means of his notion of the surplus of meaning and its consequent restoring of unintentionality as an important feature of political language. By now, a new generation of scholars has discovered the attractions of studying ideology and is advancing our understanding through detailed concrete studies and theoretical innovations. In short, a major redevelopment of political theory has been occurring and one cannot but wonder why it is that cultural and professional constraints have prevented so many American political theorists, in particular, from taking stock of these developments and from addressing them.

The study of liberalism as a concrete and contextualised set of discourses presented in part 1 needs therefore to be read with the morphological features of ideologies, on which I have increasingly focused, in view. The diverse languages of liberalism—and of any ideological family—are not an aberration, nor are all but one of these variants a deviation from a discursive and ideational norm established by a "correct" version. Liberalism's boundaries are permeable because its mainstream is negotiable at its edges and, occasionally, closer even to its core. The boundaries of an ideological family depend on the family resemblances that a given cultural perspective emphasises rather than on objective criteria that emanate from within the ideology itself. Green eyes, obesity, the Habsburg chin, or musicality are different bases on which to classify family membership, and over time and space they may be allocated variable significance as a classifying criterion. For that reason the case of eugenic thought is a particularly revealing one. An intellectual (or for some, anti-intellectual) current of thought typically believed to lie outside the liberal domain may be seen to labour in a difficult but not impossible relationship with liberalism.

[5] J. Tully, ed., *Meaning and Context: Quentin Skinner and his Critics* (Cambridge, 1988); Q. Skinner, *Visions of Politics*, 3 vols. (Cambridge, 2002).

[6] E. Laclau and C. Mouffe, *Hegemony and Socialist Strategy* (London, 1985).

[7] For a major interpretative article juxtaposing recent analyses of ideology see A. Norval, "The Things we do with Words—Contemporary Approaches to the Analysis of Ideology," *British Journal of Political Science* 30 (2000): 313–46.

The Challenge of Ideological Boundaries

The viability of ideological boundaries is the puzzle addressed in chapter 7. Eugenics had for a long time a pedigree associating it only with right-wing debates. Programmes relating to the breeding of superior races and the sterilisation of the physically and mentally unfit dominated public perceptions. That perception must still stand, and its revival through nazism has irredeemably tainted eugenics with the brush of iniquity. But careful ideological analysis reveals the extraordinary adaptability of eugenist views. If we begin to think of eugenist positions as coalitions of disparate ideas that are only held together by dint of very specific decontestations accorded to each of their components, there emerges a different range of ideational possibilities and related political practices. Components such as human and social improvement could be tweaked to relate to the body as well as the mind or the social environment. Equality of opportunity could be introduced as a prerequisite to the eugenic improvement of all. And the interdependence of the group could be invoked to emphasize altruistic virtues, the eugenic protection of the social whole—the community—and the need for benevolent social control.

Through eugenics, both liberalism and socialism explored some of their borders—ethical, conceptual, and political. They discovered that those borders could be extended, but that—unsurprisingly—such distension also brought in its wake the problems of dilution and of a reduced capacity for safeguarding the meanings that key concepts possessed within a liberal semantic field. Whether liberal ideology was engaged in a colonising activity that attempted to constrict external illiberal claims on the science of heredity, or whether liberalism was giving vent to an internal illiberal latency in its midst, is a question that has perturbed later scholars.[8] But that is really the same question from two vantage points, and it illustrates the fragile relationship between the interpretative role of the scholar and the interior architecture of any given ideological position.

The progressive flirtation with eugenics relates to one important mode of ideological decontestation: the endeavour to legitimate specific ideological constructs through invoking scientific authority. The search for scientific underpinning may or may not settle arguments among scientifically inclined ideological producers but, as noted in part 1, it has always been employed as a tactic to promote an ideological product among populations at large. Eugenics struggled to attain scientific status within the biological and social sciences. Its popularity relates to the hold the various

---

[8] See, e.g., D. J. Kevles, *In the Name of Eugenics* (New York, 1985); Diana B. Paul, *Controlling Human Heredity : 1865 to the Present* (Atlantic Highlands, NJ, 1995).

forms of Darwinism had on the public imagination, and it was rubber-stamped by conservatives eager to pronounce human inequality as natural and to remove from society elements believed to inhibit the accomplishments of the rest. But progressives demonstrated the malleability that conceptual indeterminacy inevitably bestows on any arrangement of political ideas. They did so by offering different interpretations not only of each concept, but also of the conceptual configurations that were available to ideological innovators. Scholars are now beginning to acknowledge that eugenics is an intricate ideological construct.[9]

The example of eugenics also illustrates the complex layers of the target audiences of an ideology. To begin with, eugenics involved a debate among specialists. Quickly, however, the political potential of this issue was discovered by members of the political intelligentsia for the purposes of advancing the mainstream ideological positions to which they were committed. Specialists were then brought into the debate but the language was simplified through pamphlets, articles in general periodicals, and popularising books. Ideologies need first and foremost to communicate with the broader audiences they seek to mobilise. Eugenics, to be more accurate, was not an ideology but an ideological segment that could be slotted into different macroideologies. It performed very different roles for socialism, liberalism, conservatism, or fascism. For the latter, it was closely adjacent to the core but for the others it occupied a peripheral place. It was linked to particular issues concerning real or imagined degeneration of the human stock, to questions of immigration and class, and it invited or commended practices such as limiting the right of some groups to reproduce. But it never secured a sufficiently strategic position within the first three ideological families to have a serious impact on core concepts and beliefs. The shock waves eugenics produced were countered by robust conceptual structures that, ultimately, gave it insufficient opportunities for challenging the semantic fields it attempted to penetrate.

I have dwelt upon chapter 7 because it provides a study in ideological failure, but also a study in the legion possibilities of ideological fragmentation and recombination. It might assist us in reinforcing our understanding of political thought not only as a site of ethical pronouncements and identity-bestowing narratives, but also as a site of imaginative creativity, of ideational experimentation, of contestation over meaning and influence. It demonstrates that the actual political thinking taking place in a society does not present itself in blocks or closed packages, but is—certainly at its edges if less frequently at its core beliefs—the subject of continuous renegotiation and reformulation. That of course mirrors the

---

[9] See in particular M. A. Hasian, *The Rhetoric of Eugenics in Anglo-American Thought* (Athens, GA, 1996).

political processes that occur in healthy polities and it brings home an important lesson to remember when analyzing ideologies. The very readiness of liberalism to explore new areas, even hostile territory, sets it apart from the dogmatic and doctrinaire ideologies that have ravished Europe and parts of Asia in the twentieth century. Those totalitarian versions constrained the development of ideological language through the relentless exercise of power, with its attendant penalties. Totalitarian ideologies, however, are not the norm but the exception to normal ideological performance—artificially superimposed conceptual arrangements that deliberately avoid reflecting the variety of political thinking a society produces. Itself a product of modernism, totalitarianism thwarts the diversity that is the hallmark of modernism. Whereas for the special case of liberalism diversity is part of the valuing of pluralism and difference and is vital to social, moral, and intellectual flourishing, for the general case of ideologies diversity is an inevitable aspect of modern ideological morphology and microstructure.

CONFIGURATIONAL MALLEABILITIES

Chapters 8 and 9 are, at the time of writing, explorations of relative ideological success. In focusing on the British social democratic tradition, one that includes New Labour as its most recent manifestation, they illuminate some of the chapters in part 1 in a more temporally comparative light. For one, it reaffirms that the new liberalism was no idiosyncratic or fleeting phenomenon. Whether or not contemporary scholars are acquainted with its innovative goals and legislative details, it may be rediscovered as a central component of modern social democratic programmes and thinking, certainly leaving strong traces in New Labour. Alertness to that heritage is precisely the outcome of the new approach to the internally complex morphology of ideologies. It testifies to the ability of ideologies to recombine their components—themselves always capable of rereadings—in attempts to become more politically relevant or attractive. And it raises a host of challenging questions: What are the ideological spaces available for ideologies to expand into? How are ideological boundaries sealed—historically as well as conceptually? Why are some combinations propitious for the survival and transformation of a given ideology, and others inauspicious? And the overarching question, to which I shall return below: What makes us decide that a particular field of ideas and conceptual combinations is an ideology—a decision crowned by the act of naming it? Undoubtedly, such naming or classification is no mere academic exercise. It is itself part of a society's ideological struggle over its identity or, more precisely, over the range of competing identities from which it must choose.

Confronted with the problems that engaged socialists—poverty, class, inequality, and the marginalisation of large sections of the population—liberalism offered a plethora of solutions weighty enough to be incorporated into future progressive thinking. Liberalism injected the social democratic tradition with sensitivity towards issues of liberty, the fair treatment of the underprivileged, and the harnessing of individual initiative for the social good. These issues became a non-negotiable component of progressive thinking, even if they appeared in multiple variants. Liberalism was steered in a social democratic direction—as, to a lesser extent, were some French and German liberal or progressive ideologies—for a number of reasons. Some were institutional, such as the extension of the franchise and the capture of many newspapers by crusading social reformers. Some related to the prominence of certain individuals in political debate, politicians and intellectuals who secured the ears of a nation while discovering the virtues of collective action. The liberalisms that did not tread that path were condemned to irrelevance or to abduction by the family of conservatisms. That was, for instance, the fate of the more individualistic, nonregulatory, and merit-oriented variant that assumed the title of libertarianism. Hayek, famously, asserted that liberal social democracy was the false pretender, the deviant from the right path of libertarianism—a degenerative process he located in as early a thinker as Mill.[10]

For an ideology such as liberalism the path of internal development lay through adapting its core concerns—liberty, individuality, progress, rationality, a concern for the general good, accountable and restricted power—to changing understandings of social structure; to the impact of mass democratisation; to new economic theories; to the growing potential of benevolent state legislation and regulation; to emerging technologies of social and actuarial risk pooling; and to alternating ethical standpoints concerning individual and social responsibility. The dominant progressive semantic field underpinning the welfare state was therefore positioned between voluntarism versus compulsion, wants versus needs, the individual versus the community, élitist expertise versus popular participation.[11] It is a feature of ideological morphology that available decontestations of every one of these notions permit these potential dichotomies to find a modus vivendi of compatibility. Social insurance offered individual thrift

[10] See F. A. Hayek, *New Studies in Philosophy, Politics, Economics and the History of Ideas* (London, 1985), pp. 129–30.

[11] See M. Freeden, "The Coming of the Welfare State," in T. Ball and R. Bellamy, eds., *The Cambridge History of Twentieth Century Political Thought* (Cambridge, 2003), pp. 7–44.

over and above a base of enforced contributions. The possibility of personal choice in a capitalist setting was reasonably constrained by inviting people to prefer some choices over others, and by refusing to allow a totally free market in potentially life-sustaining choices such as health. Individual growth and expression were decoded as possible only through exposure to the assets a cultural and political community possessed qua community, assets it was obligated to share among its individual members as of right; while the well-being of the community itself relied on the diverse vitality of those members, separately and in interaction. Meanwhile, the demands and requirements of rising social classes were tempered by the custodians of science and social wisdom, although the uses to which such knowledge was put were continuously subject to the verdict of public approval.

Depending on our point of view, we can treat this as the evolutionary story of a particular ideology, or as a case study in the assembling of any ideology from a pool of components, components that themselves acquire meanings only when put in a particular juxtaposition with others. Those meanings are hence fundamentally modifiable, formed as they are at the interface between logic, culture, and happenstance. Internal (logical) constraints built in to any concept meet external (cultural, social, and incidental) constraints that any concept confronts in its idea-environment. Each set of constraints—internal and external—has a number of options at its disposal in adjusting to the other set of constraints it encounters.

One lesson gleaned from conceptual historians is that from our current perspective we are more likely to trace current social democracy back to liberal roots. The reason for that is not necessarily because those roots are the authentic and correct ones (there is no way of arguing that they have a monopoly of influence, any more than grassroots working-class culture does). Rather, it is because the self-definitions and self-understandings of key social democratic figures—Tony Blair included—have incorporated key features of the liberal tradition, and because it now behoves us to make sense of the progressive twentieth century as the emergence of liberal welfarism (one of many twentieth-century stories, needless to say). This is not to claim that liberalism was destined to develop in that direction. It patently was not, for the inner logic of any ideological pattern is always multipathed, and necessarily leads in innumerable directions, some of which are incompatible, and many of which are simply weeded out through the social imposition of cultural preferences. There was no logical reason to preclude welfare solutions that involved a total privatisation of welfare, or that encouraged—as with right-wing eugenics—the voluntary elimination of the genetic input of individuals with assumed hereditary defects. Some versions of liberalism entertained such solutions, but they lost the cultural, not the logical, battle for legitimacy in an idea-environment that promoted communal ethics. Communal ethics themselves, however, could be paternalist or enforced, but these variants, too, were weakened—though not eliminated—through the vigorous injection of liberal values into public policy.

The study of British social democracy alerts us to the durability of ideological segments that have seemingly been vanquished or become obsolete. But they never seem to die, nor even fade away. Rather, they emerge in new guises, often invisible as such to the wearers themselves, never the most informed about the traditions they inhabit. New labels and a slightly rearranged conceptual content—say Crosland's revisionist socialism, or Titmuss's combination of altruism and social care with market choice, or the "Third Way"—are sufficient to impress upon an inadequately sophisticated public of ideological consumers that a new product is at hand. And of course they are new in an important sense, for maybe that is precisely what typical ideological innovation looks like: not a radical, as yet unencountered view of the social world (Marx may have come near to offering that) but a rejigged configuration of ideas that have already been around, fine-tuned in an attempt to capture the latest high ground of political language and symbolism. And undeniably, ideologies rely on the inevitable disillusionment that all political systems produce as they routinise or falter, through appealing to a vision of hope and betterment, or to feelings of fear and mistrust, that prompt citizens perennially to seek alternative solutions. Invariably, those solutions remain ideologically indeterminate. If they are as yet untested—the projections of progressives—the contextual constraints that operate on them are unforeseen. If they are allegedly tested—the comfort of conservatives—the contextual constraints operating on them will not be replicated exactly. Ideological intentions never equal ideological outcomes, let alone the ideological interpretations of the scholar aspiring to disinterestedness.

Chapter 9, explicitly, combines specific political commentary with a broader purview of ideological investigation. Exploring ideologies requires micro- as well as macroanalysis. Examining a synchronic discourse with diachronic moorings is one part of the microexercise, as conceptual historians have rightly instructed us. Another part is the detailed alignment of particular policies on an ideological periphery, in order to chart the interchange between political practices and exigencies and the fluid core of an ideology. A third aspect is to explore the different levels at which an ideology is articulated in terms of the causes it seeks to serve and the audiences it seeks to engage. Political language interweaves between the philosophical, the rhetorical, and the realm of political analysis, commentary, and program, though each may serve as a minor key to the others' major tune. Arguments can be presented in parallel conceptual morphologies in order to maximise their desired effect, or because cultural patterns of understanding direct and channel modes of expression; or they may even contain these multiple dimensions in the same sentence and be consumed simultaneously by discrete groups. Meaning is often assembled with purposive care and, if not, is still redolent with deep significance.

A fourth consideration is to identify the four Ps of an ideology: proximity, priority, permeability, and proportionality.[12] The case study of New Labour demonstrates how a particular ideological family can be redesigned while maintaining sufficient semblance of continuity to avoid overly alienating supporters, while increasing its mobilising power. Ideas redolent of traditional socialism, such as nationalisation or class, were removed from proximity to the core, while private choice and individual rights were locked into notions of welfare and the importance of the family. In assessing the conditions for proper community life and for individual conduct vis-à-vis law and order, the demand for responsible behaviour towards others was prioritised over other claims that could be made in the name of community or of individual activity, such as need-fulfilment or self-expression. Ideological permeability was illustrated through the heavy intermixture of concepts such as equality of opportunity, social duties, or the significance of work. Each of these concepts can be found in other ideological families, where the work they discharge may be different from that enlisted in the cause of New Labour. They are clearly not peculiar to any given ideological family. Finally, proportionality invokes the salience of a theme or cluster of concepts within an ideology. In the case of New Labour, the initial emphasis on an élite-delivered modernity took up an inordinate amount of space in the ideological construct that was assembled, at the expense of participatory politics and respect for the socialist past from which New Labour emerged—both of which were crowded out of the political agenda. The inevitable loss of the millennium as an iconic future-oriented symbol of *New* Labour has not been replaced by an equivalently potent linchpin.

WHEN IS AN IDEOLOGY AN IDEOLOGY?

Both New Labour and the instance of nationalism as an ideology, addressed in chapter 10, should remind us that verbal and written messages are not the only, and not even always the most effective, means of conveying ideological messages. The recent salience of "spin" alerts us to the packaging of an ideology. The inundation of jingles and visual images to

---

[12] For greater detail see M. Freeden, *A Very Short Introduction to Ideology* (Oxford, 2003), pp. 60–65.

which we are subjected highlights the function of marketing techniques applied to the political arena as a fast, attention-grabbing means to mobilise support. And the role of emotion in political thinking is one of its most underappreciated features, augmented by the disdain most political philosophers have shown for emotive argument, or for an appeal to the allegedly volatile passions.

Nationalism raises a number of crucial issues in ideology research. The expression of emotion is overtly, not implicitly, accepted by nationalist thinkers as a praiseworthy trait when directed at the nation and its advancement, and it is often redefined as patriotism. But through an examination of nationalism we may be able to reassess the vital place strong feeling has in any political vision, as well as accept it as a normal component of attitudes and beliefs in politics. Excluding emotion from political discourse is to render it schematic and emaciated—indeed, to misrepresent it. Nor is there a law that determines that emotion necessarily clouds reason, when rational arguments can be, and are, passionately advocated, as noted in chapter 1.

In addition, nationalism is an example of a "thin" ideology, a distinction I deem to be important.[13] Ideologies are only as comprehensive as they need to be, and the narrowness of coverage that nationalism imparts to the spectrum of issues that macroideologies—such as liberalism or conservatism—address reflects once again the pliability of an ideology as an effective political device. In the case of nationalism, its "natural" habitat is related to the specificity of the task it tackles—the creation or enhancement of nationhood. Because nationalism refers to salient, often dramatic, political action and to the establishment of political identity in ways that have traditionally excited popular support, it is a prime instance of the action-oriented features of ideologies. But we should not be taken in by assuming that such rough and ready political activism is typical of ideologies. Indeed, as chapter 10 shows, nationalism is usually to be found as a segment in a host-ideology that impresses on the former many features of the latter.

The question of "thinness" also applies to Green political thought, which often appears as the ideational equivalent of a pressure group rather than an inclusive political party. Green theory concentrates on a field that, while interrelated to conventional concerns of the macroideologies, refuses to address some of their key issues, preferring to regard these as consequent upon solving ecological and environmental challenges.[14] Part of that may be ideological immaturity, reflecting the newness of Green political theory and the absence of major foundational thinkers in

---

[13] See M. Freeden, *Ideologies and Political Theory*, pp. 485–87.
[14] Ibid., pp. 526–54.

its trajectory of development. Another part may also be the impatience of this strange mix of radicalism and conservatism with mainstream political thinking and policy. Chapter 11 raises a quizzical eyebrow not at the aims and intentions encapsulated in Green ideology but at the reluctance of Green theorists to examine critically their own intellectual enterprises, and to detach themselves from the oversimplifying paradigms some of those theorists have loosely and casually assimilated into their own arguments. It attempts to apply some of the concerns already represented in previous chapters in this collection to a burgeoning, yet occasionally fragile, intellectual enterprise.[15]

Behind these problems looms the more fundamental issue: what *is* the conventional garb and framework of an ideology? Can we throw a net over any combination of communal, politically engaged thinking and call it an ideology? Why do some ideological formulations attain the status of "families"? Can we break up the conventional macroideologies and confer the status of ideology on any of its segments, or on any recombination of such segments? Yet again, we are confronted by a host of impediments in so doing. To begin with, there is convention—the historical accumulation of significance attached to political movements-cum-ideologies that accrue a momentum of their own, one that is handily used as a signpost or shorthand for political positions in acute competition and that consequently has a considerable degree of staying power. To that may be added historical and political credibility, inasmuch as certain macroideological families have an impressive track record of achievements and even of failures—interwar fascism's failures were monumental and shocking in their perverse way, but the menace of fascism is still believable. Then there is self-definition—the credence we accord to individuals' ideological identity as understood by them. Most such descriptions reinforce each other, though the degree of political self-awareness and sophistication will vary. The margins of these political identities, however, can be very problematic. In particular, the misappropriation of another ideology's features has often been characteristic of devious ideologies such as national *socialism*—a case of conceptual stretching and stolen clothes if ever there was one. Or the struggle over a label may split even self-definers into largely incompatible groups. Liberalism is itself a prime instance, with the libertarian new right appropriating—though not categorically misappropriating—liberalism's family name in the face of left-liberal protests. Finally, the issues of heuristic convenience or of scholarly interpretation suggest the possibility of reconstructing traditions retrospectively. One such example is the revival of republicanism as a tag under which to regroup

---

[15] For a sophisticated analysis of Green ideology see G. Talshir, *The Political Ideology of Green Parties* (London, 2002).

many populist and democratic ideological segments that had previously been attached to other ideological families.[16]

The end result of all these considerations on ideology requires quite a few modifications in perspective. One of the most important is this. Rather than rise to the typical historical challenge of explaining change, we ought to rephrase the question: given the permanently fluctuating pool of ideas assembled in any ideological phenomenon, what accounts for the temporary *stability* of ideologies? More appositely, how is the illusion of stability produced and managed? All this demands not only ethical and sociological probings of political communities, but also a new epistemological appraisal, one that incorporates a semantic holism in the decoding of ideologies, but a holism of variable interdependencies that impacts back on the notion of community itself, in its physical, emotional, and intellectual aspects.

The closing chapter of this collection adds some reflections to my earlier investigations into the theory of ideologies. Why are we, as political theorists, dogged with the problem of practice? How can non-Marxists as well as Marxists address the spurious gap between what people think and what they do? How can we begin from the other end, reading back ideological decontestation into collective political acts? And can political thinking be a practice? This may lead us to a reassessment of the nature of political theory itself: what makes a political theory *political*? I hope to devote some attention to this in future. For the time being I would like to suggest that its construal as ideology, in the senses conveyed through these pages, may have something to do with this. In no particular order, stability, typicality, communicability, influence and mobilisation of support, creative experimentation, decontestation and its opposite, ambiguity—these are among the main attributes of political thinking and language, and they crave the kind of serious scholarship currently largely siphoned off to political philosophy.

All this, significantly, draws us back in the final section of chapter 12 to the new liberal tradition, not as a solution to the questions raised, but as a carrier of political interpretations and practices that can be crucially enriched by drawing on other intellectual understandings. That itself may be a liberal conclusion. The circle may not be closed, but it thickens and becomes more solid with the progress of human understanding.

---

[16] See the discussion of Sandel in chap. 2, above, as well as P. Pettit, *Republicanism: A Theory of Freedom and Government* (Oxford, 1999); J. W. Maynor, *Republicanism in the Modern World* (Cambridge, 2003).

CHAPTER SEVEN

Eugenics and Progressive Thought: A Study in Ideological Affinity

EUGENICS AS AN INSTRUMENT OF REFORM: DIVERGENT VIEWS

The issues raised by eugenics are of more than passing interest for the student of political thought. In itself a minor offshoot of turn-of-the-century sociobiological thought that never achieved ideological "takeoff" in terms of influence or circulation, there was certainly more in eugenics than nowadays meets the eye. The following pages propose to depart from the oversimplistic identification of eugenics, as political theory, with racism or ultraconservatism and to offer instead two alternative modes of interpretation.[1] On the one hand, eugenics will be portrayed as an exploratory avenue of the social reformist tendencies of early-twentieth-century British political thought. On the other, it will serve as a case study illustrating the complexity and overlapping that characterise most modern ideologies. While recognising, of course, the appeal of eugenics for the right, a central question pervading the forthcoming analysis will be the attraction it had for progressives of liberal and socialist persuasions,[2] with the ultimate aim of discovering the fundamental affinities the left had, and may still have, with this type of thinking.

Some difficulties relating to the definition of the field already point to ensuing problems. The coiner of the term "eugenics," Francis Galton, who established it as a specific area of study with scientific aspirations, defined it as "the study of agencies under social control that may improve or impair the racial qualities of future generations, either physically or mentally."[3] This definition was, however, only arrived at after lengthy debates by a committee that included Karl Pearson, the biometrician. Galton himself had preferred a definition he had forwarded during the first large-scale discussion of eugenics, under the auspices of the newly established Sociological Society, at the London School of Economics in 1904: "The science which deals with all influences that improve the inborn qual-

---

[1] See, for example, J.B.S. Haldane, "Eugenics and Social Reforms," *Nation*, 31.5.1924; Ashley Montagu, *Man's Most Dangerous Myth: The Fallacy of Race* (5th ed. New York, 1974), p. 236.

[2] I am using the term "progressive" as an abbreviation for liberal social reformers and moderate socialists, while recognising that they are not an ideologically monolithic group.

[3] F. Galton, *Memories of My Life* (London, 1908), p. 321; D. W. Forrest, *Francis Galton: The Life and Work of a Victorian Genius* (London, 1974), p. 260.

ities of a race; also with those that develop them to the utmost advantage."[4] The difference between the two definitions had significant bearing upon the ideological debates that shortly began to vitiate the scientific standing of this new branch of inquiry, and a number of commentators "unearthed" the latter definition, which suited their inclinations better. It included within eugenics nurture or environment as well as nature or heredity and consequently appealed to those who preferred what may broadly be termed the "socialist" or "new liberal" point of view, with its stress on the social and (to a lesser extent) physical surroundings that mould human nature.[5]

As against categorical statements, such as Pearson's, that the influence of environment was one-fifth or one-tenth that of heredity,[6] two basic claims were opposed. The first made much of the perception of society as a complex originating in social transmission,[7] but as this argument ignores the question of eugenics as such it is outside the scope of this chapter. The second—continuing the late-nineteenth-century debate—stressed the relative weight of environment in comparison to heredity. Havelock Ellis spoke of "a real underlying harmony" of the two.[8] The biologist J. A. Thomson, also an active eugenist, referred—when delivering the second Galton Lecture in 1915—to the "pruning shears . . . in the hands of the environment" and summed up: "As eugenists we are concerned with the natural inheritance and its nature, which is fundamental, as men we are also concerned with our social heritage, which is supreme."[9]

Most progressive eugenists, however, carried their argument a great deal further. In the words of one of them, S. Herbert: "We have the environment acting, as it were, like a sieve, separating the fit from the unfit and selecting those who are best adapted to their surroundings. Every change of environment necessarily alters the incidence of selection, the type of the survivors in each instance being determined by the survival-value."[10] This was developed by Julian Huxley, who not only decried the antagonism between the environmentalist and the eugenist but later came to hold emphatically that genetic improvement "can only be realized in a

---

[4] F. Galton, "Eugenics: Its Definition, Scope and Aims," *Sociological Papers* (London, 1905), p. 45.

[5] In the nondoctrinaire sense. See M. Freeden, *The New Liberalism: An Ideology of Social Reform* (Oxford, 1978), chap. 2.

[6] K. Pearson, *Nature and Nurture: The Problem of The Future* (London, 1910), p. 27.

[7] See L. T. Hobhouse, *Social Evolution and Political Theory* (New York, 1911), p. 54.

[8] H. Ellis, "Individualism and Socialism," *Contemporary Review*, 101 (1912): 526. Reprinted with revisions in H. Ellis, *The Task of Social Hygiene* (London, 1912).

[9] J. A. Thomson, "Eugenics and War," the second Galton Lecture, *Eugenics Review*, 7 (1915): 6, 14.

[10] S. Herbert, "Eugenics and Socialism," *Eugenics Review* 2 (1910): 122.

certain kind of social environment, so that eugenics is inevitably a particular aspect of the study of man in society."[11] Elsewhere he succinctly summed up the two factors of environment: "We can alter the expression of those inborn qualities which exist, and we can alter the selection which presses differently on different genetic types in different environments."[12]

C. W. Saleeby—perhaps the best-known propagandist and popularizer of eugenics for over twenty years—raised the issue in a series of articles in the *New Statesman* (writing under the pseudonym "Lens"). To counter the objection to including nurture within eugenics he not only invoked Galton's 1904 definition, but also observed simply: "We desire not fine germ-cells, but fine human beings."[13] And the *New Statesman*'s founder, Sidney Webb, had already written in 1910, in a sympathetic reference to eugenics, that its object was "not merely to produce fine babies but to ensure the ultimate production of fine adults." Therefore "we cannot afford to leave . . . bad environment alone. . . . The 'survival of the fittest' in an environment unfavourable to progress may . . . mean the survival of the lowest parasite." The typical and all-applicable Webbian conclusion was in effect the assimilation of eugenics into the following formula: "It is accordingly our business, as eugenists, deliberately to manipulate the environment so that the survivors may be of the type which we regard as the highest."[14] H. J. Laski, too, in an article published when he was only seventeen, had praised eugenics while precociously reminding his readers that "man cannot be separated from his environment, and it is well that we should render it as healthy as we can."[15]

These views certainly do not bear out the sole association of eugenics with an extreme "anti-environmentalism," whose position was, as the psychologist J. M. Cattell wrote, "If the congenital equipment of an individual should prescribe completely what he will accomplish in life, equality of opportunity, education and social reform would be of no significance."[16] The many progressives who understood that to be the eugenic viewpoint were appalled by the idea that, in the words of the liberal weekly *Nation*, eugenics conceived of social justice as self-defeating because social justice allowed the multiplication of the least worthy members of a society. Consequently, "the danger of the inverted view is that

[11] J. Huxley, "The Case for Eugenics," *Sociological Review* 18 (1926): 289; "Eugenics and Society," *Eugenics Review* 28 (1936): 13.

[12] "Eugenics, Socialism and Capitalism," *Eugenics Review* 27 (1935): 113. J. Huxley in debate at members' meeting.

[13] Lens, "Imperial Eugenics, V. Nurtural Eugenics," *New Statesman* 26.2.1916, p. 489.

[14] S. Webb, "Eugenics and the Poor Law: The Minority Report," *Eugenics Review* 2 (1910).

[15] H. J. Laski, "The Scope of Eugenics," *Westminster Review* 174 (1910): 30.

[16] Quoted in W. E. Castle, *Genetics and Eugenics* (Cambridge, MA, 1916), p. 266.

social reforms destined to the noblest objects of succouring the weak and caring for the backward in the race may be thwarted by the argument that the loser has himself to blame, and that it is his stock that should be extirpated."[17] Saleeby felt called upon to dissociate himself from such characterisations and expressed the hope that: "Time and truth will rescue eugenics from its present state as a class movement and a cover for selfish opposition to social reform."[18] In sum, for many adherents of eugenics reform was at the very least a complementary, and often integral and essential, component of the eugenic outlook. It was thus, as will be clarified below, not too far a step to proceed from a eugenics that insisted upon extensive social reform to a social reformist perspective that utilised, among other kinds, physical and racial improvement to realise its vision of a good society.

Other fissures in the eugenist ideology would further corroborate the existence of pluralistic elements that eventually led off in different directions. Indeed, in one sphere the British variant of eugenics rarely displayed tendencies manifest in its European, especially German, and even American counterparts. This was on the question of the breeding of a single type of superman. Not only popular views, but some scientific opinion as well, regarded eugenics as aiming at moulding "the whole human race . . . into a homogeneous society which shall progress toward a standard, previously determined, of a noble humanity."[19] Images of "stud farms" in which men would be bred like cattle abounded. Alternatively, Bernard Shaw, whose written and dramatised eccentricities caused much alarm, entered a plea to save democracy by creating a Democracy of Supermen.[20] As Havelock Ellis remarked, however, whereas men bred animals solely to secure advantages to the breeders, "there is as yet no race of supermen, who are prepared to breed man for their own special ends."[21]

Indeed, most British eugenists would have rejected out of hand the "Prussian glorification of the 'blonde beast.' "[22] Already in 1915, J. A. Lindsay expressed his opinion that the Nietzschean superman was con-

[17] "The Dangers of Eugenics," *Nation* 13.3.1909.

[18] Lens, "Imperial Eugenics, VI. The Racial Prospect," *New Statesman* 4.3.1916, p. 516. See also Lens, "Two Decades of Eugenics," *New Statesman* 17. 5. 1924, pp. 154–55.

[19] L. T. More, "The Scientific Claims of Eugenics," *Hibbert Journal* 13 (1914–15): 355.

[20] G. Bernard Shaw, *Man and Superman: The Revolutionist's Handbook and Perfect Companion* (London, 1971), pp. 751, 755. Even eugenists regarded his support with unease. Galton wrote to Pearson on 26.2.1910: "Bernard Shaw is about to give a lecture to the Eugenics Education Society. It is to be hoped that he will be under self-control and not be too extravagant" (K. Pearson, *The Life, Letters and Labours of Francis Galton* 3 vols. [Cambridge, 1930], 3. 427). His fears were founded, for Shaw caused a furore in the press, which responded with sensational headlines about free love and lethal chambers.

[21] H. Ellis, "Eugenics and St Valentine," *Nineteenth Century* 59 (1906):780–81.

[22] See editorial comment, *Eugenics Review*, 12 (1920): 40, quoting from Dr. C. G. Seligman.

trary to the teachings of biology, for genius was a rare mutation not under scientific control.[23] As J. Huxley made quite clear:

> No eugenist in his senses ever has suggested or ever would suggest that one particular type or standard should be picked out as desirable, and all other types discouraged or prevented from having children . . . it takes all kinds to make a world. . . . It will be time enough after a thousand or ten thousand years of this to look into further questions such as the precise proportion of poets, physicists, and politicians desired in a community, or the combination of a number of different desirable qualities in one human frame.[24]

Leonard Darwin, the longtime president of the Eugenics Society and fourth son of Charles, observed that "we should now, and perhaps for ever, abandon the hope of creating a superman."[25] In fact, by the late 1920s an important element in the eugenic creed had become "the improvement of the whole population, not . . . any one section of it." Eugenics was recognising "the paramount importance of the great mass of the more or less mediocre and the relative insignificance, in a eugenic sense, of the small minorities of the extreme types; the eminently superior and the abjectly inferior."[26] A. M. Carr-Saunders, the population expert and member of the Eugenics Society, explained that positive eugenics—the promotion of the propagation of desirable types—was "not an attempt to breed a race of supermen, but to raise the fertility of those who are not definitely subnormal until at least they replace themselves."[27] All this is not, of course, to deny that class eugenics, in the sense of securing the predominance of a specific social group or cultural type, was a central motif (though, as shall be seen below, definitely not alone in the field). Rather, this is a dismissal of the myth that eugenics aimed at the creation of a dominant race of men with unassailable qualities that would bring with it a solution to the problems of humanity.

What, then, was the ideal of British eugenists? No doubt, a good number of them had clear-cut notions about the attributes of a socially desirable type, which would correspond to those of the respectable, solid, middle-class citizen, with an extra dose of health for good measure. The influential conservative churchman, publicist, and eugenist Dean Inge en-

[23] J. A. Lindsay, "Eugenics and the Doctrine of the Super-Man," *Eugenics Review* 7 (1915): 258–61.

[24] J. Huxley, "The Vital Importance of Eugenics," *Harper's Monthly Magazine* 163 (1931): 330–31.

[25] L. Darwin, "The Future of our Race: Heredity and Social Progress," *Eugenics Review* 16 (1924): 96–97.

[26] R. Austin Freeman, "Segregation of the Fit: a Plea for Positive Eugenics," *Eugenics Review* 23 (1931): 207.

[27] A. M. Carr-Saunders, "Eugenics in the Light of Population Trends," *Eugenics Review* 27 (1935): 11–12.

visaged a new nobility with "rules for health, rules of intellectual culture, rules of honourable and heroic conduct . . . [and] a somewhat austere standard of living"—something of a transmutation of the Protestant ethic! Typical of the conservative eugenists was his remark: "We certainly do not want a society so plethoric in altruistic virtue, and so lean in other goods, that every citizen wishes for nothing better than to be a sick-nurse to somebody else."[28]

But, again, not all eugenists were prepared to regard with equanimity the advent of these new Victorians. As one progressive eugenist commented, "we cannot know what types ought to survive until we know individually what surroundings they live in."[29] Others dissociated themselves from an obvious class-based definition of characteristics, and between the wars this had become the rule, as may be seen from the preference of C. P. Blacker—a future secretary of the Eugenics Society—for qualities such as good health, vitality, intelligence, character, and psychological robustness over wealth or social position.[30] A group of leading biologists of the 1930s, including Crew, Darlington, Haldane, Hogben, Huxley, Needham, Dobzhansky, and Waddington, in a statement entitled "Social biology and population improvement," came up with a specification quite opposed to Inge's: "The most important genetic objectives, from a social point of view, are the improvement of those genetic characteristics which make (a) for health, (b) for the complex called intelligence, and (c) for those temperamental qualities which favour fellow-feeling and social behaviour rather than those (to-day most esteemed by many) which make for personal "success," as success is usually understood at present."[31] This last item displays an unmistakable bias towards the progressive ideology that liberals and socialists had been espousing from the turn of the century, but did not contradict eugenic ideas then current.

Alternative Compatibilities: Opportunity, Community, and Planning the Future

Having established certain divergences of opinion on eugenic principles, we can now proceed to examine the main issue—the compatibility of eugenics and socialist, social reformist and social liberal thought. To put it

[28] W. R. Inge, "Some Moral Aspects of Eugenics," *Eugenics Review*, 1 (1909): 28, 32.

[29] J. Lionel Tayler, "The Social Application of Eugenics," *Westminster Review* 170 (1908): 418–20.

[30] C. W. Saleeby, *Parenthood and Race Culture* (London, 1909), p. 230; M. Eden Paul, *Socialism and Eugenics* (London, 1911), p. 13; C. P. Blacker, "Citizenship and Eugenics," *Journal of State Medicine* 42 (1934): 135.

[31] "Social Biology and Population Improvement," statement printed in *Nature*, 16.9.1939, pp. 521–22.

bluntly, the question is, How could a socialism stressing environmental influences and devoted to the doctrine of the inherent equality of man; a social reform policy whose intention was to preserve the weaker elements of society; and a liberalism that emphasised the right of every man to attain free and maximal development and that regarded questions of procreation as entirely private—how could these progressive ideologies cohabit with eugenics? The obvious answer would be that they could not and, as a rule, did not. Yet what is interesting is the exception rather than the rule, for in establishing which elements of the progressive ideologies were able to assimilate eugenics, we may both be able better to understand some of their characteristics and to estimate the chances for eugenic views to resurface once the trauma of nazism abates.

There are basically three claims to be made about the relationship between social reformist and socialist tendencies, on the one hand, and eugenics, on the other, and these may be placed in an ascending order. First, it was possible to maintain, at the very least, that here were two separate but complementary approaches to the improvement of human society. Secondly, socialism could be presented as a necessary condition for eugenics. And, finally and most interestingly, there existed within the eugenic creed elements common also to the socialist and reformist mentalities.

The "separate but complementary" position was usually a sop thrown to the environmentalists by the "hard-line" eugenists, often expressing explicit hostility to current methods of social reform. Thus Dean Inge could write that "humanitarian legislation, or practice, requires to be supplemented, and its inevitable evil effects counteracted, by eugenic practice, and ultimately by eugenic legislation." And Leonard Darwin thought that more attention should be devoted to the separate study of heredity and environment, the dividing line being concern with future generations, on the one hand, and aiding one's own generation, on the other. The socialist S. Herbert also maintained that the principles involved should not be obscured "because Eugenist and Reformer have separate fields . . . it becomes necessary to supplement the method of the former, which is essentially a selection for parenthood, with that of the latter, which aims at the protection of the parent and his offspring."[32]

Most appraisals of environmental reform as a sine qua non for eugenic measures revolved around the issue of social mobility. As a correspondent to the *Eugenics Review* explained, "we should try to arrange that there should be an equal chance for all to succeed, so that we might have the best possible chance of finding inherited talent which is now submerged

---

[32] Inge, "Some Moral Aspects of Eugenics," p. 29; L. Darwin, "Heredity and Environment," *Eugenics Review* 8 (1916): 112; Herbert, "Eugenics and Socialism," p. 121.

by lack of opportunity."[33] This, too, was J. Huxley's position: "We must equalize environment upwards . . . before we can evaluate genetic difference."[34] For some eugenists the obvious conclusion was the provision by the community of economic and social conditions that could create approximately equal opportunities. This was often considered the only valid basis for estimating and comparing the intrinsic worth of individuals.[35]

But to appreciate the meaning attached to "equality of opportunity" one must understand some nuances in the liberal reformist tradition. A pattern of thought had been set by Benjamin Kidd's 1894 bestseller, *Social Evolution*, which had justified the promotion of equality of opportunity as enabling true and efficient rivalry—a refined competition in which ability would be pitted against ability.[36] The social result would be, of course, an unequal society in which the fitness of an individual could be correctly ascertained and made the basis of social organisation. This argument naturally appealed to conservative, class eugenists, but was in fact adopted by many progressives as well. Thus a socialist eugenist could claim that "we socialists . . . maintain that there should be equal opportunity from birth for all members of the community. That is a very stable and, I think, a very shrewd form of competition." And Herbert had written already in 1910 that socialism would, "by giving equal opportunities to all, create such social conditions as would lead to the automatic and natural survival of the types most desired."[37] Could this not be interpreted as a legitimising of the struggle for survival, now unencumbered by hindrances to its effective conduct? The link Kidd had forged between equality of opportunity and calculating social efficiency was carried on into socialist theory, as the following lines, first printed in the *Labour Leader* in 1911, demonstrate: "By the perfection of our social environment under Socialism, the effects of bad inheritance [will] become the sole factor in producing inefficient and anti-social members of the community. A Socialist Commonwealth which should allot to all such defectives a share of the communal product, without imposing any restrictions on their right to perpetuate their kind, would deserve all the evil that would ensue."[38] Socialist shades of Kidd, indeed!

Social mobility and equality of opportunity were by their very nature intimately linked with the issue of class. The class conception of worth,

[33] J. R. Baker, "Eugenics and Snobbery," letter to the editor, *Eugenics Review* 23 (1932): 379.

[34] Huxley, "Eugenics and Society," p. 18.

[35] "Social Biology and Population Improvement."

[36] B. Kidd, *Social Evolution* (London, 1894).

[37] S. Churchill in "Eugenics, Socialism and Capitalism," *Eugenics Review* 27 (1935): 3; Herbert, "Eugenics and Socialism," p. 123.

[38] Paul, *Socialism and Eugenics*, p. 13.

as expounded by conservative eugenists—a typical representative of whom was W.C.D. Whetham—denied the importance of social mobility as the condition to giving natural selection full play. This, Whetham held, was an almost universal fallacy because the social risers tended to postpone marriage so as not to hamper their advance. It was far better, he observed, displaying an aristocratic if not Platonic bent of mind, "to hold before each man's eyes as his natural goal a leading position in his own class . . . to give ability its due advantage within certain defined limits, but not to make it too easy for those limits to be passed."[39] On the whole, however, even conservative eugenists were not opposed to social mobility, though their arguments differed noticeably from those of the progressives. L. Darwin pointed out that men of exceptional strength and ability were constantly being selected out of the poorer ranks and transferred to the richer, while failures among the rich kept falling down into the lower economic ranks.[40] In other words, mobility ensured real eugenic differentiation, for the richer strata would thus contain a higher proportion of "inherently superior types." This free-for-all conception of social mobility was highly individualistic, whereas the progressive notion of social mobility was a socially controlled one, according to criteria that were not primarily biological.

Most eugenists, however, had come to reject the brutal struggle for existence while not relinquishing its end. The progressives among them would have adopted the new liberal and socialist refinement and humanisation of competition as a struggle for excellence after survival had been guaranteed. Equal conditions were thus the necessary condition for the emergence of true quality, and this was evidently contrary to the class conception of worth expounded by conservative eugenists. But eugenists in general desired to supersede natural selection and were loath to accept its remorseless casualty rate. Indeed, this is a cardinal point, for it goes some way towards explaining the attraction of eugenics for progressives. Its promise lay in the rational control of man over the natural laws of evolution to which he was hitherto subjected. New liberals such as L. T. Hobhouse and J. A. Hobson had welcomed this rationalisation as confirming the supremacy of the human mind and defining the path of social progress.[41] Eugenics, after all, was not merely a counterbalance to the halting of selection caused by newly accepted modes of social aid, but could speed up the processes of selection in order to attain desired ethico-social goals. And if there was no agreement over those goals, eugenics as a science could still be harnessed to different ideological ends. Hence,

[39] W.C.D. Whetham, "Eugenics and Politics," *Eugenics Review* 2 (1910): 246.
[40] L. Darwin, "Quality *not* Quantity," *Eugenics Review* 8 (1916), 305.
[41] See Freeden, *The New Liberalism*, pp. 73, 89–91, 185–56.

with the filtration of the cooperative version of social Darwinism into current sociopolitical theories, eugenics could be employed to serve the conception of an altruistic and social man. This was the view of J. A. Thomson:

> Survival and success are also to those types in which the individual has been more or less subordinated to the welfare of the species. Part of their fitness is in being capable of self-sacrifice. . . . Thus we cannot accept the caricature of Nature as in a state of universal Hobbesian warfare. . . . Especially among the finer forms of life do we find . . . less and less frequently an intensification of competition, . . . more and more frequently something subtler, some parental sacrifice, some co-operative device, some experiment in sociality.[42]

With the increasing penetration of ideas concerning the social nature of man and concerning the distribution of eugenic worth among all social sectors, the common attempt—typified by F.C.S. Schiller,[43] Oxford don and philosopher—to correlate fitness with class membership and a "natural nobility" was challenged. Saleeby warned that "directly the eugenist begins to talk in terms of social classes (as Mr Galton has never done), he is skating on thin ice."[44] The lack of a connection between social rank and degeneration was stressed and later reinforced by scientists. In fact, some eugenists went so far as to argue that the poor might be eugenically superior, because "among the poor struggling crowds of labouring masses . . . the weakest are rigorously weeded out in the battle of life."[45]

Nevertheless, the case for a progressive eugenics cannot rest solely on the issue of class, and this for the simple reason that a number of liberals and socialists themselves valued the intrinsic worth of some classes more than others. Bertrand Russell's radicalism did not prevent him from assuming that the intellectual average of the professional classes was somewhat higher than that of most other classes. This claim was given scientific dressing by R. A. Fisher, referring to the slightly wider term "middle class," who were characterized "by all the qualities which make for successful citizenship"—enterprise, prudence, character, and intellect. Fish-

---

[42] Thomson, "Eugenics and War," pp. 7–8.

[43] F.C.S. Schiller, "Eugenics and Politics," *Hibbert Journal* 12 (1913–14): 244, 249.

[44] Saleeby, *Parenthood and Race Culture*, p. 118. What Galton had intended was again a moot point. Some pointed out that Galton, unlike Saleeby, had wanted to build up a sentiment of caste among the naturally gifted and to create class consciousness within each social group (J. A. Field, "The Progress of Eugenics," *Quarterly Journal of Economics* 26 [1911–12]: 11).

[45] See, for example, S. Herbert, "The Discovery of the Fittest," *Westminster Review* 175 (1911): 39–41, 43; Carr-Saunders, "Eugenics in the Light of Population Trends," p.14; "Social Biology and Population Improvement," ibid.; J. A. Hobson, *Free-Thought in the Social Sciences* (London, 1926), pp. 214–15.

er's concern for the future of this class derived from his observation that the two biologically independent variables of qualities making for social and economic success and qualities making for low fertility were positively correlated. Though Fisher himself was no progressive, his observation was accepted by J. Huxley.[46] The preference for a certain kind of person and for a certain class became well-nigh indistinguishable.

We now enter the realm of elements common to progressives and to eugenists of all persuasions. The most salient among these was the idea of social responsibility, usually linked to the concepts of community or race[47]—in the sense of the supreme human entity to which allegiance was owed. For whereas the notion of equality was a meeting ground between some eugenists and some progressives—a possible but not necessary connection—the interest and solidarity of the social body was the ultimate appeal for all eugenists, socialists, social reformers, and new liberals. For the conservative Montague Crackanthorpe, a barrister and essayist who was president of the Eugenics Education Society from 1909 to 1911, the study of eugenics produced in Burkeian fashion "a sense of the solidarity of our race, of the debt we owe to it in the past, and of the duty we owe to it in the future."[48] A committee on Poor Law reform of the Eugenics Education Society claimed in 1910 that "the fundamental problem in social reform is . . . how to make stocks responsible to the community."[49] This was coupled with a rejection of doctrinaire individualism for, from the eugenic point of view, as Saleeby remarked, "each individual [is] . . . merely the temporary host of the continuous line of germ-cells which constitute the race." Hence he concluded that the interests of the individual and of the race were one—both because the individual, too, was concerned with the future of his progeny and because the methods of negative eugenics, limiting the propagation of the unfit, would secure the greatest happiness, liberty, and self-development for those to whom they were applied, such as the feeble-minded.[50] In similar fashion, Herbert wrote: "Eu-

---

[46] B. Russell, *Marriage and Morals* (London, 1929), pp. 261–62; R. A. Fisher, "Family Allowances," *Eugenics Review* 24 (1932): 90; Huxley, "The Vital Importance of Eugenics," 328–29. In a note to a review Huxley had written a few years earlier about L. Darwin's *The Need for Eugenic Reform*, the editor of the *Sociological Review* had taken exception to Huxley's tendency to accept conventional criteria of success in life too much at their face value ("The Case for Eugenics," p. 279).

[47] It must be emphasised that "race" was not primarily used in the now common sense of biologically exclusive determinants, but applied, as G. Watson has shown, to a "community of cultures" ("Race and the Socialists," *Encounter*, November 1976, 16).

[48] M. Crackanthorpe, "Eugenics as a Social Force," *Nineteenth Century* 63 (1908): 966. See also A. White, "Eugenics and National Efficiency," *Eugenics Review* 1 (1909): 109.

[49] "Report of the Committee on Poor Law Reform," *Eugenics Review* 2 (1910): 170.

[50] C. W. Saleeby, *Heredity* (London, 1905), p. 6; idem, *Parenthood and Race Culture*, pp. 12, 203.

genic teachings are . . . essentially communistic in spirit. It is the common interest of each social unit with the whole, which the Eugenist wishes to evoke as the central motive power in society. And it is just here, in the most vital part of its programme, that the eugenic ideal shows complete identity with that of the Socialist."[51]

A practical ramification of the hope of eugenists of all creeds to subordinate human behaviour to social considerations was their treatment of marriage. This was only a logical conclusion to the progression of socialist and social liberal thought. The gradual assumption by the community of responsibility for the well-being of its members—be it for humanitarian reasons or from the perspective of social self-interest—had initiated a series of incursions into the sphere of family life, previously considered sacrosanct. Compulsory education and the establishment of state and municipal responsibility for the nourishment of children had deprived parents of the right to be sole arbiters of their children's fate. Now the reformer's gaze alighted upon the quantitative and qualitative control of procreation. Laski maintained that to regard marriage as a private affair was antisocial, for "the time is surely coming in our history when society will look upon the production of a weakling as a crime against itself."[52] This observation added an interesting note to the eugenic argument. Whereas prevailing conceptions of poverty until the late nineteenth century had regarded pauperism as a crime arising out of defects of individual character, this judgment was now applied to irresponsible propagation of the species.[53] Laski, however, did not go to the extreme of suggesting direct public intervention in the selection of partners. Indeed, very few British eugenists did (Shaw as usual acting the devil's advocate on this issue),[54] for that was "a conception of the eugenic ideal which can rightly be left to such professional jesters as Mr Chesterton."[55]

Views similar to those of Laski were held by Russell, who reiterated what many birth-control supporters were realising, namely, that parenthood was now voluntary and that the reproductive function was hence distinguishable from that of sexual union. For Russell, this entailed refraining from social intervention or moral ruling on matters of love without reproduction. This, he thought, would enable social control to be applied exclusively to the question that really concerned the community: "The procreation of children should be a matter far more carefully regu-

---

[51] Herbert, "Eugenics and Socialism," p. 123.

[52] Laski, "The Scope of Eugenics," p. 34.

[53] C. W. Armstrong, "The Right to Maim," *Eugenics Review* 16, no. 1 (1924–25); Webb, "Eugenics and the Poor Law," p. 240.

[54] G. Bernard Shaw, written communication to symposium on "Eugenics: Its Definition, Scope and Aims" *Sociological Papers* (London, 1905), pp. 74–5.

[55] Laski, "The Scope of Eugenics," p. 34.

lated by moral considerations than it is at present."[56] Socialists, in fact, could recognise their own innermost thoughts coming from the conservative Dean Inge: "A community which makes itself responsible for the education and maintenance of all who are born within it must claim and exercise some control over both the quality and quantity of the new human material for which it will have to provide."[57]

The link between socialism, social reform, and eugenics was thus obviously forged on the plane of state intervention as well as of social solidarity. Webb and H. G. Wells were outspoken on this theme: in Webb's impassioned cry, "No consistent eugenist can be a 'Laisser Faire' individualist unless he throws up the game in despair. He must interfere, interfere, interfere!"[58] And Wells, though rejecting, as did Laski, state breeding and compulsory pairing, wrote:

> The State is justified in saying, before you may add children to the community for the community to educate and in part to support, you must be above a certain minimum of personal efficiency . . . and a certain minimum of physical development, and free of any transmissible disease. . . . Failing these simple qualifications, if you and some person conspire [i.e., propagation as a crime] and add to the population of the State, we will, for the sake of humanity, take over the innocent victim of your passions, but we shall insist that you are under a debt to the State of a peculiarly urgent sort, and one you will certainly pay, even if it is necessary to use restraint to get the payment out of you."[59]

These ostensibly utopian threats were echoed by conservative eugenists as well. L. Darwin illustrates the typical divide on this question. In 1916 he thought that "State and charitable aid to the poor as a class will often be harmful as regards racial qualities" in the fields of social reform. In 1926, introducing the policy statement of the Eugenics Society, he drew especial attention to the proposal that "the State should be regarded as having the right to exercise a limited amount of pressure in order to promote family limitation."[60] This, as the policy statement itself explained, would mean limitation of aid or actual segregation. Here, again, individualistic leanings denied the state the role of positive promoter of welfare but granted it the negative role of guardian of racial, national, or social interest: the regulation of the "less fit." In other words, though the utilisation of the state to attain social goals was not ruled out, it was perceived more in its traditional role of implementer of social control. An explana-

[56] Russell, *Marriage and Morals*, p. 270.

[57] Dean Inge, "The Population Question," *Eugenics Review* 16, no. 1 (1924–25).

[58] Webb, "Eugenics and the Poor Law," p. 237.

[59] H. G. Wells, *A Modern Utopia* (London, 1905), pp. 183–84.

[60] Darwin, "Quality *not* Quantity," p. 308; "The Eugenics Policy of the Society," *Eugenics Review* 18 (1926): 92.

tion of the resistance to eugenic state intervention was forwarded by Russell: "What stands in the way is democracy. The ideas of eugenics are based on the assumption that men are unequal, while democracy is based on the assumption that they are equal. It is, therefore, politically very difficult to carry out eugenic ideas in a democratic community when those ideas take the form, not of suggesting that there is a minority of inferior people such as imbeciles, but of admitting that there is a minority of superior people." And yet it was generally granted by eugenists that private initiative was inadequate and that 'any measures of eugenic control applicable to the population as a whole are beyond the powers of voluntary associations."[61]

The convergence of eugenics and socialism-cum-social reform is evident in some key articles of either faith. This is what initially made eugenics so attractive to the new liberals. Hobhouse, who later had occasion to attack eugenics, was nevertheless very ambivalent about the relationship of the biological and the sociological. In 1904 he conceded that "the bare conception of a conscious selection as a way in which educated society would deal with stock is infinitely higher than that of natural selection with which biologists have confronted every proposal of sociology." Elsewhere he accorded eugenics a limited role within the larger framework of social legislation, a role mainly restricted to negative eugenics.[62]

Hobhouse's colleague, Hobson, returned repeatedly to eugenics throughout his writings. At the turn of the century, the restriction of marriage to the fit was interpreted by him as a manifestation of "the social will expressing itself either by public opinion or through an act of Parliament" and was indeed "as much a natural force as any other." A few years later he was openly advocating the prevention of "anti-social propagation." By 1909 he was reminding his readers of the importance of environment, side by side with the control of parenthood by the state, and could write, apparently oblivious of the contradiction, both that "the child is not everything. Each generation must lead its own life," and "the end of all politics is the parentage of the future." In 1911, in contradistinction to Hobhouse, he presented the "modern science of eugenics" as stimulating thought among those "who are beginning to recognize that industrial and political reforms are not the last and only word in human progress"—a rather startling observation by such a committed social reformer. By 1926, while admitting the value of scientific eugenics, he had launched

<hr>

[61] Russell, *Marriage and Morals*, pp. 262–63; R. Austin Freeman, "Segregation of the Fit," p. 209.

[62] L. T. Hobhouse in discussion during symposium on eugenics, *Sociological Papers*, p. 63; "The Value and Limitations of Eugenics," *Sociological Review* 4 (1911): 281–302. Reprinted as chap. 3 of Hobhouse, *Social Evolution and Political Theory*.

an attack on racial, "Nordic," eugenics, with its inegalitarianism and imperialistic leanings. With his usual perceptiveness, Hobson had picked up the early warning signals long before many of his compatriots. Yet he remained basically sympathetic and in 1932 once again commended eugenics for intending to remove questions of stock from the sphere of private individual enterprise. In theory, he remarked, eugenics should be "the first of the productive arts to come under social planning."[63]

One may, in short, locate three related ideas as common to the mentality of eugenists and reformers: the evolution of human rationality, orientation towards the future, and their concomitant—planning. It was, as Hobson put it, "Nature, in her later form of Reason" that should be "sustaining this harmony of vital interests between the individual and the race."[64] Reason and planning were the logical consequence of the Darwinian understanding of man and his place vis-à-vis the universe. With his attributes of mind and intelligence, man could control his environment and shape his destiny. One of the rare occasions on which eugenics actually occupied the national political stage was during the debates on the Mental Deficiency Bill in 1912–13. The bill proposed, among others, compulsory detention of the mentally deficient consequent to a court decision and the presentation of a medical certificate. It aroused considerable opposition in Parliament from Josiah Wedgwood, who attacked the "horrible Eugenic Society" for its flouting of individual liberty.[65] The liberal press was in part worried about the wide and vague definition of a defective. But no less significant was the support rendered to the bill by other liberal newspapers. Control and compulsion were seen to infringe upon fewer rights than freedom; a rational and scientific social reconstruction now preceded individual liberty. The final outcome of this debate was an act that narrowed the definition of a defective and made it palatable even to such critics as Hobhouse.[66] New liberals would have regarded the following statement by F.C.S. Schiller as indicative of their mood: "The difference between our present society and a rationally organized and eugenical society is, not that in the former the individual is free and in the latter controlled, but that our present organization is so largely random, aimless,

[63] J. A. Hobson, "Mr Kidd's 'Social Evolution,' " *American Journal of Sociology* 1 (1895): 309; idem, *The Social Problem* (London, 1901), pp. 214–17; idem, "Eugenics as an Art of Social Progress," *South Place Magazine* 14 (1909): 168–70; idem, "Race-Regeneration," *Manchester Guardian* 10.10.1911; *Free-Thought in the Social Sciences*, pp. 200–21; idem, *The Recording Angel* (London, 1932), pp. 71–73.

[64] J. A. Hobson, "The Cant of Decadence," *Nation*, 14.5.1910.

[65] *Hansard*, 5th Ser., vol. 38, 1468–69, 1474 (17.5.1912).

[66] For a more detailed discussion, see Freeden, *The New Liberalism*, pp. 190–93; G. R. Searle, *Eugenics and Politics in Britain, 1900–1914* (Leyden, 1976), pp. 106–11; K. Jones, *Mental Health and Social Policy, 1845–1959* (London, 1960), pp. 61–72.

inconsistent, and self-frustrating . . . while the latter would be planned, and would enable him to rise insensibly above the lurid past and to reach a harmonious development in a perfected society."[67]

It is interesting to note that when the issue of mental deficiency arose again after the war, the argument, though much muted, proceeded on almost identical lines. The question was the certification of mental defectives through disease or accident, rather than those from birth. The government had introduced a bill in 1926 which extended mental defectiveness to include vaguely a condition "induced after birth by disease, injury or other cause." This prompted the Labour MP Rhys Davies to move for its rejection. It was feared that habitual criminals could be certified under its terms; indeed, as Davies wryly remarked, "the whole of the present Tory Government might be put in an asylum at any time."[68] In 1927, however, Davies supported a new version of the bill that deleted "other cause" and restricted the secondary amentia cases within its scope to the age of eighteen. But what had excited such discussion before the war encountered only minor opposition in the House—Wedgwood once again expressing his concern and that, too, in a lower key—and the press was not drawn into any debate at all. In fact, the parliamentary reporting in the liberal newspapers was favourable to the bill while gently mocking Wedgwood's eccentricity.[69] In this field the conception of community responsibility superseding all other considerations, which had been established before the war, had become an acceptable and reasonable norm.

Still, compulsion was as a rule limited to the case of defectives, for in other instances eugenists preferred persuasion and recognised the need for balancing the claims of the race with those of individual freedom. It is important to appreciate that the determinism endemic in eugenics was countered by the factors of rational choice and of purposive manipulation of the environment. The absoluteness of the germplasm was, after all, to be harnessed to the human end of the production of as many people as possible with desirable qualities. The difference between the eugenist and the social reformer lay rather in the former's acceptance of fixed components of human nature, an acceptance that, of course, has affinities with the conservative outlook. But in his reliance on social policy to achieve social ends, the eugenist varied little from the full-fledged social reformer. Any variations discernible were of degree rather than kind, variations

[67] F.C.S. Schiller, review of M. Ginsberg, *Studies in Sociology*, in *Eugenics Review* 25 (1933): 42.

[68] Mental Deficiency Bill, 1926 [16 and 17 Geo. 5] [H.L.]; *Hansard*, 5th Ser., vol. 200, 966–69 (29.11.1926).

[69] Mental Deficiency Act, 1927 [17 and 18 Geo. 5]; *Hansard*, 5th Ser., vol. 203, 2333–39 (18.3.1927); see, for example, *Daily News*, *Westminster Gazette* and *Daily Chronicle* for 19.3.1927.

which also set apart the avowed socialist from the new liberal. These revolved round the scope and magnitude of, and faith in, proposed reforms. Boundless optimism versus guarded caution and self-imposed limitation were the poles between which the reformist mentality travelled. But reformist mentality it was.

Orientation towards the future is also indicative of the growing sense of social responsibility evinced by reformers of various schools. Conservation of the racial qualities of the nation is not merely some sophisticated elaboration of the instinct of self-preservation. It embodies in part the altruism of the social reformer because, as even conservative eugenists were quick to point out, self-sacrifice for the sake of future generations was involved—the forgoing of present gratifications and unrestricted liberty.[70] Second, not a few eugenists harboured a utopian streak and some went so far as to adopt the literary device of conjuring up a future society as a means through which to elucidate their views. Galton's clumsily named "Kantsaywhere," William McDougall's "Eugenia," Wells's forays into the future, and of course frequent references to Plato's *Republic*, are but some examples.

Obviously, utopian does not necessarily imply socialist, but a shared preference for elaborate and often unrealistic blueprints exists. Some utopias are conceived as methodological critiques of the present rather than as attainable futures. Others envision that a bridge could exist between present and future. The eugenic utopia, as also the socialist commonwealth, seemed within human reach.[71] Yet it is precisely on the question of the future that the divide between social reformer and conservative eugenist re-emerged. The responsibility towards the future was frequently coupled with indifference towards the present, notwithstanding Inge's claim that the present and the future counted for the same and should not be sacrificed for each other.[72] Not many of the eugenists, when confronted with the future incarnate—children—supported extensive legislation for their benefit. Vague statements such as Havelock Ellis's that "we are the keepers of our children, of the race . . ." and that it was "within our grasp to mould them" referred in the main to their conception, after which the more extreme eugenist no doubt assumed that quality would hold its own.[73] This is once again the central nature-versus-nurture issue, with progressive eugenists professing concern over the bringing up of children and over their health, safety, and education as well.

[70] M. Crackanthorpe, "The Friends and Foes of Eugenics," *Fortnightly Review* 92 (1912): 746; Darwin, "Quality *not* Quantity," p. 298; Armstrong, "The Right to Maim."

[71] Saleeby, *Parenthood and Race Culture*, p. 149.

[72] Inge, "Some Moral Aspects of Eugenics," p. 27.

[73] H. Ellis, *The Problem of Race-Regeneration* (London, 1911), p. 50; idem, "Eugenics and St Valentine," p. 781.

INTERWAR CONCERNS: THE PRESSURES OF POPULATION

It is important to emphasize that the First World War did not basically alter the nature of eugenic thinking. Most ideas and attitudes concerning eugenics were developed before the war, as indeed many key approaches to social policy in general. But the often impractical theoretical perspectives focused after the war on a few concrete social issues (the one exception before the war having been the Mental Deficiency Act). In the 1920s, even more in the early 1930s, a twofold movement was discernible. Within the mainstream of eugenics itself—the Eugenics Society—there was a perceptible shift towards the outlook that the hitherto minority of progressive eugenists had espoused. This was perhaps most pertinently expressed by Blacker in his distinction between liberal and authoritarian eugenics.[74] Concurrently, ideas that were fundamentally eugenic and that related to population quality and heredity were entertained by progressive groups not directly associated with the eugenics movement. A focal point of this convergence was the issue of the birthrate and its control. Eugenists and progressives addressed each other on these questions and gratefully rendered mutual support in an effort to gain further respectability and national recognition for their causes.

The postwar period witnessed a confrontation between two schools of thought on the subject of population. On the one hand were the neo-Malthusians with their perennial fear that population would outstrip the means of subsistence. On the other were those who pointed, Cassandra-like, to the figures confirming an increasing decline in the birthrate that appeared to threaten the very existence of the nation. This latter view was slow to catch on despite the growing statistical evidence. During the war, Havelock Ellis repeatedly appealed to restrict the birthrate because, as a commentator on his work wrote, the governing classes were inducing the workers to multiply so as to provide "a plentiful supply of cannon food upon the one hand and of submissive wage-labour on the other." Hence Ellis saw a falling birthrate as the means to avert war. This he linked with eugenics, for "birth-control yet remains the only instrument by means of which . . . eugenic selection can be rendered practicable." Ellis believed that Malthusianism, evolution, humanitarianism, and medicine all pointed in the direction of the necessity and, indeed, inevitability of birth control. Contraception, which was slowly spreading down from the upper to the lower classes, would serve a eugenic purpose if it reached those strata that contain "the largest proportion of incapable elements."

[74] C. P. Blacker, *Eugenics in Retrospect and Prospect*, the Galton Lecture 1945 (London, 1950), p. 9.

It did not reach them yet, and this, thought Ellis, constituted a challenge to be met by the usual eugenic combination of propaganda and inducements and, failing those, compulsory sterilisation and segregation.[75]

In effect, as Ellis himself offered, the advocacy of birth control as a solution merely created a new problem for eugenists: "Neo-Malthusian methods may even be dysgenic rather than eugenic, for they tend to be adopted by the superior stocks, while the inferior stocks, ignorant and reckless, are left to propagate freely."[76] Hence the opposition between neo-Malthusians and their adversaries was often revealed to be spurious when it came to eugenic issues. The former were concerned with restricting the growth of the masses; the latter with encouraging first and foremost the better stocks. Together, they constituted the complementary measures of negative and positive eugenics. These stances appeared again and again in literature on population. In 1916 the National Birth-Rate Commission drew attention to the declining birthrate. Many of its members, such as Hobson, argued against the neo-Malthusians that there was not too much population and considered as a possible solution the restriction of the birthrate among the low-skilled and casual labourers, together with the granting of security of income to encourage it among "efficient" stock.[77] This elicited the response from the *Nation* that social reforms to ease the financial situation of such stock were a doubtful inducement "in face of the conspicuous fact that it is precisely the best-to-do, best-housed, best-educated, and most secure classes of the population that carry farthest the restriction in the size of the family."[78]

The attitude of the *Nation* is, in fact, a case in point. In the postwar period, when still under the editorship of H. W. Massingham, it triumphantly announced the collapse of Malthusian theory. Malthus, claimed the *Nation*, had postulated a correlation between an increased standard of comfort and an increasing number of children, while the postwar evidence showed the opposite was true. By limiting the number of their offspring, the "educated, professional, and skilled artisan classes" were "deliberately destroying the stock which is most likely to produce citizens of physical excellence and intellectual vigour and ambition." In 1923 the *Nation*

---

[75] "Thinking for the future," *Nation*, 23.12.1916; H. Ellis, "War and the Birth-Rate," *Nation*, 25.9.1915; H. Ellis, "Birth-Control and Eugenics," *Eugenics Review* 9 (1917): 34, 38–41.

[76] Ellis, "Birth-Control and Eugenics," p. 34.

[77] *The declining birth-rate: Its causes and effects.* Being the Report of and the chief evidence taken by the National Birth-Rate Commission, instituted, with official recognition, by the National Council of Public Morals—for the promotion of race regeneration—spiritual, moral and physical (London, 1916), pp. 282–98. Among others, original members of the inquiry included Inge, Saleeby, Hobson, and Hobhouse (who was unable to attend).

[78] "The Falling Birth-Rate," *Nation*, 24.6.1916.

accused birth-control agitators of a conservative bias, by deflecting social thought away from questions of environmental improvement. Birth control was now seen to be in the interest of capitalists, who were tired of subsidizing the consuming masses through taxation—a modern version of Speenhamland. Education and housing, rather, would operate to check the population.[79] While ostensibly diametrically opposed to Ellis's argument—that capitalists wanted more workers—there was some common ground. Many environmentalists hoped to decrease the birthrate among the poor by improving their living conditions because they considered the poor unable at present to supply adequate conditions for their children. Some held that only socialism could relieve the economic pressure that stimulated the lowest classes to "reckless propagation." As one socialist sympathizer so quaintly put it: "When people have nothing else to think about, their minds are full of sex."[80] Eugenists also hoped to decrease the birthrate, but by direct control over the ability of the poor to procreate. The question was really, Did birth control constitute an asset for the masses or the means to its exploitation? The spokesmen for the masses themselves disagreed violently on this matter.

In April 1923 the *Nation* came under J. M. Keynes's control. Despite Harrod's assertion that "Keynes made it a rule never to interfere with the editorial policy,"[81] the shift on the population question is unmistakable. Keynes was a neo-Malthusian and engaged later in the year in a controversy over population trends with W. H. Beveridge.[82] It was consequently the *New Statesman* that took up the anti-Malthusian position in an article by its editor, Clifford Sharp, who, in an extraordinary statement, denounced birth control as "one of the most dangerous movements that has ever threatened civilization." He attacked Keynes's "Malthusian moonshine," which claimed a connection between overpopulation and unemployment, and supported Beveridge's description of a declining population.[83]

The crucial aspect is that the only area of agreement among the discussants was over the importance of eugenics. For it was eugenics that frequently bridged the gap between the various sides on the birthrate question. The now neo-Malthusian *Nation* repeated the claim that contraception among the poor was essential to prevent dysgenic tendencies.[84] At

---

[79] "Malthus up to Date," *Nation*, 12.6.1920; "The Demand for Birth Control," *Nation*, 17.3.1923.

[80] H. Sturt, *Socialism and Character* (London, 1912), p. 89.

[81] R. F. Harrod, *The Life of John Maynard Keynes* (Harmondsworth, 1972), p. 396.

[82] See J. Harris, *William Beveridge: a Biography* (Oxford, 1977), pp. 341–42; Harrod, *The Life of John Maynard Keynes*, p. 397.

[83] "Malthusian Moonshine," *New Statesman*, 22.9.1923.

[84] "The Problems of Birth-Control," *Nation*, 6.6.1925.

the same time Beveridge, from the opposite end, was worried by birth control as practised by the "responsible sectors" and wrote a few years later: "As to quality—more important to encourage birth of good than to discourage birth of ordinary persons."[85] Sharp extended this concern to include not only those "who ought to be encouraged to bear children" but to prevent deterioration of the white races.[86] He was clearly infected by the Webbian type of socialism with its apparently incongruous fascination with race and class. The eugenic question underlying all debate was hence over which end of the social scale was one to worry more, not whether the population was increasing or decreasing or should do either. The issue was the fundamental one of differential fertility, still generally believed to be on the increase.

At about the same time another group joined the debate, again from a slightly different angle. This was the family endowment movement, whose central figure was Eleanor Rathbone, supported by Eva Hubback, Mary Stocks, and others. Here again is an example of the social reformist affinity with eugenics. The Family Endowment Council (later "Society") was linked, on the one hand, with the National Union of Societies for Equal Citizenship, which pressed for political and social equality for women and was, on the other hand, connected with advanced liberal circles centred round E. D. Simon and the liberal summer school movement.[87] Family endowments had developed from the prewar interest in motherhood, a theme that was also prominent in the eugenist outlook. For Saleeby this was a central issue: "Any system of eugenics . . . any proposal for social reform . . . which fails to reckon with motherhood . . . is foredoomed to failure." In language that a contemporary described as having the "touch of the prophet's fine frenzy" Saleeby waxed lyrical over "the safeguarding and the ennoblement of motherhood as the proximate end of all political action, the end through which the ultimate ends, the production and recognition of human worth, can alone be attained," and added the not imperceptive observation that "at present the most important profession in the world is almost entirely carried on by unskilled labor."[88]

The connection between eugenist and progressive was, however, in their mutual insistence on freedom of choice and economic independence for women. It was economic independence as a counterweight to the existing

---

[85] Harris, William *Beveridge*, p. 342; Beveridge papers, London School of Economics, III, 19, MS notes on "The Population Problem Today. B. The Special Problem."

[86] "Malthusian Moonshine."

[87] See M. D. Stocks, *Eleanor Rathbone* (London, 1949), pp. 84–99; D. Hopkinson, *Family Inheritance: a Life of Eva Hubback* (London, 1954), p. 134. See also M. Freeden, *Liberalism Divided: A Study in British Political Thought, 1914–1939* (Oxford, 1986), chap. 4.

[88] Saleeby, *Parenthood and Race Culture*, pp. 167, 194, 173; Field, "The Progress of Eugenics," p. 47.

social inequality, and the consequent freedom from considerations of financial gain through marriage, that would restore the model of nineteenth-century laissez-faire social interaction, with its assumed total equality: "For eugenic mating one of the primary conditions is perfect freedom of choice of the contracting parties. . . . It hardly needs saying that these conditions would be fulfilled under a Socialist scheme."[89] Short of this freedom through equalization, the "endowment of motherhood" as advocated by Fabians also made eugenic sense, though on that subject, again, views were divided. Opponents of state aid to mothers argued that "the thoughts of the physical gratification resulting from the immediate expenditure of a maternity grant might affect the fertility of the utterly degraded," and a conservative eugenist went so far as to attack the "endowment of motherhood" schemes by trenchantly remarking: "Mr Webb states that he regards the bearing of a healthy child as a public service for which the state should pay. The eugenist will be more inclined to regard the abstaining from bearing a child when no sufficient means exist for its support as a public service."[90] Supporters of "endowment of motherhood" retorted that the poorest classes were already breeding as fast as they could and that improving one's position in life led to more prudence. They demanded that parenthood be made economically easy and called for efforts at postwar reconstruction to be directed also at relieving the financial stresses of raising families. Indeed, it is illuminating, though not unexpected, to find Sidney Webb concerned about the differential birthrate and seeking encouragement for parents displaying the traditional middle-class virtues of thrift, foresight, prudence, and self-control.[91]

The Family Endowment Council continued on similar lines. During the 1920s Eleanor Rathbone repeatedly emphasized the appeal family allowances should have for eugenists. As a measure of positive eugenics they would encourage parents who were child-lovers but could not afford children. This would be, she asserted, citing Beveridge and McDougall, the best security against racial decay. In her well-known *The Disinherited Family* she also claimed for family allowances, paid directly to the mother, the opposite effect among the lower strata. Money would bring self-respect, continence, and contraception. In 1924 she lectured to the Eugenics Society on the direct maintenance of women and children as part of a

[89] Herbert, "Eugenics and Socialism," p. 120: Hobson, *The Recording Angel*, p. 74.

[90] L. Darwin, *The Need for Eugenic Reform* (London, 1926), p. 419; E. W. MacBride, review of books, *Eugenics Review* 12 (1920): 219.

[91] H. D. Harben, *The Endowment of Motherhood*, Fabian tract no. 149 (London, 1910), p. 20. See also evidence of Mary Stocks to National Birth-Rate Commission, *Problems of Population and Parenthood* (London, 1920), p. 235; S. Gotto, "The Eugenic Principle in Social Reconstruction," *Eugenics Review* 9 (1917), 194–95; S. Webb, *The Decline in the Birth Rate*, Fabian tract no. 131 (London, 1907), p. 18.

"living wage," that is, a national minimum. Both then and later she concurred with the society's policy of graded allowances and even considered stopping them after the third or fourth child.[92] The society itself adopted the nonredistributionary principle of benefit per child directly proportional to the scale of earnings of the parents, to promote the fertility of "superior types." But it later preferred "graded equalization pools" that would "equalize standards of living between parents and non-parents doing equivalent work" to exemption from income tax, and flatly rejected state payments.[93] A common approach existed, however, to "influencing the birth-rate and guiding its flow, without violating the privacies or interfering with the liberties of individual citizens."[94] Meanwhile, Eva Hubback, Rathbone's collaborator and a member of the Eugenics Society and later of its council, demonstrated again the flexibility of the eugenic argument for family allowances by claiming first that they would lower the birthrate of the poor and—when the menace of underpopulation had suddenly captured widespread attention in the 1930s—that they would prevent race-suicide.[95]

All the while the Eugenics Society itself had been moving into areas that concerned progressive social reformers—family allowances, family planning, and population research—while trying to emphasise that it was sympathetic towards the working classes, associated with social reform, and not necessarily biased in favour of conservatism.[96] In one field it even succeeded in swinging public opinion towards its (somewhat modified) views. This was on the subject of sterilisation of the unfit. The society took up in earnest the issue of voluntary sterilisation in 1929. In that year the Wood Report on mental deficiency had drawn attention to the high fertility of what it termed the social problem group.[97] It recommended that institutional treatment for mental defectives be regarded as a "flowing" lake rather than a stagnant pool, but it opposed sterilisation. Consequently, the Eugenics Society established a Committee for Legalising Eu-

---

[92] E. F. Rathbone, *The Ethics and Economics of Family Endowment* (London, 1927), pp. 112–13; *The Disinherited Family* (London, 1924), pp. 241–42; "Family Endowment in its Bearing on the Question of Population," *Eugenics Review*, 16 (1924): 270–73.

[93] "An Outline of a Practical Eugenic Policy," *Eugenics Review* 18 (1926): 98; "Aims and Objects of the Eugenics Society," *Eugenics Review* 26 (1934): 135; Fisher, "Family Allowances," p. 89.

[94] Rathbone, "Family Endowment," p. 275.

[95] Hopkinson, *Family Inheritance*, pp. 108, 135. For the underpopulation argument in the 1930s see E. Charles, *The Menace of Under-Population* (London, 1936); C. P. Blacker, *Eugenics: Galton and After* (London, 1952), pp. 147–48.

[96] See the retrospective remarks in the *Eugenics Review* 31 (1940): 203–5.

[97] Report of the Joint Committee of the Board of Education and the Board of Control, 1929. Cf. C. P. Blacker, *Voluntary Sterilization*, reprinted from the *Eugenics Review* (London, 1962), p.12; Jones, *Mental Health and Social Policy*, pp. 80–87.

genic Sterilisation in 1930.[98] Voluntary sterilisation (except in the case of low-grade defectives, when the consent of the parent or guardian and of the Board of Control—established under the 1913 Mental Deficiency Act—was suggested) was recommended as supplementary to segregation, mainly for those leaving the "lake." A Labour MP, Major A. G. Church—a member of the Committee—introduced a bill on these lines in 1931. Significantly, the motion, though dismissed, was supported by many Labour and Liberal MPs, including D. Maclean, E. D. Simon, E. Rathbone, and C. P. Trevelyan. The split among progressives was reminiscent of their ambiguous attitude to birth control—a motion backing it having, for example, been introduced in 1926 by one Labour MP and opposed by another.[99] Even an avowed antieugenist like Lancelot Hogben supported the 1931 bill, as did the *New Statesman* while commenting:

> The legitimate claims of the eugenist standpoint have been vastly weakened in this country by gross over-statement motivated by class bias. Though exponents and supporters of the eugenist movement like Major Darwin and Dean Inge have done everything that could well have been done to alienate the sympathy of the working class leaders in this country, the legitimate claims of eugenics are not inherently incompatible with the outlook of the collectivist movement.[100]

In 1934 a departmental committee on sterilisation which had been appointed by the minister of health, Sir Hilton Young, reported (the Brock Report) and recommended voluntary sterilisation on lines very similar to those of the Eugenics Society. By now the reaction was almost universally favourable. Conservative MPs welcomed the idea of eugenic sterilisation but the liberal press, too, supported its recommendations. The *Manchester Guardian* thought the report "admirably balanced and . . . admirably cautious" and accepted the voluntary sterilisation that "the eugenists soundly urge." The proposed measures, it believed, "will inflict no damage on any liberty of the individual." The *News Chronicle* thought the Brock Committee had presented the problem "with great moderation and good sense." There was a case for experimenting "for the obvious good

---

[98] For a full list of members see Blacker, *Voluntary Sterlization*, p. 11. They included Carr-Saunders, Fisher, Hubback, and Huxley.

[99] See Eugenics Society pamphlet, *Committee for Legalising Eugenic Sterilization* (London, 1930); *Hansard*, 5th Ser., vol. 255, 1249–58 (21.7.1931); *Hansard*, 5th Ser., vol. 191, 849–56 (9.2.1926).

[100] "Sterilisation of Defectives," *New Statesman and Nation*, 25.7.1931. Hogben's wife, Enid Charles, the author of the above-mentioned *The Menace of Under-Population* (previously entitled *The Twilight of Parenthood*), though herself an antieugenist, also admitted that the encouragement or discouragement of individual stocks who are valuable or retrograde was an essential feature of any project of planned ecology (p. 127).

of the community."[101] These echoes of the liberal reaction to the 1913 Mental Deficiency Act are notable in view of the growing alarm with which German legislation on sterilisation was regarded. British eugenics was clearly seen in a different light and the Eugenics Society itself went out of its way to condemn the Nazi approach. Following an initially favourable reaction to the Nazi government's plans concerning eugenics and sterilization,[102] the *Eugenics Review,* and especially C. P. Blacker, stressed "the essential differences between the aims of the eugenic movements of Germany and of this country," in particular as regards compulsory sterilisation.[103] Hence the earlier recognition accorded by the new liberals to the principle that "compulsion means simply a larger freedom" was rescinded. The recommendations of the Brock Report, however, came to nothing due to lack of governmental interest and the growing disrepute that, nevertheless, Nazi eugenics was bringing upon the field.

INTIMATIONS OF SOCIALISM

It remains to be seen how eugenists themselves regarded the connection between eugenics and socialism. There exists a familiar argument associating some versions of socialism with race-thinking or conservative eugenics. Even in Britain the Webbs would not be absolved from this charge, as a perfunctory glance at Beatrice's diaries will indicate. A somewhat more interesting case is that of Karl Pearson, who occupied the first chair of eugenics at the University of London. He started out in the 1880s as a Malthusian socialist, but saw the community primarily as an enforcement agency providing the means of social control over propagation.[104] By the time Pearson had become Britain's leading practising eugenist, there remained little room in his paternal, statist attitude for individuals. National eugenics now reigned supreme in his conception; human sympa-

---

[101] Report of the Departmental Committee on Sterilisation, 1934, Cmd. 4485. For details see Jones, *Mental Health and Social Policy,* pp. 87–90, and Blacker, *Voluntary Sterilization,* pp. 15–16. Two of its members were R. A. Fisher and the conservative eugenist A. F. Tredgold; *Hansard,* 5th Ser., vol. 286, 1179–86 (28.2.1934); vol. 291, 1824–28 (3.7.1934); "The Sterilisation Report," *Manchester Guardian,* 19.1.1934; "The Unfit," *News Chronicle,* 19.1.1934.

[102] *Eugenics Review* 25 (1933): 76–77, though immediate exception was taken to the anti-Semitic intention of the Nazi eugenists.

[103] C. P. Blacker, "Eugenics in Germany," *Eugenics Review* 25 (1933): 158–59. See also Blacker, *Eugenics in Retrospect and Prospect,* pp. 9–12; idem, *Eugenics: Galton and After,* pp. 138–46; and the socialist H. Brewer on the importance of voluntary as against compulsory sterilisation (*Eugenics Review* 26 [1934]: 85, letter to the editor).

[104] K. Pearson, *The Moral Basis of Socialism* (London, 1887), p. 21; cf. B. Kidd, *The Science of Power* (London, 1918), pp. 80–82.

thy—surely the cornerstone of ethical socialism—he saw as so exaggerated as to endanger race-survival by suspending selection. This was the stock-in-trade argument of the Social-Darwinism-as-struggle school. If this was socialism at all, it was a regimented socialism, subservient to a racial definition of national welfare and morality and devoid of humanity.[105]

The socialism singled out in this chapter was almost always of the ethical, humanitarian kind. Havelock Ellis presented eugenics as essential to the success of that socialism. It was "the only method by which Socialism can be enabled to continue on its present path."[106] One of the interesting spokesmen of this reform eugenics, Herbert Brewer, was at pains to point out "to the equalitarian that eugenic policy is not antagonistic to social reform and lessening of economic differences." Moreover, improving the health and efficiency of the population meant making social reform itself more promising. But Brewer certainly had a socialist viewpoint and one of his recommendations even drew praise from such a reluctant eugenist—but enthusiastic socialist—as J.B.S. Haldane. This was the proposal to socialise the germ plasm, to apply artificial insemination for eugenic purposes: "The establishment of the right of every individual that is born to the inheritance of the finest hereditary endowment that anywhere exists." This was "biological socialism, in the truest sense of the word."[107] Even Huxley commended this plan as heralding evolutionary improvement instead of mere tinkering, and subsumed it under the aim of substituting social salvation for individual salvation and enabling self-expression and personal satisfaction to be achieved in serving society.[108] For Brewer, it was all part of a conception of society that was anchored to service rather than to profit. Even the fact of human inequality could hence be interpreted as a guarantee of human amelioration, for positive eugenics was not to be limited to a minority but spread out so that the mass of humanity might rise to the stage gained by any one of its members. Universalising the genetic qualities of highly developed people would multiply immensely the resources of any society: "Biological inequality means not only the possibility of biological advance. It means also a fundamental requirement of a human society which values and conserves real individuality in its members. Just as a body is better and

---

[105] K. Pearson, *The Chances of Death and Other Studies in Evolution*, vol. 1 (London, 1897), pp. 246, 250; idem, *The Scope and Importance to the State of the Science of National Eugenics* (London, 1907), pp. 25, 41; idem, *The Groundwork of Eugenics* (London, 1909), p. 21.

[106] Ellis, *The Task of Social Hygiene*, p. 402.

[107] H. Brewer, *Eugenics and Politics* (London, n.d. [1940]), pp. 7, 12; J.B.S. Haldane, *Heredity and Politics* (London, 1938), pp. 123–24.

[108] Huxley, "Eugenics and Society," pp. 29–30.

more efficient for not being composed either of all brain cells, or all bone cells, or all muscle cells, so it is with the community. Democracy above all needs diversity and freedom to express diversity in every possible way."[109]

J. S. Mill's appreciation of eccentricity was joined here with the organic conception of society, a synthesis already successfully undertaken by the new liberals. In effect, the liberal maxim of variety that Mill developed was given a new lease of life by a number of eugenists. As Huxley asserted, "in these days when the worship of the State is imposing a mass-production ideal of human nature . . . eugenics as a whole must certainly make the encouragement of diversity one of its main principles." It was, he elaborated, of the utmost importance for the material and spiritual progress of civilisation that extreme gifted types (Mill's "eccentrics") should be supplied with niches by the social system.[110]

Opponents of eugenics like Chesterton accused socialism of creating an atmosphere that favoured intervention and was conducive to eugenic experiments unethical and inhuman by nature. Antisocialist eugenists saw nothing in that ideology favourable to the improvement of the race, if indeed it did not encourage the propagation of the inferior.[111] Progressives could nevertheless state that both socialism and eugenics were complementary parts of humanism. If, as Eden Paul claimed, socialists could supply the perfect social environment, only bad inheritance would account for the existence of "inefficient and anti-social members of the community." The practice of eugenics would then be essential because of the reciprocal notion of obligation between individual and community. In return for guaranteeing subsistence to all—that is, a minimum wage and the right to work—the state would insist on making "the ability to earn the Minimum Wage a precondition of the right to become a parent. . . . on Restrictive Eugenist principles, a national minimum of social efficiency will be the indispensable prerequisite to the right to parenthood." One is obviously tempted to ask where lies the humanism of this vision, for efficiency and humanity usually made strange bedfellows. Paul believed it lay in the demand that "those who will suffer or cause suffering shall not be born."[112] And, indeed, Brewer as well remarked years later, in a similar vein, that "it is unfair to any child to be born and reared by persons who cannot help being cruel to it through their own weak-

---

[109] Brewer, *Eugenics and Politics*, p. 16.

[110] Huxley, "Eugenics and Society," p. 28. See also A. C. Pigou, "Galton Lecture," *Eugenics Review* 15 (1923): 306.

[111] G. K. Chesterton, *Eugenics and other Evils* (London, 1922), pp. 7, 146, 165; Crackanthorpe, "Eugenics as a Social Force," p. 971; R. Austin Freeman, "The Sub-Man," *Eugenics Review* 15 (1923): 383.

[112] Paul, *Socialism and Eugenics*, pp. 11, 13, 15, 17.

nesses."[113] This, more than anything else, was the humanitarian argument that supported sterilisation.

The odd thing about the nevertheless predominant "strange opposition" between eugenists and socialists was perhaps not so much that eugenists were not socialists,[114] but that, in the astute observation of Dean Inge, more socialists were not eugenists.[115] As state interventionism in the cause of social reform became a fact of life, eugenists were far more eager to market their ideas as progressive than were the progressive circles to take them too seriously. But the lack of interest seems to have been a question of priorities rather than of principle. For the moral of this story is not that eugenics can be legitimised with ease even in its worst excesses, nor that its salient antiliberal and often fascist leanings can be obfuscated. Rather, it has been to illustrate the inappropriateness of approaching ideologies, or segments of social thinking, in black-and-white dichotomous fashion.

British eugenics certainly is such a case. For many, it was a new and worthwhile experiment in the field of social reform—a field that in the first half of this century invited and encouraged innovations in ideas and practice. For a few, its aims appeared to be socialist ones and, as I have tried to argue, many of its fundamental precepts were shared with socialism. But above all, many enlightened progressives accorded it respectability, even in the face of persistent attempts to discredit it entirely or to associate it with undiluted racialism, chauvinism, imperialism, fascism, or conservative individualism. They dallied with it at one time or another, they spoke of it favourably, they accepted invitations to speak at the Eugenics Society, they even became members of that body. How else can one explain that Keynes was the treasurer of the Cambridge Eugenics Society before the First World War and a member of the Eugenics Society's council upon his death? How else can one explain that the central annual event of the Eugenics Society, the Galton Lecture, was given by progressives such as Huxley, Keynes and Beveridge? Keynes remarked at the 1946 Galton Lecture: "Galton [was] the founder of the most important, significant and, I would add, genuine branch of sociology which exists, namely eugenics."[116] Herbert Samuel, one of the leaders of the Liberal Party and close to new liberal circles, wrote in 1937, while nazism was rampant, about the "new science of Eugenics": "As the means are discovered by which the physical qualities of the human race may be improved generation by generation, to make use of those means will rank as a

---

[113] Brewer, *Eugenics and Politics*, p. 10.
[114] Herbert, "Eugenics and Socialism," p. 116.
[115] W. R. Inge, "Eugenics," *Edinburgh Review* 236 (1922): 47.
[116] J. M. Keynes, quoted in *Eugenics Review* 38 (1946–47): 68.

duty. . . . To put debased money into circulation is an offence, but to put degenerate men and women into circulation is an offence far graver."[117] Richard Titmuss, though he always stressed the greater importance of environment and of social improvement, was an active member of the Eugenics Society for many years and occasionally addressed it. He justified eugenic conclusions in the light of turn-of-the-century knowledge and drew attention to findings concerning dysgenic trends.[118] Graham Wallas in his *The Great Society* and G. Lowes Dickinson in his *Justice and Liberty* recommended eugenic measures.[119]

In recent years eugenics has become increasingly the domain of geneticists and less of social scientists, social philosophers, or politicians. The biological breakthroughs promised us by scientists, coupled with renewed interest by laymen in questions of heredity and human quality—a normal development as the atrocities of nazism recede into the past—will no doubt raise again many of the themes touched upon here. That these themes can be pursued by the type of thinker considered representative of Western social democracies I hope to have demonstrated in this chapter.

[117] H. Samuel, *Belief and Action* (London, 1937): pp. 149–50.

[118] R. M. Titmuss, *Poverty and Population* (London, 1938), pp. 44–46; "The Social Environment and Eugenics," *Eugenics Review* 36 (1944): 56–57.

[119] G. Wallas, *The Great Society* (London, 1914): p. 59; G. Lowes Dickinson, *Justice and Liberty* (London, 1908), pp. 39, 46, 137.

CHAPTER EIGHT

True Blood or False Genealogy: New Labour and British Social Democratic Thought

WHEN TONY BLAIR traced some of the ideational roots of New Labour back to early- and mid-twentieth-century liberals, as well as when he put out organisational feelers of cooperation toward the Liberal Democrats, he dared make explicit a central feature of British progressivism. In contrast to the overt politics of confrontation and the tactics of exclusion that have typified the public face of British political culture, with its assumption of a one-to-one association between party and political values, the ideology of social and political reform has cut across party boundaries ever since Labour was formed. Although liberalism and social democracy have frequently displayed diverging subcurrents, they have been for the past century overwhelmingly involved in a complex series of intertwined relationships, overlaps, and parallel growth. This mutual succour has created a peculiar blend of ideas and programmes distanced both from classical liberal and from continental socialist positions. Within this broad family there have evidently been unhappy partnerships, black sheep and even conscientious objectors. Indeed, its resemblances are far more obvious to the external analyst than they have been to most of its members.

But this raises a problem with regard to the relationship between New Labour and its heritage. The iconic status that Blair has accorded liberal thinkers and practitioners such as Hobhouse, Lloyd George, Beveridge, and Keynes suggests that their input into the progressive tradition from which New Labour draws has been a crucial counterweight to the statist and group-oriented character of British socialism. To the contrary, as will be shown here, the work of assimilating some of the most advanced ideas of liberalism had already been accomplished by central social democrats *within* the Labour movement, in the spheres of personal liberty, economic cooperation between state and individual, theories of human welfare and growth, and the mobilising of a democratic and regulatory, not bureaucratic and overbearing, state.

The problem is, however, slightly more complex than that. It is not a question of establishing a common ground between liberal and social democratic positions; on a superficial level that can be demonstrated to the satisfaction of all but the most rigid students of politics. The real issue is the identification of a large number of common-ground configurations in which the notions of community, liberty, welfare, and the sphere of the state are mutually related. Each little shift in emphasis, in prioritising one value over another, in associating some of these ideas more closely and separating others results in a different ideological balance. Within this rich field of interpretations and influences, an open society can choose from a plethora of social democratic constructs, and it is against that kind of backdrop that New Labour must be evaluated.

The so-called centre left position of New Labour's "Third Way" is hardly new in its desire to stake out a common ideological ground among apparently disparate political convictions, but it is entirely misguided in implying that such a common ground is monolithic and clearly defined and that, consequently, New Labour can appropriate the totality of its substance. The emerging issue is in fact rather different: if at all, New Labour is positioned somewhat outside the field of the welfare state progressivism that has been Britain's most notable ideological contribution to the political thinking of the twentieth century. To that extent it has abandoned key facets of the social democratic inspiration emanating from its own past ranks by moving *away* from the liberal and, no less significantly, the communitarian tenets on which even British liberals had prided themselves.

THE PROGRESSIVE CRUCIBLE

Strictly speaking, then, there is of course no such thing as social democracy, if by that label is meant a singular fixed list of beliefs and practices. Nor has social democracy been a term much in favour in the history of British Labour thinking. Rather, Labour appropriated the term "socialism" because in the British context socialism had already been tamed and domesticated. Before the advent of the Labour Party in 1900 it had not even been a party-political word. It signified instead the recognition, shared among progressives in general, that society was an interdependent structure and that the regulated coordination of social life was essential in order to abolish, or reduce, unacceptable material conditions. The Rainbow Circle, one of the most important discussion groups to straddle the ostensible divide between liberalism and socialism and a vital crucible of progressive thought, illustrates this ideological compound admirably. In the early years of its formation, employing a rhetoric that uncannily resonates with that of New Labour exactly one century later, Herbert Samuel identified a "third social philosophy" located between the liberalism of Bentham and Adam Smith and the socialism of the Social Democratic Federation and the Fabians. The root idea of this "New Liberalism" was "the unity of society—complex in its economic, cooperative, ethical and emotional bonds"—and a view of the State as a partnership.[1] The Rainbow Circle was no stranger to the view that divisions among progressives were institutional, not ideational; that "the cleavage between the new Liberalism & Socialism is not to be found in their ideas of property but in the ordinary political possibilities of the two parties."[2] On the eve of the founding of the Labour Party, J. A. Hobson reminded the Circle, in the presence of one of its most illustrious members, Ramsay MacDonald, that the principles upon which a joint Progressive Party should be based "are already in evidence in the form of widely held intellectual affinities which as a matter of fact place the leaders of the Radical, the Socialist & the Labour groups much nearer to each other than their followers imagine."[3]

The liberalism that John Stuart Mill bequeathed to his intellectual successors was based on the free development of individuality, on a specific configuration of these three concepts in a mutually sustaining framework. It focused on the centrality of responsible human choice in a setting of personal growth, one that acknowledged the constraints of social life as well as the dual benefits to society and to the individual of nourishing differences. Some of the features of social democracy emanated from the logic of liberalism itself: an increasing sense of sociability, the rational desirability of social harmony, and the promise of continuously improving control over the conditions of human development—a possibility attached to a hopeful view of social evolution and of the future. It was also located at a crucial transformative juncture when human nature was no longer perceived solely in terms of action from which unreasonable hindrances had to be removed, but also in terms of processes of intellectual, moral, and emotional development that had both to be unblocked and enabled, by means of individual endeavour as well as external assistance. As we saw in chapter 2, Hobhouse had put this succinctly when he located the sphere of liberty in "the sphere of growth itself" and considered the theory of collective action to be no less fundamental than that of personal freedom.[4]

WELL-BEING AND WELFARE

Combined with these emerging features of advanced liberalism was a subtle but persistent shift in the language of utilitarianism—a theory by no means dead with the fall from grace of Bentham's hedonistic calculus

---

[1] M. Freeden, ed., *Minutes of the Rainbow Circle, 1894–1924* (London, Royal Historical Society, 1989), p. 28.

[2] Ibid, p. 29.

[3] Ibid., p. 68.

[4] See chap. 2, above, p. 52; see also L. T. Hobhouse, *Liberalism* (London, 1911), pp. 124, 147.

and maximisation of individual pleasures. Utilitarianism had recognised human beings as loci of fundamental interests and needs that required satisfaction, and this heritage underwent refinement as its core idea moved from pleasure to happiness and well-being, and finally to welfare. Moreover, this discursive change was interlinked to the rise of the "social" as an analytical unit, so that social welfare and even the welfare state gradually entered the progressive vocabulary.

Here already was ample room for the fertile pluralism of British progressive thought. While the old Hobbesian understanding of liberty as the absence of impediments to individual action had been severely truncated, progressives in the main transplanted liberty into a soil nourished either on the idea of natural human growth, or on the idea of social self-expression. The first remained focused on the benefits liberty conferred on an individual, but did not rule out any intervention genuinely conducive to removing barriers to personal growth and welfare. The second concentrated on the benefits liberty conferred on society, developing the Marxist notion of emancipation to include human realisation only through a full immersion in social life.

Concurrently, the concept of welfare was locked into a dual ideational environment. On the one hand, it was linked in three senses to pervasive images of health. First, the rhetoric of rights was intriguingly married to an extensive range of individual functional requirements that included personal health. Second, social entities were discovered to have needs partially separate from those of their members. Third, those needs were addressed in terms of structural and relational normalities, and came to be best described in the language of health and disease. This intellectual cocktail lay at the root of welfare thinking as it developed in early-twentieth-century Britain. On the other hand, welfare was linked to intricate notions of community. These could in turn be broken down into a harmony of individual welfares, a focus on raising the material welfare of the dispossessed as central to the process of bestowing full social membership on them, or an emphasis on the flourishing of collective life. The confluence of welfare and health could, however, also be retained as a second-order issue, one which could only be addressed indirectly by removing bad housing, enforcing reasonable working hours, and protecting against dangerous trades. Behind that lurked a far more instrumental view of personal health as conducive to individual wealth-production.

Hints of this conceptual indeterminacy within progressive ranks may again be detected through the Rainbow Circle minutes. The discussants disagreed on whether the presence of materialist arguments weakened or strengthened social democracy; on whether the same concept of property was entertained by liberals and socialists; on whether society could or could not be described as an organism; on whether individuals sensitive to social needs were the most valuable and whether communal benefit was most furthered by placing individuality at its disposal; on whether progress was attributable to individual achievement or whether such achievement resulted from what society had placed at the disposal of such individuals; on whether the ideas of fraternity and equality were distinctively socialist; on whether nationalisation would reduce efficiency or be replaced with physical, moral, intellectual, and artistic efficiency. But these variations were all accommodated within agreed parameters of reformist political discourse: they constituted competitions over the correct combinations of the elements to be found in a shared pool of ideas.

SOCIAL DEMOCRATIC STRANDS

The Fabians

British socialism in the meantime, arriving on the scene while liberalism was undergoing significant internal change, was itself a multilayered phenomenon, although already well-attuned to its native culture. Calls for aesthetic and ethical fellowship, demands for radical changes in the conditions of life and labour, an insistence on workers' control through nationalisation and a crude economic reading of Marx filled the space of public debate, edging out the more revolutionary continental rhetoric of class conflict and social upheaval. The language of socialism introduced some additional notions into the public domain: equality as a material rather than legal concept; labour as a human attribute and expressive requirement, not merely an activity; and the existential situatedness of individuals in groups, to the point where some groups were seen to adopt a persona of their own. It is striking that the ideological architecture of British socialism contained much of the structure of its advanced liberal counterpart even if, as emphasised above, the internal configuration of ideas varied from ideological family to family, and from case to case, and their application could follow different routes.

Three of the socialist strands between the 1880s and 1930s are of major consequence in the mainstream ideological development of the social democratic tradition in Britain: the Fabians; the views initially epitomised by Ramsay MacDonald, which underwent further modifications as the century progressed; and the pluralists in the interwar years. The Fabians were social democratic in a number of senses: First, though they were notoriously élitist in organisation and in the role they assigned to expertise, they were democratic in their pioneering recognition of mass political education and the need to convince an electorate of the rightness of their programmes rather than the wisdom of their political leaders. Second, they assimilated the dominant cultural icon of evolution into the notion of gradualism, expecting a transformation through the ballot box. Third, they discarded individualistic atomism in favour of a concern with social categories. This involved the redefinition of individuals as constituting clusters of group attributes, rather than vehicles of narratives of growth. Fourth, and here the Fabians shared a crucial belief with other socialists as well as with the new liberals, they regarded the state as the agent of reform and social justice, the only social agency, in fact, possessed of the power, the prestige, the benevolence, and the disinterested nonsectarianism that could attract political loyalty, transcend conflict, underpin citizenship, and effect the redistribution of wealth required to repair the social costs of the Industrial Revolution. Sidney Webb referred to the "fourfold path of collective administration of public services, collective regulation of private industry, collective taxation of unearned income, and collective provision for the dependent sections of the community."[5] For many socialists, though not for all, the logic of state activity was conceptually attached to the nationalisation of key public resources and services, but it could concurrently be employed to enlist state supervision and control of other important social practices. Notably, the liberal concern with the state as a source of potentially arbitrary and unaccountable power was largely removed from Fabian understandings.

State Socialism

MacDonald's socialism well illustrates the common discursive field with liberalism, as well as one particular arrangement of social democratic concepts. For MacDonald, the organic analogy was attractive for the same reason that new liberals had adopted it: not merely because it focused on groups, but also because it made one think "of the whole of Society as well as of the separate individuals who compose it." It was in fact, he insisted, capitalism whose productive processes imposed a deadening uniformity, allowing less play for individuality: "Nothing is, indeed, more absurd than an argument in support of the present state of Society, based on the assumption that as we move away from it in the direction of Socialism we are leaving individuality and individual liberty behind."[6] Individuality was conjoined in a social framework with well-being, and MacDonald gave prescient expression to the evolving concerns of social democracy when he speculated that "it appears to be the special task of the twentieth century to discover a means of co-ordinating the various social functions

---

[5] S. Webb, "Modern Social Movements," in *The Cambridge Modern History of the World* vol. 12 (Cambridge, 1910), p. 760.

[6] J. R. MacDonald, *Socialism and Society* (London, 1905), pp. xviii, 7–8.

so that the whole community may enjoy robust health, and its various organs share adequately in that health. But this is nothing else than the aim of Socialism."[7] MacDonald's socialism shared with liberalism an abhorrence of class as a divisive sectionalism, ripe for replacement by national and communal growth, and it even retained a vision of "civil society"—smaller groups such as trade unions, churches, and families—whose importance would increase as safeguards of material and spiritual needs.[8]

On the question of equality it is even more difficult to prise MacDonald away from broadly liberal and pluralist notions. Socialists, he argued, understood by the concept "that the inequalities in the tastes, the powers, the capacities of men may have some chance of having a natural outlet." This would ensure both, in liberal terms, that for the individual personality "opportunities should be given to it to advance in certain directions" and, in socialist terms, that each may have "an opportunity to contribute their appropriate services to society"—a foreshadowing of R. H. Tawney's views on social function.[9] In standard Millian terms, MacDonald linked individual growth and welfare by interpreting equality as " 'I have an equal right with you to self-development' and even that is limited to a development upon lines consistent with individual and social well-being." Hence, also, MacDonald argued the case for limited private property "in those things which personality requires for its nourishment," objecting mainly to the misuse of monopolistic concentrations of property as constraining individual liberty, a well-rehearsed liberal argument harking back to nineteenth-century liberalism.[10]

It was, however, on the issue of liberty that fissures between the socialist and liberal traditions could be seen. MacDonald diverged from his liberal colleagues in the Rainbow Circle by setting liberty more firmly than they would have dared within a communal framework. The result was a curious fusion, employing developmental language to insist that the liberty of socialism was the "liberty of a man to fulfil his true being—the being which has ends that are social, that relate to Society, and that are not merely personal."[11] This left little space between the concepts of individuality and community, a lack of space reproduced in Amitai Etzioni's communitarian views and their intimations of social control and social duty, which have been influential in New Labour circles, and of which more in the following chapter.

[7] Ibid., p. 9.
[8] Ibid., pp. 131, 185.
[9] J. R. MacDonald, *The Socialist Movement* (London, 1912), p. 139.
[10] J. R. MacDonald, *Socialism and Government* (London, 1910), pp. 155, 158.
[11] Ibid., 152–54.

The Pluralists

Nevertheless, the seeds of social democracy had been sown, and the ensuing diet of the Labour intellectual tradition was identifiably one from which liberals had partaken. Similar themes are present in the writings of Tawney and G.D.H. Cole. Tawney ascribed a powerful sense of altruistic fellowship to an ethically construed idea of community. But he also insisted that the free disposal of personal possessions was the condition of a healthy and self-respecting life and sought to distribute property rights more widely, though property had to be accompanied by special obligations and was hence conditional.[12] This followed because human activities and practices were valorised, not only as expressions of self, but also in terms of the social functions they performed. Here one can identify the early hint of a motif that New Labour have replicated, but only up to a point: the grounding of reward and remuneration on the basis of service to the community. The liberal appreciation of excellence in performance was closely associated with a recognition of the community as the ultimate norm-setter for what counted as useful work.[13] Nevertheless, throughout his writings Tawney not only paid tribute to aspects of the liberal tradition but insisted that the only version of socialism that stood a chance of success was the one that accepted liberal notions of fair play: personal liberty, freedom of speech, tolerance, and parliamentary government.[14] Individualism and voluntarism were key concepts for both Tawney and Cole. Indeed, as has recently been argued, their notion of function entailed little more than the socialist emphasis on human productivity but lacked the primacy organic perspectives assigned to serving distinct social needs.[15] And whereas liberal and socialist organicists were confident about the state's ability to act as the guardian of human interests, the guild socialists—quite contrary to the Fabians, and more typical of the old liberals than the new—displayed a fear of the state's unadulterated power.

Socialism for Tawney was henceforth social democracy. And beyond this "political" liberalism, as Tawney stated in 1949, was an "ecumenical liberalism" that "profoundly affected" socialists. For, although they rejected the "arid provincialisms" of the Manchester School, socialists acknowledged as the goal of political effort the free development of human

---

[12] R. H Tawney, *The Acquisitive Society* (London, 1921), pp. 25, 94–95.

[13] For a development of this argument see M. Freeden, *Liberalism Divided: A Study in British Political Thought, 1914–1939* (Oxford, 1986), p. 315.

[14] R. H. Tawney, *Equality*, 3d ed. (London, 1938), p. 266.

[15] M. Stears, "Guild Socialism and Ideological Diversity on the British Left, 1914–1926," *Journal of Political Ideologies* 3 (1998): 289–305.

personality, unimpeded by class, capricious inequalities of circumstance, or arbitrary despotism. The moral challenge to socialism was therefore "to work out a new social synthesis which may do justice both to the values of the Liberal era and to equally important aspects of life, to which that era, for all its virtues, was too often blind." Here was already the mark of another "third way," located between capitalism and communism. Specifically, Tawney positioned social democracy in an area hewn out between the denial of political liberty by both fascism and communism, and the denial of equal economic opportunities by the plutocracies of the West.[16]

Revisionism as Mainstream: Crosland

A generation later, Anthony Crosland, reacting to the temporary rise of Marxist arguments in the 1930s, attempted to revise the socialist creed. That revision was in effect a reassertion of mainstream British social democracy; it was, as Crosland himself admitted, "hallowed by an appeal to the past."[17] Crosland vaguely recognized a crucial feature of ideological structure, namely, that what one group may assert as first principles, another will regard as contingent and ephemeral expressions of deeper core concepts. Thus, he identified a contest between nationalisation of the means of exchange and the labour theory of value as merely reflecting "the underlying aspiration towards equality."[18] Echoing the views of interwar centrist liberals, Crosland resurrected the importance of incentives as a psychological constituent of human activity. Previous socialists had objected to profits as corrupting, or at the very least had kept quiet about them. But once profits were subsumed under the broader category of incentives, they could not be singled out from practices that social democrats—as distinct from Marxists—would be willing to endorse.[19] The "psychologisation" of profit thus redeemed it as an aspect of human nature that respect for individual needs would have to legitimate.

Crosland had already reflected the process of narrowing the concept of welfare that is so conspicuous in New Labour language. He bracketed the welfare state together with the paternalist tradition, a categorisation that would have disturbed new liberals: the state had certain responsibilities towards its citizens for preventing poverty and distress. Paternalism was a response to a series of demands for social security and a guaranteed national minimum. Social welfare was now targeted at a specific deprived

---

[16] R. H. Tawney, *The Radical Tradition* (Harmondsworth, 1964), pp. 146, 161–62, 166.

[17] C.A.R. Crosland, *The Future of Socialism*, rev. ed. (New York, 1963), p. 62.

[18] Ibid., p. 42.

[19] Ibid., pp. 54–57.

sector of the population, rather than interpreted as a general attribute of human flourishing. The fundamental needs that welfare had to satisfy were reduced to addressing need in the sense of primary and secondary deprivation, thus significantly decoupling welfare from a broader idea of equality underpinned by the free and universal provision of social goods.[20] Nevertheless, Crosland defined a socialist as one who accorded welfare exceptional priority over other claims. That is to say, welfare retained a prime position in the conceptual configuration of social democrats, but only as an etiolated redistributive version of the fuller concept available to them.

In addition, individual rights for workers had replaced more participatory applications of the socialist concepts of work and community, the latter being demoted to "an ideal of fraternity and co-operation" and to the practice of "collective responsibility." The mixed economy was signalled by the refusal to dismiss capitalism, merely its inefficiencies. Yet the state was still the prime mover: government had to allow space for private corporations, but it needed to manage them as a reflection of democratic responsibility and popular control.[21] Liberty was simply taken for granted, for "it would never have occurred to most early socialists that socialism had any meaning except within a political framework of freedom for the individual."[22] But which conception of liberty? Crosland offered a glimpse in the conclusion to his book, in which he advocated a more expressive view of liberty, supported by a culturally qualitative increase in the choice of lifestyles—in effect a pluralist version of the Millian avowal of self-development. Taking on the Fabians, Crosland observed that much legislation in matters sexual and in the area of censorship "should be highly offensive to socialists, in whose blood there should always run a trace of the anarchist and the libertarian, and not too much of the prig and the prude." Socialism was not about the sacrifice of private pleasure to public duty. Neither was it, importantly, about the suppression of dissent.[23]

HEALTH AS LIBERATION: TITMUSS

Finally, some brief reflections on Richard Titmuss, whose contribution to British social democratic thinking has not been adequately recognised. Returning to the theme of welfare as health, Titmuss persevered with the metaphor of society as an organic whole composed of interdependent

---

[20] Ibid., pp. 80–91.
[21] See also A. Crosland, *Socialism Now* (London, 1975), pp. 33–35.
[22] Crosland, *The Future of Socialism*, pp. 49–50, 67–68, 76.
[23] Ibid., pp. 354–57.

parts, with its corollary that many human needs were social in origin and collective in the means for their satisfaction.[24] But he was also sensitive to the claims of individual liberty, which he specifically applied to the relationship between patient and doctor. Titmuss related liberty to two major factors. The first was that of lifestyle choices, inasmuch as health had now been reinterpreted by radical reformers not merely as social well-being but as a subjective constituent of an individual's own understanding of his or her capacity to function.[25] Liberty was consequently linked to psychological states of mind that required recognition and assistance through the fundamental altruism of others. Need, welfare, and liberty were connected at a more basic level than the motivation for incentives. The second was that of power relationships, now discovered in the internal logic of professional structure. Whereas liberty had traditionally been conceived as the emancipation of classes from the very idea of class, or as the limitation of state intervention in the private sphere, Titmuss transferred its focus to new ground. He was alert to the mixed blessings of professional expertise. Science may have encouraged the growth of a critical spirit, but it also was fast becoming a technology with new authoritarian implications. The current linchpin of the medical profession—the general practitioner—was in danger of being squeezed between the bureaucratic demands of socialised medicine and the power of the medical specialist. Hence this crucial group of GPs, on which free access to medicine depended, had itself to be allowed to exercise its own judgment, which the development of science had opened up. In other words, where knowledge had become the province of a few, its free and fair dissemination was a function of according new rights to its middlemen.

In the language of such rights, doctors required and secured the freedom to choose which medical technologies to administer, as well as to choose the nature of their association with the state. Concurrently, patients obtained access to health services for all who wanted to use them. Hence for Titmuss, health care was not only a question of *equal* access for all, but of *free* access, including the freedom to choose which health services to use and whether to use them.[26] The defining classical liberal choice-right had reappeared: "The emphasis on the social rights of all citizens to use *or not to use* as responsible people the services made available by the community in respect of certain needs which the private market and the family were unable or unwilling to provide universally."[27] This liberal aspect of Titmuss's creed prioritised individual choice over the social insistence on

[24] R. M. Titmuss, *Essays on "the Welfare State"* (London, 1963), p. 39.

[25] Ibid., p. 134.

[26] R. M. Titmuss, *Commitment to Welfare* (London, 1976), p. 237; *Essays*, p. 141.

[27] Titmuss, *Commitment to Welfare*, p. 129. My italics.

the scrupulous discharge of a duty to be healthy. Both doctors and patients were therefore endowed with the essence of liberal interaction: the possibility of opting in and out of constitutive social relationships. The intention of Titmuss's argument was not, however, to reintroduce a new exclusivist contractualism into such relationships. Titmuss rightly regarded—as did progressive liberals and social democrats—the emergence of these rights not as the product of a conflict between individualism and collectivism, but as reflecting a dispute over different degrees of freedom. And, as did so many of those progressives, Titmuss aspired to "release the individual (whether, in this context, doctor or patient) from unalterable dependence on any particular social group."[28]

New Labour and Liberty

The analysis of some of the theoretical constructions of British social democracy has of necessity been selective, though far from arbitrary. It does however assist in adumbrating certain parameters of the field within which New Labour professes to be located. Party rhetoric, instructive and central as it is to understanding how a political system works, rarely aspires to the heights of complex ideological arguments, nor can it if it is to act as an effective mobiliser of public opinion. But New Labour rhetoric is ambitious, and it has laid claim to being the inheritor of a social liberal, or centre left, position in British politics. And it is on that claim that it has to be judged as a set of ideological and philosophical positions.

The focus on liberty has for a while been notable in Labour discourse, in the writings of Roy Hattersley and Bryan Gould, authors of books that were entitled respectively *Socialism and Freedom* and *Choose Freedom: The Future for Democratic Socialism*, as well as in the official voice of Neil Kinnock, whose statement "at the core of our convictions is belief in individual liberty" graces the preface to the Labour Party's 1992 manifesto. To be sure, Kinnock positioned liberty firmly in the context of equalising social and economic opportunities provided by the community, but he distinctly prioritised it. Although the role of liberty in the social democratic tradition has been acknowledged in New Labour writings and speeches, that emphasis on liberty has been muted. Talk of self-development and growth has been replaced by a more minimalist notion of equality of opportunity, of life chances, moving away from the emancipatory tone of many past British socialists. The recognition of social interdependence as a mechanism of releasing individuals from socioeconomic fetters

---

[28] Ibid., pp. 238, 242.

gave way to limited promises of a Freedom of Information Act, which then disappeared from the governmental agenda.

Free will, on Blair's understanding, is associated with religious under-tones of individual responsibility, not the growth of personhood.[29] Inter-dependence may still relate to employing collective power to advance indi-vidual interest but this is "an enlightened view of self-interest [that] regards it, broadly, as inextricably linked to the interests of society."[30] Gone is the libertarian space carved out by Crosland and the emphasis of the pluralists on individual personality; back comes the fusion preferred by MacDonald. There is nothing on individuality in Blair's preface to New Labour's 1997 manifesto, except a reference to the abilities of indi-vidual pupils; the preferred and fundamental social unit is the group, the British people, the community, the family (albeit a modernized family in which women are equal to men). Only one individual activity is singled out—that of "successful entrepreneurs." Significantly, liberty is not lo-cated in proximity to self-development, as in new liberal and much social democratic argument. Instead Blair wishes to retrieve from an older and more capitalist version of liberalism "the primacy of individual liberty in the market economy."[31] As maintained in the next chapter, that places individual liberty on a path instrumental to employability, rather than on a path that connects it to autonomy.

THE PARTICULARISATION OF COMMUNITY

The concept of community has undergone the most intriguing changes of all. On one dimension, it has lost its inclusive, organic features typical of mainstream social democracy and has become startlingly majoritarian. One of the most allusive passages of the manifesto talks of "a government that will govern in the interest of the many, the broad majority of people who work hard, play by the rules, pay their dues and feel let down by a political system that gives the breaks to the few, to an elite at the top." But the subtext of this passage, borne out in other utterances, is that there may also be others, on the marginalized outreaches of society, who do not—in the language of socialist expectations—work hard, who do not—in the language of conservative conventionalism—play by the rules, and who do not—in the language of liberal contractarianism—pay their dues. Communal membership is not ascribed, but earned; it is not a status but a virtuous activity.

[29] T. Blair, *New Britain: My Vision of a Young Country* (London, 1996), p. 61.
[30] T. Blair, *Socialism* (London, 1994), p. 4.
[31] T. Blair, *The Third Way* (London, 1998), pp. 1, 13–14.

This is spelled out more unequivocally on a second dimension. "The assertion that each of us is our brother's keeper has motivated the Labour movement since the mid nineteenth century," thus Blair. Individual responsibility is linked not to autonomy but to duty to others and to the community, it is "a value shared." Indeed, the potential pluralism of social democracy recedes before the establishing of a "sense of values, of common norms of conduct." A singularity of moral purpose spells out a holism, not an organic unity of parts: "The only way to rebuild social order and stability is through strong values, socially shared, inculcated through individuals and families."[32] This rhetoric of unified and virtuous authority represents a breach with the conceptual structures of social democracy, even with Fabian dirigisme. In its echoing of the "one nation" of paternalistic conservatism, its rediscovery of natural harmonies and the decent institutions that underpin them, and its contraction of the role of politics, it jettisons the mechanically segmented, yet statist, nature of Fabianism. A plethora of rights gives way to a new emphasis on obligations-cum-responsibilities, not of others towards yourself but of yourself towards others, and a community is understood as the local repository of culturally inherited and preserved ways of life to which compliance is required. Sometimes this notion of mutual rights and responsibilities is expressed as a market relationship, "a modern notion of social justice—'something for something,' "[33] a rather starker rendition of Tawney's functionalism. Being human is comprehended neither in liberal terms of development nor in socialist terms of nourishing fundamental needs, but in terms of responsible conduct. The fundamental unconditionality of full social membership is hence repudiated.

More often, though, as seen through the revealing phrases of New Labour's principal ideologues, the balance tips heavily in favour of the community away from the permissive, individualist, and loosely regulatory fraternity of Crosland: "New Labour builds on the traditional Labour ideal of social cooperation and expands it into a more dynamic view of the need for a strong society and an active community to help people succeed. This new tough concept of community, where rights and responsibilities go hand in hand, enables New Labour to reclaim ground that should never have been ceded to the right."[34] It therefore intersects with liberty as a value constrained not only by harm to others or by socioeconomic obstacles, but by shared values "promoting tolerance within agreed norms."[35]

<hr />

[32] Blair, *New Britain*, pp. 238, 43, 61, 208.

[33] Ibid., p. 298.

[34] P. Mandelson and R. Liddle, *The Blair Revolution: Can New Labour Deliver?* (London, 1996), p. 4.

[35] Blair, *The Third Way*, p. 12.

A Partnership of Equals?

The mixed economy emerges in an altered form under New Labour. It is centred around an ambivalence concerning human nature, the site of a fragmented self unrecognisable to earlier progressives. That nature is co-operative as well as competitive, selfless as well as self-interested. People require groups—families and local communities—as a nourishing bed of their moral powers, and multicultural differences must be acknowledged within a framework of equal human worth. Government appears not as a manager and overseer but as a coequal, arguably even minor, partner with business and industry, in order to promote the aspirations of individuals. The partnership is no longer one in which pockets of private enterprise are permitted as long as they do not unduly serve private ends. The social democratic state that demanded compliance, indeed subservience, to democratically established social aims has vanished. Instead, New Labour fully recognises that "the private sector, not government, is at the forefront of wealth creation and employment generation." Competition is the norm where possible, regulation the reserve restraint where necessary.[36] Or, put even more succinctly, "New Labour welcomes the rigour of competitive markets as the most efficient means of anticipating and supplying consumers' wants, offering choice and stimulating innovation."[37] The internal balance of the social liberal and social democratic ideational configurations have been discarded. Any hint of a struggle between the public and private sphere, or of their different functions and purposes, is elided. The battle is declared over. Instead, a politics that combines "ambition with compassion, success with social justice,"[38] is mooted. New dichotomies are formed, but their synthesising mechanisms are assumed rather than constructed. The "stakeholder" phrase, redolent of "shareholder," signifies a society in which seizing opportunities, achievement, and merit are the main bases of social justice, while need is a secondary criterion. In this vision of boundless property owners, wealth is crucially spread, not redistributed—a term that New Labour avoids if at all possible.

The Constriction of Welfare

How is the notion of welfare interpreted in New Labour understandings? Here again, important slippages have occurred in relation to the social democratic tradition. In the visionary heights of that tradition, welfare

---

[36] Ibid., p. 10.
[37] Mandelson and Liddle, *The Blair Revolution*, p. 22.
[38] Blair, *New Britain*, pp. 107, 213.

evolved as a view of optimal human and social flourishing alongside the idea of citizenship as an attribute of the entire community participating in and prospering on a full range of social goods. New Labour, however, has pressed further with the shrinkage of welfare back to the more modest and minimalist conception that has run in parallel to that major theme. The particularism of welfare is evident in a number of ways. It is limited in the population it addresses, aiming "to provide for those at the bottom." It has refocused on poverty, as the main form of social exclusion, and on care for vulnerable groups such as the elderly. It sees the virtues of the welfare state as transformative for the less well-off but also as cost-effective. It is defined, as Giddens has put it, as "a pooling of risk rather than resources."[39] It has adopted a critical perspective concerning welfare dependency, replacing it with the aim of making people more independent and responsible and regarding welfare as functional for wealth creation. It has scrapped Titmuss's faith in human altruism and in the liberating force of welfare for all. Curiously, it sees as part of the welfare brief the "insecurity of middle income Britain"—that insecurity being a fear of crime. And most tellingly, because welfare is no longer thought of as universal but has been reduced to a "hand-up" to the poor, it has conceptually assimilated the American notion of workfare in the phrase "from welfare to work"—thus indicating a dichotomy that cuts loose from the more inclusive socialist views of work as welfare, as the essence of well-being, and redefining the status of welfare as instrumental to other ends.[40]

DENATIONALISING CITIZENSHIP

While pride in and allegiance to the welfare state is still tendered, the concatenation of "welfare" and "state" causes an additional difficulty for New Labour. One finds the odd glimmering of the role of government through providing work and education to help people to help themselves,[41] but even that falls short of former social democratic aspirations. More often, the ascending revival of civil society, not only as a supplement but a substitute for state activity, signals a reallocation of institutional power and responsibility. This differs, however, from MacDonald's approval of the role of voluntary groups. New Labour has ceased to believe in big, centralised government as the framework within which civil society operates. It would dissociate itself from MacDonald's assertion that "the

---

[39] A. Giddens, *The Third Way* (Cambridge, 1998), p. 116.

[40] Blair, *New Britain*, pp. 142–43; idem, *The Third Way*, pp. 5, 14; interview in *The Guardian*, 17.1.1998; Mandelson and Liddle, *The Blair Revolution*, pp. 72–73, 142–43; Giddens, *The Third Way*, p. 117.

[41] Blair, *New Britain*, p. 302.

Socialist considers that the State is as essential to individual life as is the atmosphere" and that the evolution of political democracy was directed at creating "a state which could respond to the common will."[42] New Labour's state is not only a partner, but also an institution that no longer wishes to assert universal control over the various spheres of society. Indeed, public-private partnerships are identified as a distinct way of establishing citizenship itself, of "reconnect[ing] people to the political system." Community is firmly detached from both state and government rather than expressed through them. Localisation suggests an emphasis on communities rather than an overarching community.[43]

New Labour thinking, as the next chapter will show, certainly cuts across ideological and party boundaries, but its reinterpretation of key social values and the patterns in which they are packaged represents the strongest deviation from the social democratic tradition of mainstream British progressive thought to date. Its belief in human improvability was initially located not in an open-ended view of social evolution but in the belief that the future had already arrived, courtesy of New Labour. That chiliastic language disappeared with the advent of the year 2000, the moment the impending millennium could no longer be exploited to signify the end of history and the final attainment of modernity. Its Fabian dirigisme is expressed not in its love of state bureaucracy but in its claim to the monopoly of political wisdom, to conceptual and epistemological certainty. Its view of society is less organic and more structurally (though not value) pluralist, but some of that organicism is displaced to smaller units such as the family as motors of social coordination, while the direct link between individual and society is toned down. Social rewards are handed out less for good citizenship or for a life of service, and more for achievements in fields of material productivity and independence from social support. Its nod in the direction of individual choice is vitiated by its transferral of bureaucracy to the level of civil society itself, with its new managerial ethos of the competitive assessment of professionals. New Labour is undoubtedly centre left, as it is unquestionably reformist. But its parentage cannot simply be sought in the century-old social liberal tradition nourished in Britain, a tradition that now appears to have been both rich and vulnerable.

---

[42] MacDonald, *Socialism and Society*, pp. 133–34.
[43] Blair, *New Britain*, pp. 261, 298; Giddens, *The Third Way*, pp. 78–86.

CHAPTER NINE

The Ideology of New Labour

In march 1998 Tony Blair addressed the French parliament in its native language to general applause. But Martine Aubry, the French employment minister, was annoyed by Blair's speech. As the *Independent* reported: "Among other things, he had said ideology was dead; all that counted in government was that policies should work. Ms Aubry told colleagues that she found his address 'lamentable.' "[1]

What is lamentable about Blair's reported view is not the "fact" that it ostensibly announces but the illusion it promotes. Marx held ideology to be dissimulative, a distortion of the relations of the material world. Now, however, we are more likely to contend that a declared disavowal of ideology is a colossal act of self-deception. Forty years ago, the shaking off of ideology and the proclamation of its death reflected the confidence of the Western world in the converging economic and social policies encouraged by states and governments propelled by Keynesian theories. Since then, it has become necessary not to abandon ideology but to look for it in more subtle, and frequently more fragmented, manifestations.

Sidestepping the State

At the end of the twentieth century we are facing a curious crisis of confidence, not *in* the state but *of* the state. New Labour is unsure whether it is the role of the state to innovate, except in the specific and traditionally political area of constitutional reform; it is even uncertain to what extent the state *can* innovate and provide, rather than merely facilitate and protect, in the face of both global and subnational forces. Instead, businesses, families, communities, voluntary associations—anyone, preferably, but the state—are entreated to set examples, take a lead, and stamp their authority on social conduct. In parallel, New Labour theorists such as Tony Wright and Anthony Giddens have welcomed the prospects of a new civic culture,[2] and have called upon the government to "help repair the civil order" among local groups, while contending also that "a healthy

---

[1] *The Independent*, 27.3.1998.
[2] T. Wright, *Why Vote Labour?* (Harmondsworth, 1997), p. 110.

civil society protects the individual from overwhelming state power."[3] This stance has been picked up by Blair himself.[4] The state is reduced to the status of one actor among many, both internationally and domestically, appearing as pathetically subservient to global economic forces, unwilling to generate policies through its bureaucracies because it no longer believes in the power of politics as a central force for change. Societies have simply become too complex for wielders of political power and authority to manage. To take one example, not only economics but also medical technology is granted a privileged position in articulating social policies. Rather than reasserting social and humanitarian values in view of these developments, state-organised social welfare—the pride of domestic state activity for much of this century—is in danger of shrivelling away in the bright light of the exploding genetic information that encourages redefining human beings as insurance risks.

Of course, the downplaying of the *state* must be distinguished from the centralizing tendencies of the Labour *government* and Labour *party*. Understandably for an administration forged on re-entry from the wilderness with a huge majority, Labour in power are determined to keep control of the reins, to minimise internal dissent through exercising their power of nondecision making (that is, of preventing alternative views within the Labour movement from vocal expression), and to override any opposition with firm and slightly impatient insistence. But they do all that while extending the range of interests consulted and brought in to manage social, economic, and cultural projects. In Britain the role of government now is to direct this reallocation of power and functions, while reserving the last word for itself. It thus pursues openly what Thatcher's administrations pretended not to do. Moreover, the Thatcher revolution succeeded in achieving one thing more than any other: in redefining the concepts of political language, in replacing "state-citizen" relations with "provider-client" ones. This redefinition, it appears, has now become entrenched in the new world of Labour, with the proviso that additional defining social relationships have been introduced: cultural innovators and the instruction-thirsty populace, style-setters and the enthusiastic trend-worshipers, ethical guardians and the guidance-seeking perplexed. These relationships are then wrapped up in an unspecific notion of community in much the same way as Hegel endeavoured to check the necessity of a fissiparous civil society through an overarching framework of national ethical solidarity.

[3] A. Giddens, *The Third Way* (Cambridge, 1998), pp. 78–82, 85. The latter argument, calling also for state containment of civil society to protect individuals, mirrors the view of the French social liberal thinker, Émile Durkheim.

[4] T. Blair, *The Third Way: Politics for the New Century* (London, 1998), p. 3.

An Ideological Narrative

All this is, of course, an ideological position. The age in which we live, far from being postideological, is one of ideological experimentation, of the resurrection of past principles combined with new attitudes. On the macrolevel, the demotion of politics as an arena of planning, social responsibility, and public welfare is its main feature. On the microlevel, current labourism is, above all, ideologically eclectic, but it is emphatically not ideologically dormant. Indeed, it is brimming with complex ideas, values and practices that draw on all the major British ideological traditions. Paradoxically, the reputedly nonideological Blair has in the past been keen to attach himself to British ideational movements, though it is frequently liberalism, and not socialism, that has been chosen in this reinvented narrative. Significantly, in a much publicised lecture in 1995, Blair did not deny the existence or importance of ideology. Rather, he claimed that Labour ideology was "out of date," having been in the past too narrowly construed around "one particular strand of socialist thinking, namely, state ownership." The task he now set his party was "to reconstruct our ideology around the strength of our values and the way they are expressed. And then to create an organisation to match and reflect the ideology." One aspect of that "ideological re-foundation" of the party had already been achieved: the revision of Clause Four, with its dogmatically perceived linkage of socialism and nationalisation.

Blair went on to associate his political beliefs with David Lloyd George, L. T. Hobhouse, William Beveridge, and J.M. Keynes—icons of British liberalism and its pioneering work in clearing the ideological ground for the welfare state—and not only with stalwarts of Labour social democracy such as Aneurin Bevan and Anthony Crosland. Tellingly, he adopted a phrase that had become particularly salient in Labour vocabulary over the previous ten years—"the aim of socialism is to give greater freedom to the individual"—though, as suggested in the previous chapter, that conception of freedom was rather loosely associated with liberal theories of individuality as personal development and diversity. Blair consequently drew attention to the affinity between Labour and "its progressive liberal cousin." He was particularly appreciative of a liberalism wedded to "a credo of social reform and state action to emancipate individuals from the vagaries and oppression of personal circumstance," intent on creating through collective cooperation a quantity of social wealth to be employed for social purposes. That reflected, as it did with the new liberals, a notion of individual interdependence necessary for human flourishing.[5]

[5] T. Blair, *Let Us Face the Future* (London, 1995), pp. 4, 11–12. For the views of the new liberals see M. Freeden, *The New Liberalism: An Ideology of Social Reform* (Oxford, 1978).

Themes, Labels, Numbers

The present Labour allegiance to the new liberal values that emerged at the outset of this century has recently been explored by Andrew Vincent, who has detected many unconscious as well as conscious themes in current Labour thinking. Among those are a rediscovery of markets as tools of egalitarian choice, and an emphasis on the ethical virtues of participatory citizenship, dressed up in the mutually complementary and quasi-contractual language of rights and obligations.[6] On the other hand, David Marquand has intriguingly suggested that we know what New Labour is not: "It is not socialist. It is not even social democratic or social liberal. It has abandoned the tradition once exemplified by such paladins of social democracy as Willy Brandt, Helmut Schmidt, Ernest Bevin and Hugh Gaitskell. It has also turned its back on Keynes and Beveridge."[7] They are both right, first in the sense that certain components of Labour thinking reverberate strongly with progressive themes, and second in the sense that New Labour cannot be neatly boxed in a hermetically sealed ideological family.

One way to begin this investigation is to enquire whether the New Labour project deserves the descriptor "Third Way" it now so avidly seeks to popularize. For there to be a third way there has to be a first and a second. The first appears to be the modified social democracy that typified labour from the 1950s to the 1980s, the second the neoliberalism (or, more accurately, neolibertarianism) of the 1980s. But something is wrong with this arithmetic. The temptation for some politicians to stop counting at the magic number three is irresistible. If the first way was nourished on the new liberal tradition of the early part of this century, from which Blair has consciously drawn, it also coexisted with a number of British socialist currents that cannot be reduced to social liberalism: Fabianism, ethical socialism, and a trade union–oriented labourism. If the second way is loosely coextensive with Thatcherism, it overlooks the robust Tory beliefs that have sustained much of middle England in the recent past, and still do. All this is worth mentioning not as an historical quibble but precisely because New Labour has assumed aspects of all these traditions at once.

One dismissive response to the "Third Way" has been to point out that in the twentieth century, in Britain as well as elsewhere, a host of "third" and "middle" ways have emerged. "So what's new?" these detractors ask. The novelty is that these different middle ways have not been positioned between the same two extremes, if extremes they are. Other "Third

---

[6] Andrew Vincent, "New Ideologies for Old?" *Political Quarterly* 69 (1998): 48–58.
[7] David Marquand, "The Blair Paradox," *Prospect* (May 1998): 19.

Ways" have not had to choose between neoliberalism and social democracy. Harold Macmillan's 1930s middle way saw itself choosing between capitalism and socialism—a somewhat different pairing, in which a strong Toryism and a putatively hardcore socialism locked horns.[8] Labour's "Third Way" shares a similar *rhetoric* with other attempts to ditch perceived ideological dualisms, but it is quite different in *content* from those "Third Ways."

Perhaps all this could be put slightly differently. The ideological amalgam of New Labour includes liberal, conservative, and (how could it be otherwise!) specifically socialist components as well. In addition, ideational imports from the United States have added a flavour of their own. But New Labour ideology is not identical with any one of the above categories and it deviates from every one of them in crucial areas. Some people, of course, deny that the "Third Way" is an ideology at all. That is a misconception. Ideologies do not have to be grand narratives; they certainly do not have to be closed, doctrinaire, and abstract systems. Ideologies are recurrent, action-oriented patterns of political argument, and it can be empirically demonstrated that New Labour is definitely endowed with those. Moreover, ideologies are not simply superimposed upon practices, but also embodied in them. What distinguishes New Labour ideology, as indeed any ideology, are the distinctive configurations it forms out of political concepts, the occasional new meanings it assigns to political words in common currency, and the innovative manner in which it blends ideas both external and internal to its traditions. To what extent, then, can Blair's claim that "our values do not change" be affirmed?

WHICH COMMUNITY? WHOSE RESPONSIBILITY?

Early in 1998 Julian Le Grand published a spirited endorsement of the "Third Way."[9] He detected four components of the distinctive New Labour route between the Scylla of neoliberalism and the Charybdis of social democracy: community, accountability, responsibility, and opportunity. Whichever way one interprets these contested and multilayered concepts, they come attached to some heavy baggage. Each of these concepts rotates around a full axis of different meanings, but no matter where that rotation is halted, the fourfold combination does not signal a *new* way, or a *new* ideology. There is little in the principles and values underlying Labour's "Third Way" that hasn't already been given expression in other places, at other times.

---

[8] H. Macmillan, *The Middle Way* (London, 1938).
[9] Julian Le Grand, "The Third Way Begins with Cora," *New Statesman* 6.3.1998.

The meaning of community for Le Grand is split between a geographical entity, a locality, and a solidaristic spirit of cooperation. He also contends that community implies contracts between people and government, and partnerships between individuals and local organisations. But the idea of a social contract is a classical liberal one, suggesting a weak—and possibly commercial—human relationship. Instead, community is also reflected in broader traditions. For new liberals, community had strong organic connotations, according to which social membership was a constituent of individuality, and society as a whole had interests and needs of its own, the fulfilment of which would be crucially conducive both to social and to individual welfare. For many conservatives, community suggests a residue of the one-nation Britain, in which the more fortunate were paternalistically entrusted with the welfare of the less advantaged. For the American sociologist Amitai Etzioni, a former guest of pro–New Labour circles, community entails a form of social control in which neighbourhoods regulate the conduct and morals of their members, demanding support for established norms and less individual assertiveness. To which version does New Labour subscribe? Certainly not to pure forms of the first or the second, but there is more than a hint of the third.

Accountability, a classic component of the liberal rule of law, is interestingly directed towards both local and national communities, though there is far less evidence to endorse its foundational status in Labour discourse. Responsibility, however, has a greater resonance with Etzioni's contrasting of rights with responsibilities. He sees rights as individual claims that are fundamentally confrontational and egoistic, many of them burdensome to society, especially when they threaten the values cherished by a community. At one point, Etzioni called for a moratorium on new rights, because in the balance between individual and community he comes down firmly in favour of the individual responsibility to maintain the social fabric, and because he assumes that communities are repositories of a shared moral language and practices. The moral voice of the community (notably couched in the singular) is expressed by what he sees as the transmitters of correct conduct—the family and the schools—with their shared spaces, causes, and futures.[10] In the New Labour vision, this is reflected in the insistence on parents facing up "to their responsibility for their children's misbehaviour,"[11] in a tough attitude to crime and "antisocial behaviour," and in a strict policy of controlling school standards.

In particular, New Labour has adopted Etzioni's preference for guided persuasion over coercion: clean hands in public life, self-discipline, the

---

[10] A. Etzioni, *The Spirit of Community: Rights, Responsibilities, and the Communitarian Agenda* (London, 1995).

[11] *New Labour: Because Britain Deserves Better* [1997 Labour Party Manifesto] (London, 1997), p. 23.

enhancement of social cooperation. Individual virtue is tantamount to not being a nuisance to others, whether in terms of demanding money, eliciting effort, or challenging values. It is particularly exemplified in the opposition to the "dependency culture," seen as a distorted aspect of the welfare state, rather than the socialist ethic of actively creating networks of interdependent social support. The overriding assumptions are unity in plurality, gentle yet persistent regulation, the existence of a single, beneficent, moral universe transcending the diverse communities of which society is formed—all epitomised in the reassuring paternalism of Britain's new leadership: "Trust us! We know what is good for you. Have patience! We will give you what you want." This extraordinary blend of moderate American conservatism, elitist British Fabianism, and populism has resulted in a deficit of the liberal capacity for choice New Labour wishes elsewhere to encourage.

AMERICAN ATTRACTIONS

The impact of American public policy is discernible in two other major areas, embodying practices that have contributed to the shaping of New Labour ideology. The first is "zero tolerance"—a phrase to be found in the 1997 manifesto, and a dramatic linguistic repudiation of the core liberal value of toleration. Recently, surpassing the term's association in the United States with an uncompromising approach towards crime (frequently expressed as "a third strike and you're out"), the term has been applied in Britain also to underperforming schools. Such schools are quasi-criminalised by implication. In a culture where individual death penalties have been ruled out as unacceptable, schools are potentially subject to an institutional death penalty: "ministers will order a 'fresh start'—close the school and start afresh on the same site."[12]

The second area is "workfare," which in the United States has been linked to deterrent social policies, aimed at reducing social security bills and implementing a work ethic amongst the "underclass." Notably, New Labour have reformulated this policy as a movement from welfare *to* work—a phrase laden with ideological significance. As Blair put it in an interview, the welfare state was created "to give the first parts of opportunity to people. . . in a society and labour market that doesn't exist any more . . . If you were to talk to people and ask them what they think the welfare state should do . . . their concept of welfare is the relieving of poverty and the help of people in need."[13] In the past, the concept of

[12] Ibid., p. 7.

[13] Hugo Young, "Vision for our Future" [interview with Tony Blair], *The Guardian*, 17.1.98.

welfare in socialist thought pertained to human flourishing and well-being, to the ethical end of optimising human creativity and eliminating human alienation. It was closely linked to the egalitarian pooling both of human resources and of social goods. In current jargon, however, it has been reduced to support services for the marginalised, the handicapped, or the unlucky—those who are unable, rather than merely unwilling, to provide adequately for themselves. In many senses this refers to no more than an escape from poverty, a minimal rather than optimal view of human happiness, to which a minority are unequally condemned. That echoes the very social exclusion New Labour has loudly denounced, notably in the establishment of a Social Exclusion Unit. As indicated in the previous chapter, welfare and work are counterpoised, as if work were not, in mainstream social democratic as well as socialist views, the epitome of human welfare itself.

THE MORAL MARKET

All the above is indicative of a new dichotomy: on the one hand stands an unreciprocated catering for basic human needs, rather grudgingly elicited but nevertheless recognised as a humanitarian duty; on the other, a contributory investment of labour in the social and economic fabrics, as an expectation of responsible citizenship, and the replacement of the socialist "right to work" with a puritanical "duty to work," amidst references to human beings as a resource, or as capital. The state still maintains a shadow of the substantive enabling functions that earlier progressive theories accorded it but, as Raymond Plant has pointed out, one of its main roles is the re-skilling of individuals not in order to develop their autonomy and well-being but so as to equip them with employability skills and improve their position in the market.[14] Markets are no longer seen as subservient to governments, but as coequal with them in a new synergetic relationship.[15] Welfare has emphatically been removed from the core position it had attained in European socialist thought. Labour aspirations may still be communal and integrative; its political phraseology suggests otherwise.

Is the liberal deficit made good by Le Grand's fourth watchword: opportunity? Does it ensure the predominance of a social liberal ideology to which Blair seemed committed, especially the optimisation of development-enhancing choices as advocated by liberals? This remains unclear. In Le Grand's reading of Labour values, opportunity is provided for a

---

[14] Lord Plant, *New Labour—A Third Way?* (London, 1998), p. 34.
[15] Giddens, *The Third Way*, pp. 99–100.

specific activity: for work rather than for the realisation of personal potential. Work is seen not in the socialist terms of human creativity, not even
in the social liberal terms of a quid pro quo for services granted by the
community, with its sense of a common enterprise, but as the far starker
assumption of individual responsibility for financial independence, and
as an activity subservient to the economic and productivity goals established by market forces. In particular, as Le Grand observes, this version
of opportunity dispenses with egalitarian distribution as a linchpin of social justice.

It remains to be seen how New Labour relates to socialism—ironically
the most discomforting word in its current vocabulary. The term "socialism" does not appear in the 1997 manifesto. Instead, it is alluded to via
code words such as "outdated dogma or doctrine" or the "old left."[16]
When Blair has used it, it appears, carefully unpacked, in the form of
"social-ism." In a speech given to the Fabian Society in 1994, Blair recognised the multiple strands of socialism, and stressed the importance of
revitalizing its ethical tone, "not a break with its past or its traditions but,
on the contrary, a rediscovery of their true meaning" in order to distinguish it from the "neo-conservatism of the left."[17] "Social-ism" identifies
what is generally accepted as one of the core concepts of socialism: "Individuals are socially interdependent human beings. . . . individuals cannot
be divorced from the society to which they belong."[18]

For Blair, this kind of communitarianism signifies the recognition of the
duties individuals owe to one another and to society, as well as a view of
collective power whose aim is the pursuit of the good and interests of
individuals, a formulation familiar to the new liberals a century ago. But
it is also linked with a further set of core concepts: social justice, cohesion,
the equal worth of each citizen, equality of opportunity. The meaning
of socialism has been retained by emphasising cooperation and mutual
responsibility, but contained by combining it with a particular vocabulary
of fairness towards individuals, greater productivity, consumer choice,
and, especially, identifying an economic *public* interest in which the market plays a key role. Socialism could thus be diverted away from the old
clichés of nationalisation and towards a more complex notion of a society
acting in concert to regulate and encourage individual enterprise. This
project had of course been set in motion at a far earlier stage of Labour
Party history, but the crucial linguistic and conceptual turns now effected
by New Labour had then been politically inconceivable—not least among
them its designation by Blair as centre left.

[16] *Because Britain Deserves Better*, pp. 2–3.
[17] T. Blair, *Socialism* (London, 1994), pp. 2, 7.
[18] Ibid., p. 4.

In Blair's personal ethic, though not in New Labour more generally, there is also a significant Christian strand that underpins his understanding of community as a relationship of mutually respecting and responsible individuals. The sacrament of communion, suggestive of community, is conjoined with an undertone of social sin—"a purely libertarian ethos"—and punishment for failing one's social duties. That failure is notably one of free will, of willing bad rather than good acts, made all the more culpable in a cohesive society that offers opportunities to individuals as long as they embody "common norms of conduct" in a "strong and decent" community.[19] When the substantive value-content of citizenship fails to match the formal and legal dimensions in which it can be expressed, the question of ideological pluralism is left dramatically unresolved.

AN IDEOLOGY REASSEMBLED

The ideological map of New Labour now looks something like this. It is located between the three great Western ideological traditions—liberalism, conservatism, and socialism—though it is not equidistant from them all. Liberalism has always concentrated on the pursuit of liberty, on the development of individuality, on human rationality, on open-ended progress, on limiting state power, but also on some notion of the common good. From that ideology New Labour has extracted ideas concerning private choice, the enhancement of human capacities, the furtherance of legitimate individual interests, a respect for individual rights, and a concern with human well-being pursued in part by a welfare state but in the main through the exercise of personal responsibility. These are underpinned by what Blair identifies as "talent and ambition . . . aspiration and achievement."[20] It has, however, rejected the extreme libertarianism affiliated with some forms of liberalism. The socioeconomic practices associated with these liberal components include the rule of law, a mixed economy with both the managerial and consumer-orientated efficiency it is presumed to entail, and the encouragement of mutually beneficial contractarian relationships between state and individual, and between individuals and the institutions of civil society. Indeed, the 1997 election manifesto is strikingly contractarian in the quasi-legal language of its commitments to the electorate.

Conservatism has always concentrated on the regulation of social and political change, by permitting only their organic and continuous versions, as well as on a range of appeals to the extrahuman bases of the

---

[19] T. Blair, *New Britain: My Vision of a Young Country* (London, 1996), pp. 39, 57–61.

[20] Ibid., pp. 299–300; Blair, *The Third Way*, p. 4.

social order: God, history, nature, and, intermittently, economics. In Britain its Thatcherite version regarded the economic sphere as the prime arena of self-regulation, in which the laws of an impersonal market channelled the aggression, competition, and even greed vital to its success. These qualities are, however, lethal in other areas of social life. Hence the family is entrusted with functions of social control (which it frequently fails to exercise), and the police exist to enforce respect for the norms without which the social order will collapse. From that ideology New Labour has extracted ideas concerning productivity and material well-being, the moral authority of a single order of common social norms, the notion of overriding individual duties towards society, the denunciation of crime as a failure, not of society, but of the smaller social units that should have prevented it, the importance of directive political leadership, and a romantic engagement with lost values.[21]

If some of those ideas are not directly derived from conservative influences, they nevertheless show a marked ideological affinity with them. But New Labour has rejected the conservative respect for past customs and its marginalisation of concerted, planned, enabling political action. The socioeconomic practices associated with these conservative components include the strict regulation of public institutions (in particular educational ones) in terms of the production of desirable social goods, the insistence on the reconstruction of stable family values—introducing, for example, curfews on children in the evenings, "zero tolerance" policies for social deviants, and an inflated view of the role of government as the guardian (though not direct implementer) of the social interest. As Giddens has put it, a new radicalism must incorporate a philosophical conservatism that focuses on a "retrieval of suppressed moral concerns." But it is difficult to see how some of these practices are also to be reconciled with his idea of recapturing a liberal civic public space.[22]

Socialism has always concentrated on the group nature of the social relationship, on the centrality of work, labour, and creativity, on an ethos of social and economic egalitarianism, on human welfare and the improvement of the material conditions of life, and on a view of history as ensuring future and beneficial change. From that ideology New Labour has extracted the first core concept concerning the structural significance of the group, though it has translated it into a view of groups operating at different levels: from the norm-setting society to which we owe duties, to the family that functions as a socialiser, and the locality in which partic-

---

[21] On this latter point see Wendy Wheeler, "Dangerous Business: Remembering Freud and a Poetics of Politics," in M. Perryman, ed., *The Blair Agenda* (London, 1996), p. 102.

[22] A. Giddens, *Beyond Left and Right* (Cambridge, 1994), pp. 249–50; Giddens, *The Third Way*, pp. 68, 106–7.

ipatory and identity-shaping goods are to be found. Tellingly, the notion of a group is also employed to equate New Labour with New Britain, that patriotic group of groups and focus of a new national identity that is replacing the failed collectivist projects of the past. Conspicuously, it has eradicated the conception of group as class from its lexicon: sometimes ideological silences are as evocative as brash utterances. It has retained the notion of labour, but less as an act of self-expression and more as a further duty owed to the community, both in terms of productivity and in terms of individuals standing on their own two feet, the latter through the practice of workfare. It has reformulated welfare as mutual individual responsibility plus a safety net for the genuinely needy. It has reduced the concept of equality to its less radical, and fundamentally liberal, interpretation as equality of opportunity, fairness, and a modest redistributionism incorporating freedom from want,[23] though it has also contributed to raising the status of women in the political arena (unless they fall into the morally ambivalent category of lone parents!). The socioeconomic practices associated with these socialist components include measures of redistribution to reduce poverty and hardship, the retention of free and universal services within areas crucial to human functioning such as health and education, and the attempt to break up or reform some inegalitarian or privileged structures such as the "underclass" or the House of Lords.

THE ALLURE OF THE NEW

Most intriguingly, New Labour has refashioned socialist transcendentalism and future-orientation through an obsessive focus on modernising, on change and renewal, which constitute its main claim to radicalism.[24] Socialism required a patient belief in historical laws of evolution that New Labour can no longer afford. New Labour has developed a notion of historical time that moves away from past constraints, that will not be "shackled or intimidated" by the lessons of its history.[25] That is why it is "New," why novelty and youth are crucial ideological signifiers, and why, in so far as the European Union is perceived as dynamic, New Labour will want to be part of it. Moreover, New Labour has had the good fortune to come to power on the verge of the millennium. For the millennium represents not only the bright new future that is already upon us—a future present—but it resonates with utopian undertones that fit a New Labour agenda far more than they did a conservative one. New Labour *is* the

[23] Blair, *Let Us Face the Future*, p. 6.
[24] See Wright, *Why Vote Labour?*, pp. 24–27.
[25] Quoted in Perryman, *The Blair Agenda*, p. 3.

future and, as befits a realised utopia, it is an end-state. As Blair has put it, "the process of what is called 'modernisation' is in reality, therefore, the application of enduring, lasting principles for a new generation."[26] This dialectical conflation of the enduring and the new reflects a belief in a future that is here to stay, a future that is ipso facto conservative. Yet one linguistic aspect of New Labour modernising is the ephemerality of its catchwords. The "stakeholder society" of 1996 has already been forgotten. Even "New Labour" is now being ditched in favour of the "Third Way," and the shelf-life of that latter phrase should not be capable of outlasting its empirical inaccuracy. The future in which we are currently living requires constant reaffirmation in order to prevent it from sliding back into the past.

Ultimately, the ideology of New Labour can only be understood as an internal arena of competition, indeterminacy, and uncertainty over the key meanings of the political values and concepts with which it engages. This is not a criticism; indeed, a healthy, nondoctrinaire ideology is always in a state of flux and conceptual change within certain confines, and some of the patterns of New Labour's thought-practices are clearly visible amid that change. Its core concepts include community, responsibility, equality of opportunity, and liberty. These core concepts are contained in a looser framework than those constructed by some of the more rigid ideologies of the past, though they have mostly been interpreted in a manner that ensures their mutual compatibility.

But two problems remain. First, the core concepts are themselves inevitably prone to multiple meanings, and New Labour (again, inevitably) bends them in certain directions rather than others. A second, compounded problem is that in a number of areas incompatible meanings of the concepts *adjacent* to those in the New Labour core still exist side by side: organic community versus directed community; freedom from want and for individual development versus freedom of market choices; welfare as the provision for need versus welfare as the routinisation of dependency; rights as an expression of human dignity versus rights as an expression of human egoism. Even in the relatively successful sphere of constitutional reform, the grammar of democratic devolution as applied to Scotland and Wales, and possibly to Northern Ireland, is countered by the practice of democratic centralism as realized in England, and the grammar of democratic accountability as applied to the Labour leadership or the House of Lords is countered by the practice of controlled coordination of the entire legislative process in the best British manner, linked to Blair's own high profile in what has frequently been described

---

[26] Blair, *New Britain*, pp. 221–22.

as a hegemonic enterprise. As long as these tensions between incompatible elements persist, clear-cut policies in those areas will be impossible. In order to enable policies to be made, New Labour will face further choices as to which forks to take in the ideational roads it has constructed. Some of these may yet lead to the land of pluralist social democracy, but others may locate a once evolutionary socialist party in a very strange terrain.

CHAPTER TEN

Is Nationalism a Distinct Ideology?

THE CATEGORISATION of nationalism as an ideology is a matter of some confusion in contemporary political analysis. Textbooks on political ideologies adopt widely different positions. Thus Adams regards nationalism as an ideology, however flawed, observing that "among modern ideologies, nationalism is the simplest, the clearest and the least theoretically sophisticated, but it is also the most widespread and the one with the strongest grip on popular feeling."[1] On the other hand, Ball and Dagger note that "nationalism and anarchism take so many forms and are so entwined with so many different ideologies that we think it better not to treat them as distinct ideologies."[2] Heywood straddles these poles, stating that "strictly speaking, nationalism is not an ideology at all in that it does not contain a developed set of interrelated ideas and values" but nevertheless has a chapter on nationalism in his book.[3] Recent political theorists, by contrast, avoid the question whether nationalism is an ideology by focusing on different issues: investing nationalism with ethical concerns or attempting to construct a model of nationalism that would find favour with contemporary political philosophers, often substituting for it terms such as "nationality" or "nationhood."[4] Yet their readings of their subject matter may themselves, from a very different methodological perspective, contain clearly ideological features.

For the student of ideologies this state of affairs is far from satisfactory. Given the current interest in nationalism and the rapid increase in scholarly writing on the topic, the question whether or not nationalism is a political ideology needs posing and requires the development of criteria to enable the formulation of a response. Not surprisingly, such a response turns out to be a complex one. It hinges on an approach that relates to ideologies in the concrete world, not as phenomena that ought not to exist, or as occurring on a truth-falsehood dimension, or as essentialist. Ideologies, as we have already seen, are those actual and composite thought-patterns of individuals and groups in a society that relate to the

---

[1] I. Adams, *Political Ideology Today* (Manchester, 1993), p. 82.

[2] T. Ball and R. Dagger, *Political Ideologies and the Democratic Ideal* (New York, 1991), p. 18.

[3] A. Heywood, *Political Ideologies: An Introduction* (London, 1992), p. 136.

[4] See, e.g., D. Miller, *On Nationality* (Oxford, 1995); M. Canovan, *Nationhood and Political Theory* (Cheltenham, 1996).

way they comprehend and shape their political worlds, that supply us with crucial clues for understanding political conduct and practices, and that are contextualised on time and space continua. Hence nationalism, too, may be understood as embodying clusters of conceptual configurations that accord any of its specific instances a particular set of identifying meanings.

For nationalism to be an *established* ideology within a loose framework of family resemblances it will have to manifest a shared set of conceptual features over time and space. On the basis of observed linguistic practices those features will be able to be organized into general core concepts—without which an ideology will lose its defining characteristics as well as its flexibility—and adjacent and peripheral concepts and ideas that colour the core in different ways. The latter include the conceptualisation of perimeter practices, through which ideologies interact with, and shape, the concrete world. These structures of conceptual interdependence fix, or limit, the meanings conveyed by the ideological system in toto. This is accomplished by different arrangements of proximity and priority accorded to the constituting concepts of an ideological family.

But in addition, in order to be a *distinct* ideology, the core of nationalism, and the conceptual patterns it adopts, will have to be unique to it alone; and in order to be a *full* ideology it will need to provide a reasonably broad, if not comprehensive, range of answers to the political questions that societies generate. Ideologies compete over the "correct" meanings of political concepts, and they tend to abhor conceptual vacuums and to address all the political concepts to be found in a prevailing political language or discourse. They do so by offering recommended routes through the conceptual clusters they utilise, while ignoring or prohibiting other possible routes.

NATIONALISM AS A THIN-CENTRED IDEOLOGY

How does all this help us to make sense of nationalism? For nationalism to be an ideology, it would have to display one of two structures. It could exhibit a full morphology, containing particular interpretations and configurations of all the major political concepts attached to a general plan of public policy that a specific society requires. That fullness exists either by design, or by default as a reaction to the challenges of ideological rivals. Alternatively, it could exhibit a thin-centred morphology, with a restricted core attached to a narrower range of political concepts.

A thin-centred ideology is one that arbitrarily severs itself from wider ideational contexts by the deliberate removal and replacement of concepts. The consequence is a structural inability to offer complex ranges of argument, because many chains of ideas one would normally expect to find stretching from the general and abstract to the concrete and practical, from the core to the periphery, as well as in the reverse direction, are simply absent.[5] Thus if nationalism entertains neither practices nor conceptual fundamentals pertaining to welfare policies—a feature of all major ideological systems—a shrinking of the political is inevitable. A thin-centred ideology is hence limited in ideational ambitions and scope. That type of narrow nationalism often abandons mere persuasion in favour of a resort to force exercised over political language and over the practices involved with that language. The power struggle engaged in by narrow nationalism enforces the selection, prioritisation, and combination of certain political concepts and the elimination of others. The exclusionism directed against concrete individuals and groups that many scholars see in extreme nationalist practice is paralleled in its ideological morphology. Because this requires a form of legitimisation, it necessitates some explanation for why circumstances can justify the exclusion, suppression, or neglect of other concepts, and why its limited political programme is a sufficient one. That may be presented simply as a question of urgency, or it may be one of elevating nationalism to the apex of political expression.

If, on the other hand, nationalism is not an ideology, we would expect to find its conceptual arrangements as a component in another, broader ideological family. In that case, it is not that nationalism needs to be "filled out by other idea-systems" as that it helps to fill them out.[6] We must certainly resist the temptation proffered by the suffixes of the English language to assume that every "ism" is ipso facto an ideology.

My contention is that nationalism fails to meet the criteria of a comprehensive ideology. Its conceptual structure is incapable of providing on its own a solution to questions of social justice, distribution of resources, and conflict-management that mainstream ideologies address. At best, as Lord Acton noted of theories of nationality, "they cannot serve as a basis for the reconstruction of civil society, as medicine cannot serve for food; but they may influence it with advantage."[7] Indeed, it has been asserted with some justification that "nationalism is clearly an extremely poor ideology and no match whatsoever for the great bodies of thought that constitute socialism or liberalism."[8] Instead, nationalism oscillates between

---

[5] For the notion of thin-centred ideologies, two of which are feminism and green political thinking, see M. Freeden, *Ideologies and Political Theory: A Conceptual Approach* (Oxford, 1996), chaps. 13–14.

[6] A. D. Smith, *Nations and Nationalism in a Global Era* (Cambridge, 1995), p. 150.

[7] Lord Acton, "Nationality," in Lord Acton, *Essays on Freedom and Power* (Cleveland and New York, 1955), pp. 143–44.

[8] P. Alter, *Nationalism* (2d ed. London, 1994), p. 118. See also B. Anderson, *Imagined Communities* (London, 1991), p. 5: "It would, I think, make things easier if one treated

the second and third possibilities—between being a distinct thin-centred ideology and being a component of other, already existing ideologies. The very different conceptual configurations of nationalism allow its polysemic variants to develop in these diverse directions. This is no simplistic dualist assertion. Rather, it is the conceptual parallel to Smith's observation that nationalism displays "a chameleon-like ability to transmute itself according to the perceptions and needs of different communities."[9] The existing literature on nationalism is full of broadly dichotomous distinctions between liberal and radically illiberal, liberal and conservative, moderate and aggressive, risorgimento and integrative nationalisms. A morphological approach shows these either to be generalisations from what actually happens in nationalist discourse or tangential to it. There are indeed overarching family resemblances, but they do not capture the internal nuances of a multidimensional set of arguments.

THE CORE STRUCTURE OF NATIONALISM

What, then, is the core of nationalism, the components all users of nationalist language actually employ, and without which that semantic field is unsustainable? First is the prioritisation of a particular group—the *nation*—as a key constituting and identifying framework for human beings and their practices. The realised condition in which this occurs is called "nationhood." Second, a *positive valorisation* is assigned to one's own nation, granting it specific claims over the conduct of its members.[10] Third, the desire to give *politico-institutional expression* to the first two core concepts.[11] Fourth, *space* and *time* are considered to be crucial determinants of social identity. Fifth, a sense of belonging and membership in which *sentiment* and *emotion* play an important role.

As with all sets of political beliefs and ideological families, we must not expect the core concepts of nationalism to be sufficient to account for the *complexity* of all forms and instances of nationalism, or to bear

---

[nationalism] as if it belonged with 'kinship' and 'religion,' rather than with 'liberalism' or 'fascism.' "

[9] Smith, *Nations and Nationalism in a Global Era*, p. 13.

[10] Alter suggests that "disrespect for and animosity towards other peoples" is a common structural component of nationalism, but there is no evidence that this is a necessary component (see Alter, *Nationalism*, p. 3.). Rather, the emphasis is on what Breuilly has called the celebratory "quality of self-reference" (J. Breuilly, *Nationalism and the State*) [2d ed., Manchester, 1983], p. 64).

[11] Some scholars also suggest that national identity or nationalism are activating principles, but that is a fundamental feature of an ideology in general—its shaping and identification of political practices. See respectively Miller, *On Nationality*, p. 24, and Alter, *Nationalism*, p. 4.

the *totality* of beliefs incorporated in any one variant of nationalism. Rather, they are necessary for identifying any given instance as *belonging* to the family of nationalisms. Its core concepts will be found at a level of abstraction that requires further concretisation through multiple, often incompatible, and hence competing, adjacent and peripheral concepts and ideas. On their own, core concepts are too vacuous to contain the meanings necessary to provide interpretations of political reality and plans for political action. Hence each core concept of nationalism—as shall presently be demonstrated—logically contains a number of possible meanings. These meanings are established by adjacent and peripheral concepts that radiate out from the core, forming interpretative paths, each path constituting a different pattern of conceptual combinations in conjunction with the core concept.

In order to endow an essentially contestable core concept with a decontested meaning, however, a choice among these paths has to be made. That choice will depend on cultural, social, and historical preferences for surrounding the core with a given set of political concepts from among the competing configurations. The core concepts of nationalism may hence be attached to as many adjacent and peripheral concepts and ideas as there are interpretations of nationalism, though both nationalists and students of nationalism may prefer to bunch together the ensuing multiple nationalisms in clusters, whose constituents will each contain roughly similar configurations. The different adjacent and peripheral notions that comprise all these possible interpretative paths supply the varieties of nationalism with their richness, thicknesses, and irreconcilable diversities. Nevertheless, the core concepts of nationalism cannot rival the possibilities available to the mainstream ideologies such as conservatism, liberalism, or socialism—all of which have core conceptual structures that permit a far fuller range of responses to sociopolitical issues. Whether or not the nationalist core will then constitute a thin-centred ideology or be assimilated into existing ideological families will reflect the extraneous proximities forged by sociocultural factors. Having a distinctive core does not as such rule out being a segmented component of a broader political ideology.

The first core concept already allows for different readings: the nation as a group may be homogeneous, it may be holistic, or it may be pluralistic. A homogeneous group refers to its perceived scope and singularity, and the nationalism concerned will relate to an "imagined community" called the nation-state (or aspiring to become a nation-state), and will be reluctant to accept national diversity. A holistic group refers to the intensity of the constituting tie between it and its members, and the nationalism concerned will contain certain assumptions about the nation's independent attributes and will be reluctant to accept the detachment of individuals from national aims, though different degrees of holism may apply. If the group is both homogeneous and holistic, the chances are that we are facing an organic theory in which the individual is subservient to a monolithic set of values attached to national wills and purposes. If, however, the group is conceived as pluralistic, the nation is at least partially defined and interpreted through relationships among spatially proximate groups, whether ethnic, religious, or cultural (though one group may be dominant); another political concept, usually the state, is called in to provide a political framework as a form of supranational identity, or as a substitute for it. Thus the goal of full citizenship may, as with aspirations of blacks in the United States, be the route to and expression of membership in a nation.[12]

The second core concept also allows for different readings. One familiar distinction occurs when the positive valorisation is also a privileged one, bringing into play adjacent concepts of loyalty demands directed at members and superiority claims directed at other nations. This interpretation will, of course, gain support from a holistic decontestation of the first core concept. The ensuing externalisation of nationalism—its frequent engagement in the international arena—is mainly a function of the high salience its core concepts acquire in a world in which nations are the dominant actors. Nationalism operates at its best in the international sphere because its conceptual structure fits in well with a simplified political world focusing on nation-states, who acquire a prominence and power they rarely do in national fora. For the same reason its domestic agenda is weak, as it has to contend with a multiplicity of complex social structures, principles, and priorities that dissipate the salience of its core. The nation as ideological construct has a sharper definition in competition with other nations. When it appears as a thin-centred distinct ideology it will struggle against other instances of the same ideological family—other nationalisms, as witnessed in the Northern Ireland situation. When it is an adjunct to other ideological families, such as liberalism, socialism, or fascism, it will compete against other ideologies not as nationalism, but as part of a broader ideological structure, and it will then relate to the broader concerns of the ideologies it attacks. Yet another path from the core is possible when, as Hall has suggested, "nations can develop together in a positive sum game."[13] Patriots may extol their nation without denigrating others.[14]

The third core concept relates to the close association between a sense of nationhood and the desire to create a political forum through which it

---

[12] H. von Amersfoort, "Institutional Plurality: Problem or Solution for the Multi-Ethnic State?" in S. Periwal, ed., *Notions of Nationalism* (Budapest, 1995), p. 166.

[13] J. A. Hall, "Nationalisms, Classified and Explained," in Periwal, ed., *Notions of Nationalism*, p. 18.

[14] On the relationship between patriotism and nationalism, see below.

can be represented. The most obvious form is the state for, as MacCormick has contended, this may well be a function of "a context in which the dominant politico-legal culture asserts the unity of state and nation."[15] That contextualism is the precise reason for proffering the nation-state combination as one conceptual proximity among many. Other quasi-autonomous or federalist solutions have been mooted, and national aspirations can also attach themselves to varieties of imperialism. When the first two core concepts of nationalism have attained a high degree of salience within a political culture, the result is often an understanding of the political, and its institutional forms, as tantamount to the implementation of nationalist ends. *All* types of nationalism seek institutional recognition, however.

The fourth core concept involves the privatisation of, and often exclusive control over, stated space and time parameters. It constitutes a type of particularism that can be justified in terms of competing notions of national space—geographical, linguistic, cultural, biological. These are generally reinforced by an association of space with time: the continual occupation of land, the inherited ties of family in possessions and blood, the evolving cultural domain of language. Time is usually constructed as an invented continuity designed to cover fragmentary historical evidence. It is occasionally attached to a founding myth and an ultimate destiny,[16] that is, to fixed points in past and future, or it may be evolutionary and open-ended. Moreover, even within one nation diverse constructions and myths about time and space may compete over exclusive legitimacy.

The fifth core concept refers to sentiment and emotion as the bases for sociopolitical ties.[17] Philosophers often aspire to be free of the nonreflective emotionalism seen to characterise ideological thinking. All ideologies, however, carry emotional attachments to particular conceptual configurations, both because fundamental human values excite emotional as well as rational support, and because ideologies constitute mobilising ideational systems to change or defend political practices. Emotive argument is a crucial shortcut to attain rational ends, and then to support them without having to reopen the debate.[18] In nationalism, however, the role of emotion becomes an overriding *consciously* desired value, which is why it contains such useful sets of ideas when recruitment to the flag and

[15] N. MacCormick, "Liberalism, Nationalism and the Post-sovereign State," *Political Studies* 44 (1996): 553–67, quotation on 565.

[16] Cf. E. Balibar and I. Wallerstein, *Race, Nation, Class: Ambiguous Identities* (London, 1991), pp. 86–87.

[17] The two concepts overlap sufficiently to consider them as one for the purposes of this argument.

[18] For a helpful assessment of the role of sentiment in nationalism—and the message this comports to political philosophers—see Miller, *On Nationality*, pp. 15, 56, 64.

sacrifice are predominant political ends. Nationalism is a rare instance of Enlightenment-generated rational political thought that acknowledges the political importance of emotion when pointed in certain directions. Nationalism institutionalises and legitimates emotion as a motive force of political, not just private, life.

MULTIPLE NATIONALISMS

The core concepts of nationalism are too indeterminate to make sense on their own. They require further proximate concepts to enable us to appreciate how these geographical, linguistic, cultural, or biological spaces, and memories, sequences, and events are transformed into supportive structures for nationalism. Adjacent concepts such as democracy, power, political obligation, ethnicity, liberty, community, and state are now brought to bear on the core in a wide range of combinations. The choice among and configuration of these concepts also affect the political arrangements sought, which vary from statehood to a federal status to forms of regional or cultural autonomy. Once we understand the microstructure of ideological morphology, the semantic field of nationalism begins to unfold.

As noted above, conceptual indeterminacy permits the construction of alternative interpretative routes through logically possible configurations of the core, adjacent, and peripheral concepts pertaining to nationalism. We may, for example, surround the concept of the nation (decontested as one of many identity-constituting groups) with the adjacent concepts of democracy (decontested as the equal participation of all in the running of a community), liberty (decontested as the pluralistic choice over the expression of one's group identity, or liberation from external oppression), power (decontested as control over one's national policies), and citizenship (decontested as the recognition of individual membership as a complex of duties and rights), and with perimeter practices concerning the ability to opt in and out of national membership without loss of standing, and the accessibility and development of shared cultural artefacts. But a cultural choice to pursue other logical paths may create a very different semantic field within the family of nationalisms. We could decontest the nation as inherently superior to its members, and surround it with the adjacent concepts of hierarchical authority (decontested as the sole location of national will), community (decontested as a homogeneous ascriptive group whose membership features are involuntary and natural), liberty (decontested as the release of the nation from constraints in attaining whatever ends its leaders, representing the national will, set for it), and power (decontested as necessary to assert the superior national interest against a host of potential internal and external detractors). We could then add perimeter practices concerning the restriction of immigration, the enforcing of language on all members of the nation, the positive valuation of compulsory military service, and the development of rituals in which emotional ties to the nation are given priority over other bonds. Of course, there are countless other conceptual variations. Crucially, political concepts acquire meaning not only through accumulative traditions of discourse, and not only through diverse cultural contexts, but also by means of their particular structural position within a configuration of other political concepts.

Let us examine this more closely. The concepts of liberty and democracy can account for different nationalist variants. Historically, the liberty dimension of nationalism preceded its democratic dimension. Many theorists of nationalism attach a positive understanding of national identity to the desire to encourage the growth of liberty, whether through the wish to throw off the shackles of tyrannical regimes and to enable a population to rule itself—an aspiration voiced by J. S. Mill and Mazzini[19]—or as a valuable form of patriotism as the love of one's people. But in many such cases the promotion of nationhood is merely a means to the enhancement of liberty and a range of humanist Enlightenment values. Nationalism is a subservient and partial component of broader ideologies.

To understand the separate growth of nationalism, as a narrow doctrine, another conceptual path must be taken that highlights a specific ideational overlap between liberty and democracy. One of the components of liberty is the removal of restraints over the making of choices concerning one's life plans. One of the components of democracy is the removal of restraints over the choice making of a group. The common component is often called self-determination. In neither case is this a total characterisation of either liberty or democracy. But once the self-determination component of liberty is emphasised (rather than the opportunity, or growth, components), and once the self-determination component of democracy is emphasised (rather than the equality, or the more republican participation, components),[20] both liberty and democracy risk being taken over entirely in the cause of the self-determination argument. A particular kind of nationalism may flourish by underplaying the equality and participation elements of democracy and overemphasising the self-determination ones, with their egoistic and atomistic connotations,[21] reflecting as

[19] J. S. Mill, *On Liberty* (London, 1910), p. 67; J. Mazzini, *The Duties of Man* (London, 1907), pp. 53–54.

[20] See Canovan, *Nationhood and Political Theory*, p. 87.

[21] See also J. Keane, "Nations, Nationalism and European Citizens," in Periwal, ed., *Notions of Nationalism*, p. 197.

they do a social individualism in the intersocial sphere. Various nationalisms can extract these particular usages of liberty and of democracy in ways that support the core concepts of nationalism. In so doing they employ a plethora of conceptual arrangements, ranging from promoting the self-determination of all nations (retaining an egalitarian component) to promoting the self-determination of the nation over that of its members (jettisoning the egalitarian and participatory components altogether).

As we move among different nationalist morphologies, the object from which liberation occurs alters as well. It shifts from the oppressor, the coloniser, the tyrannical government, to the foreigner, the stranger, the alien. In extreme illiberal forms, nationhood is *defined* by means of artificially imposing outsider status on *any* unwanted group, thus excluding that group from social and citizenship benefits. An arbitrary criterion—race, religion, occupation, culture—is invented, or grossly distorted, which by definition removes the preferred values and practices of the "outsiders" from the imposed ideological morphology, from nationally monopolised social space and time, and from dominant political languages. Liberty becomes extrication from contamination; democracy becomes the expression of the innermost "soul" of the nation.

NATIONALISM AND COMMUNITY

The link between democracy and various conceptions of community may either assist or impede nationalist arguments. Democracy and nationhood become proximate not only via the route of self-determination, but also via the alternative route of group interests and consciousness. The appeal of democracy contains among others the element of membership in an egalitarian whole. This can be swung in the direction of aggregative views of individualistic human relations (as in utilitarian theories) or in that of various theories of interdependence. At this point many notions of community may emerge that in turn feed into different variants of national identity. "Community," however, should not be treated as a constant, undifferentiated concept, but one that evokes many levels of intensity and embeddedness.[22] Thus, conceptions of the common good may be merely cooperative, or they may invoke organistic theories. Socialists such as Otto Bauer may claim that "only socialism will give the whole people a share in the national culture," via control over the means of production.[23] Indeed, we may note the victory of the term "nationalisation" over the term "socialisation" in socialist language to denote the retrieval by the

[22] Cf. chap. 2 above, and Freeden, *Ideologies and Political Theory*, pp. 247–59.
[23] O. Bauer, "The Nationalities Question and Social Democracy," in O. Dahbour and M. R. Ishay, eds., *The Nationalism Reader* (Atlantic Highlands, NJ, 1995), p. 185.

community of its own property. The nation signifies the repository of social goods and values. But the semantic field of nationalisation is closely controlled by being held adjacent to the core socialist concepts of equality and community. Contrast these conceptions of community with Treitschke's observation: "Every nation over-estimates itself. Without this feeling of itself it would also lack the consciousness of being a community; as Fichte truly said, 'a nation cannot dispense with arrogance.' "[24] Here the meaning of community-cum-nation was secured through its adjacency to an exclusionary superiority.

Canovan has persuasively argued that liberalism builds upon the tacit assumption that nations are given, that emotional solidarity, power relationships, and cultural identity constitute the unconscious presuppositions of contemporary political theory.[25] Tamir has shown that nationalism can provide liberals with the "national virtue of embeddedness" that liberalism otherwise is believed to lack.[26] The complexity of ideological morphology must, however, also heed that the presence of community in an ideology does not necessarily indicate that it has been introduced via nationalism alone.[27] There are trends in Western political theories and ideologies that attempt to isolate the concept of community from time and space. Some of these are outside the family of liberalisms: thus Marxist species-being, not national being, is an essentialist category of human nature.[28] Some appear within current political philosophy, claiming that human beings are embedded in a community, but again this is couched in terms of a suprahistorical, universalist, and generic statement of philosophical anthropology.[29] Others emphasize the voluntarist nature of a national community, constituted by analogy as a liberal *political* community.[30] Yet others point to the strength of sentiment in forging a common national identity, while allowing outsiders willing to accept that identity the choice of membership.[31]

We need to note that organicist theories, models of political cohesion, and conceptions of affective ties may be gleaned from non-nationalist as well as nationalist conceptual configurations. The notion of a group, and

---

[24] H. von Treitschke, *Politics* (London, Constable, 1916), p. 284.

[25] Canovan, *Nationhood and Political Theory*, pp. 2, 41, 101, 122.

[26] Y. Tamir, *Liberal Nationalism* (Princeton, 1993) pp. 10, 33.

[27] See also the strictures in M. Billig, *Banal Nationalism* (London, 1995), pp. 167–68, who criticises the assumption in Richard Rorty's writings that the community entails the nation.

[28] K. Marx, "Economic and Philosophical Manuscripts," in D. McLellan, ed., *Karl Marx: Selected Writings* (Oxford, 1977), pp. 81–83.

[29] M. J. Sandel, *Liberalism and the Limits of Justice* (Cambridge, 1982)), pp. 62–64.

[30] Tamir, *Liberal Nationalism*, pp. 19, 87, 117.

[31] Miller, *On Nationality*, pp. 64, 130.

of group interests, may be endorsed on a variety of grounds without transporting the argument into the domain of nationalism. Conversely, liberalism may even consciously adopt a communal focus that is nationalist. In the German political tradition, liberalism typically developed a national orientation, as the German *Rechtsstaat* epitomised a concern for the rational safeguarding of the liberties of its members, yet the emancipated *Volk* afforded a more concrete interpretation of the general interest—the state containing the irrationality of the *Volk* and the *Volk* containing the impersonality of the state.[32]

THE ECLIPSE OF THIN-CENTRED NATIONALISM

When nationalism stands on its own as a dominant set of political ideas, it exhibits a distinctive kind of thin-centredness. Unlike mainstream ideologies, whether liberalism, conservatism, socialism, and unlike other thin-centred ideologies such as feminism and Green political thinking, thin-centred nationalism discards the general validity of its assertions as a universal organising principle of political ideas. It does not aspire to compete successfully with, and permeate, other political languages and semantic fields in the international arena but, frequently, to ignore them. Moreover, unlike feminist and Green ideologies, it does not have recourse to the self-contained morphologies of other ideologies in order to fill its ideational vacuums.[33] The competition it conducts over the correct meanings of political terms takes place mainly within the one, unique nation and, if internationalised, only in order to establish the superiority of the particular. Thus Treitschke's nation-state was decontested as the will to power through which the "highest welfare of the human race" could be attained.[34] War was the perimeter practice that best embodied the superiority of the state in comparison to its members: "The grandeur of history lies in the perpetual conflict of nations."[35] Treitschke's exclusionist *Völkisch* nationalism was underpinned by the strong emotion of pride: "The real German is absolutely not to be confounded with any other people."[36] And Maurras prioritised *Patrie* over mankind as an absolute value, a deified goddess.[37] In that sense nationalism finds a special affinity with fascism,

---

[32] See R. Koselleck, "Nationalismus," in O. Brunner, W. Conze, and R. Koselleck, eds., *Geschichtliche Grundbegriffe*, vol. 7 (Stuttgart, 1992); Freeden, *Ideologies and Political Theory*, chap. 5.

[33] Freeden, *Ideologies and Political Theory*, p. 486.

[34] Treitschke, *Politics*, p. 588.

[35] Ibid., pp. 21, 66.

[36] Ibid., p. 280.

[37] E. Nolte, *Three Faces of Fascism* (New York, 1966), pp. 104–5.

whose particularism and inward-looking nature distinguish it from the universalist tendencies of other ideological families.

We have, however, so far focused our attention on the core concepts of nationalism, the independent variables, and examined how a plethora of key political concepts are organized around them. That is standard procedure for the analysis of the main ideologies, which have developed a concrete and stable profile over time. The problem with nationalism is that to proceed in this fashion is partly deceptive. A number of concepts adjacent within the morphology of nationalism such as liberty, community, or democracy form the cores of *other*, mainstream ideologies. The proximity of these concepts to the nationalist principles of group, sentiment, or spatial identity may well reflect the *adjacency*, rather than centrality, of nationalist principles to the mainstream ideological structures. It is really a question of what is adjacent to what? Are, for instance, democracy and community glosses on nationhood, or are nationhood, and nationalism more generally, a gloss on ideologies in which democracy and community play a crucial part? If a notion of nationhood is indeed a ubiquitous phenomenon, as Canovan contends, this does not rule out its being located in many ideologies somewhere on the margins of significance, rather than as a deliberate or central constituting principle. Because concepts are crucially defined by their idea-environments and their meaning cannot be accessed on its own, those various features will display different meanings when placed in alternative ideological morphologies. If we adopt this perspective, nationalism as a distinct, if thin, ideology begins to collapse, even though many of its features remain in a more peripheral role within, say, liberalism or conservatism. In that case it may well be that "when nation and state are coextensive . . . all the parties are 'nationalist' in the sense that the nation they represent already has a state of its own; 'nationalism' is taken for granted."[38] More precisely, as Benner has demonstrated with respect to Marxism, nationalism "cannot be analysed . . . as a phenomenon *sui generis*."[39] Instead, it serves more fundamental goals.

There are, however, instances when nationality may become "a paramount claim"[40] even for liberals, but only in the contingent and ephemeral circumstances of liberation from national oppression, or competition over a particular space. In that curious sense, a thin-centred nationalism may arise within a broader liberal context, as well as from nonliberal contexts, but it will be time-specific, emerging only in crises when liberationist or secessionist problems occur (nation building, conquest, external threat, disputed territory, or internal dominance of a cultural or ethnic group

[38] M. Guibernau, *Nationalisms* (Cambridge, 1996), p. 62.

[39] E. Benner, *Really Existing Nationalisms* (Oxford, 1995), pp. 96, 155, 225.

[40] Acton, "Nationality," p. 155.

perceived as hostile), and the political system becomes predominantly devoted to such issues. Once the goals of nationalism are attained, however, it has, like a realized utopia, nowhere to go. It becomes obsolete,[41] or—if enduring—absorbed in ritualistic assertions of achievement, once again attached to broader universalistic ideologies. This thin-centred nationalism displays a sporadic diachrony in its separate ideological guise, and it attains longer life only when contained in larger vessels. It is, arguably, the only instance when nationalism may be identified as a separate ideology, and its tenuousness and ephemerality speak for themselves.

NATIONALISM AND ITS HOST-VESSELS

Liberalism

When nationalist ideas are found in host ideologies, they reflect the features of the host. It is therefore more accurate to talk not of a liberal nationalism but of the areas of nationalist discourse within liberal ideologies. Mill's discussion of nationality illustrates that it cannot be removed from a constraining context of "equal justice," "equal consideration," "freedom" and "concord" that takes precedence over nationality.[42] Acton—an older-type liberal, property-respecting and anti-interventionist—related it to true republicanism, "the principle of self-government in the whole and in all the parts,"[43] thus simply extending the intension of this liberal concept of self-government to include federal as well as unified nation states. Tamir's recent project aims to "plac[e] national thinking within the boundaries of liberalism."[44] Of course, the complex relationship between core and periphery in all ideologies ensures that a temporary emphasis on nationalist ideas may itself elevate them to an adjacent position from whence they may exercise influence on core liberal understandings of liberty, progress, and tolerance.[45] But this occurs within a semantic field delineated by those core features.

Nationalist concepts within liberal ideologies also reflect the universalism of liberalism. For liberals, nationalism has always included the bestowing of an equal right to national expression on a wide range of similar nations. Liberals, however, more frequently locate the concept of the nation in a morphological position adjacent to another liberal core concept; thus popular sovereignty is decontested as national self-determination;[46]

---

[41] Alter, *Nationalism*, p. 34.

[42] J. S. Mill, *Considerations on Representative Government* (London, 1910), pp. 365–66.

[43] Acton, "Nationality," pp. 147–48.

[44] Tamir, *Liberal Nationalism*, pp. 4, 12.

[45] Cf. Breuilly, *Nationalism and the State*, p. 63.

[46] See Guibernau, *Nationalisms*, p. 53.

itself an offshoot of the core concept of liberty. Nevertheless, liberalism is equipped with a variety of conceptual arrangements through which to ensure the legitimacy of the state, only one of which operates through attaching that institution to the concept of a nation. Nationalist arguments certainly do not provide sufficient conditions for such legitimation within liberalism, and often fail even to provide necessary ones.

But tensions still abound. For one, liberalism itself now reflects the universalism/particularism divide. Merely to state, as some scholars have done, that a synthesis between universalism and particularism takes place is unedifying.[47] Detailed conceptual analysis is required to establish the different kinds of synthetic mixture available. Initially, constraints on liberal universalism applied—as in the case of Acton—in the form of a desire to encourage different kinds of national expression in diverse societies. Here a pluralist liberalism as the host-ideology is dominant, and is put to the service not of freedom as self-development, but of freedom from the unnecessary intervention of government.[48] This principle was extended by liberals from individuals to groups, as in Hobhouse's reiteration of Mazzini's position that "every nation had its own peculiar function to fulfil in the life of humanity." But he also observed that national rights had to be found a place *within* the unity of the state in order to make room for diversity. Writing on Irish Home Rule, Hobhouse adopted a majoritarian view, arguing for the legitimacy of a lesser "Belfast" nationalism, but only when operating within a wider "Dublin" one.[49]

These liberal themes have been extended to embrace the new awareness of multiculturalism and multiethnicity. Nationhood is incorporated into the new pluralism of the liberal host-ideology, accepting groups and communities as formative social units, but it must often compete on equal terms with the claims of other non-national groups.[50] Nevertheless, liberals may have to deny—as Hobhouse did—what Miller terms "radical multiculturalism" and opt instead for arrangements by which minorities share in the common and larger culture and sense of identity, while simultaneously preserving formative elements of their separate identities.[51] Another perspective on the universalistic-particularistic dimension asserts the

---

[47] Cf. G. E. Rusconi, quoted in M. Viroli, *For Love of Country* (Oxford, 1995), p. 172.

[48] Acton, "Nationality," pp. 159–60.

[49] L. T. Hobhouse, "Irish Nationalism and Liberal Principle," in J. Meadowcroft, ed., *Hobhouse: Liberalism and Other Writings* (Cambridge, 1994), p. 173; L. T. Hobhouse, *Social Evolution and Political Theory* (New York, 1911), p. 147.

[50] "Under conditions of security, I will acquire a more complex identity than the idea of tribalism suggests. . . . I will be an American, a Jew, an Easterner, an intellectual, a professor. . . .When identities are multiplied, passions are divided" (M. Walzer, "The New Tribalism," quoted in Dahbour and Ishay, *The Nationalist Reader*, p. 332).

[51] Miller, *On Nationality*, pp. 130–40.

constitutive inevitability of both elements. As MacCormick has argued, since all individuals are contextualised liberalism must include respect for a sense of national identity and belonging as part of the self-understandings of individuals.[52] These positions are interestingly compatible with Kristeva's understanding of the nation both as a series of differences and as a general interest. According to that view, particular rights need to be highlighted as well as integrated, though not absorbed, into a Montesquieuian *esprit général* offering identifying space. That space is typified by defining (and hence dominant) cultural and political features, in this case the principles of the French Enlightenment.[53]

Another tension within liberalism, however, relating to political obligation, reduces the possibility of a rupturing competition between nationalism and other group allegiances. Nationalism obviates consent/promising as the preferred liberal method of settling the issues of legitimacy and obedience and offers instead nonreflective and nonvoluntarist grounds—memories, proximity, kinship, and the emotionalism of passion and loyalty—as the basis for eliciting support for state or group activity. The advent of the nation-state has established an additional level of suprapolitical obligation, not accounted for in contract theory, that strikes an uncomfortable note for liberals. Political obligation is no longer directed solely at governments and civil societies, or even at states *simpliciter*—that is, at politically responsible institutions and rational processes—and it can therefore no longer be tested in the breach. For how can civil disobedience be directed not at a government or state, but at the nation itself as the ultimate focus for, and underpinning of, allegiance? Civil and political disobedience have been couched in terms of disregard for a law or authoritative rule, not for a cultural practice, a blood tie, or a sentimental attachment. No wonder that nationalist discourse is still assigned marginal status in liberal morphologies. In that case it may yet withstand the fragmenting tendencies of postmodernist analysis.[54] In contrast, Treitschke's narrow nationalism proceeds much further on this logical route. Distinguishing between civil society—an arena of *internal* conflict endorsed by liberalism—and the state, with its "moral sanctity," Treitschke removed the realm of political obligation as contract entirely from his morphology: "In all my life I have never once thought of my moral obligations towards [civil] society, but I think constantly of my countrymen, whom I seek to honour as much as I can."[55]

[52] MacCormick, "Liberalism, Nationalism and the Post-sovereign State," p. 565.
[53] J. Kristeva, *Nations without Nationalism* (New York, 1993), pp. 41–42, 55, 60.
[54] Cf. Billig, *Banal Nationalism*, pp. 128–48.
[55] Treitschke, *Politics*, pp. 45–49.

Conservatism

The relationship between nationalism and conservatism is slightly more complex than that between nationalism and liberalism, though there is still a case to be made for subsuming nationalism within conservative core concepts. The two main core notions of conservatism concern an insistence on controlled organic and natural change, and a belief in the extrahuman origins and underpinning of the social order.[56] Both notions align easily with certain interpretations of the nationalist core concepts. The organicist conception of community, discussed above, has an important bearing on this issue. For another distinction that can now be added to that conception is the one between spatial and temporal organicism. The one refers to synchronic interrelationships, a generic condition of human interdependence at any given point in time, in real or imagined space, such as Durkheim's organic solidarity or Marx and Engels's slogan "working men of all countries, unite!"[57] Both socialisms and left-liberalisms have adopted it irrespective of nationalist discourse, though not ruling the latter out. Conservative discourse has occasionally had recourse to spatial organicism, but often of a hierarchical nature, as in the Victorian idea of "my station and its duties."

Temporal organicism is, however, more typical of well-known instances of conservatism. It refers to diachronic historical continuity, intimating the Burkean conception of natural growth,[58] and employing a view of historical time as accumulative. This perception of time can be buttressed by a reading of nationalism as incorporating "the possession in common of a rich heritage of memories," though as Renan rightly observed, those memories will include a great deal of forgetting as well.[59] Expressed differently, the less liberal the nationalism, the more insistent it will be on the construction and legitimation of a selective and singular national or folk memory that takes no account of broader historical frameworks. This particularisation of time is in marked contrast to its universalisation by other historically inspired political theories such as Hegelianism or Marxism. The group known as the nation can be constructed to reinforce the conservative conceptual configuration and support the crucial growth

[56] For an elaboration of this argument see Freeden, *Ideologies and Political Theory*, pp. 317–47.

[57] E. Durkheim, *The Division of Labor in Society* (New York, 1964), pp. 111–32; K. Marx and F. Engels, "The Communist Manifesto," in McLellan, ed., *Karl Marx: Selected Writings*, p. 246.

[58] E. Burke, *Reflections on the Revolution in France*, ed. C. Cruise O'Brien, (Harmondsworth, 1969), p. 120.

[59] E. Renan, "What is a Nation?" in A. Zimmern, ed., *Modern Political Doctrines* (London, 1939), pp. 190, 202–3.

metaphor. Even Herder, often seen as a founder of a liberal nationalism linked to freedom as a differential, pluralistic self-realisation among nations, reflected this conservative motif, by regarding spiritual and cultural unity as the basis of a natural political community, a *Volk*, over time, and drawing upon both spatial and temporal organicism.[60] "A people can maintain its national character for thousands of years. . . . For a people is a natural growth like a family, only spread more widely," he wrote.[61]

The retroactive appeal to the naturalness of nations offers important support for conservative forms of social control. The general reference to the extrahuman sanctification of the social order shields a system of government, and the social order it maintains, from unwanted criticism. If not only time evolves on a growth model, but the nation, too, is seen as natural, nationalist core ideas can powerfully uphold conservative ideologies. Maistre, for example, decreed that "no nation has ever succeeded in developing by written constitutional laws rights other than those present in its natural constitution."[62]

Fascism

Within fascism, too, a variant of nationalism emerges that is crucially supportive of a host-ideology, but only as a part of a larger whole, whose core concepts include not only the nation, but also leadership, totalitarian organicism, myth (determinist and/or antimodernist), regenerative revolution, and violence.[63] Fascism decontests the concept of the nation in a specific way precisely because of its proximity to these other core notions. Alone among the major ideological families, however, fascism recognises the nation as a core concept, although in doing so it is prone to considerable conceptual crudity. The particular attraction between fascism and nationalism lies in the fact that both locate the concept of the nation in their respective cores, though beyond that the core similarities diminish. As for the naturalness of social features, to which both conservatives and fascists appeal, this may invoke very different conceptual patterns. When

[60] Viroli, *For Love of Country*, pp. 119–20; V.A. Spencer, "Towards an Ontology of Holistic Individualism: Herder's Theory of Identity, Culture and Community," *History of European Ideas* 22 (May 1996): 245–60.

[61] J. G. Herder, "The Nation as an Enlarged Family," in Zimmern, ed., *Modern Political Doctrines*, p. 165; B. Barry, *Democracy and Power* (Oxford, 1991), p. 169.

[62] J. de Maistre, *The Works of Joseph de Maistre*, ed. J. Lively (London, 1965), p. 78.

[63] This morphology of fascism reflects and combines various approaches, such as Z. Sternhell, "Fascist Ideology," in W. Laqueur, ed., *Fascism: A Reader's Guide* (Harmondsworth, 1979), pp. 325–406, and R. Griffin, *The Nature of Fascism* (London, 1993), pp. 1–55, while suggesting that all these components are core concepts without which the historical instances of fascist ideology are incomplete.

race is employed by fascists as the constituent of community, naturalness relates to virtually impermeable physical, therefore spatial, boundaries unconducive to the moderate vista of change offered by conservative growth, let alone the quasi voluntarism evident in liberal communitarianism.

Consequently, the thought-patterns of fascism, as well as its political practices, may seem to fluctuate between appearing solely as a thin-centred nationalism and assimilating nationalist argument to broader ends. But the thinness of an independently standing nationalism suggests that the latter is the more plausible approach; indeed, the precise decontestation of the nationalist component of fascism is, as Griffin has argued, a populist ultranationalist (that is, illiberal) variety.[64] In the terms employed here, fascism attaches the concept of the nation to an extreme valorisation of one's own nation. That valorisation is constrained by markedly irrational myths that help to constitute a conception of the national group, as well as its aggressive location in space and time. Its expression necessitates the concept, as well as the practice, of violence as a manifestation of political will and power. But the fascist core cannot be contained in that form and will also include concepts of leadership, regenerative revolution, and totalitarianism absent from thin-centred nationalism, all of which appear in different fascist configurations.

NATIONALISM AND EMOTION

The core concept of sentiment and emotion—a peculiarity of nationalist argument—has differential impact on various ideological configurations. Though human emotion is often recognised by political philosophers, it has been contained—as with Hegel—in the realms of the private, the family, its immediacy considered to be inferior to mediated and reflective thought.[65] As second-wave feminists have frequently pointed out in a different context, Western modern political thought lacks the vocabulary to conceptualise emotion in the public sphere.[66] In liberal host-ideologies nationalism is the only form of acceptable emotion, carefully surrounded by other constraining concepts. Mill referred to the "sentiment of nationality," consisting of "collective pride and humiliation, pleasure and regret, connected with the same incidents in the past."[67] Acton talked of the "na-

---

[64] See Griffin, *The Nature of Fascism*, pp. 36–38. See also R. Eatwell, "On Defining the 'Fascist Minimum': the Centrality of Ideology," *Journal of Political Ideologies* 1 (1996): 303–19, for whom nationalism is one component of fascism.

[65] G.W.F. Hegel, *Elements of the Philosophy of Right* (Cambridge, 1991), pp. 199–201.

[66] See, e.g., C. Gilligan, *In a Different Voice* (Cambridge, MA, 1993).

[67] Mill, *Considerations on Representative Government*, p. 360.

tional sentiment" and "a community of affections and instincts"—though the latter have to be tamed through a framework of laws and obligations. "Self preservation," he contended, "is both an instinct and a duty."[68] Mazzini reflected the liberal mixture between the "sentiment of love, the sense of fellowship" and a rational approach to a "community of work and purpose." Within liberalism, national feeling is often referred to as patriotism, a positively evaluated term. Though conceptually and historically distinct from nationalism, this is not necessarily true of its actual usage. Patriotism accords nationalist ideas moderation and respectability and is located adjacent to core, universal liberal concepts such as liberty, limited government, and participatory self-government.[69] "I adore *my* Country," wrote Mazzini, "because I adore a Country in the abstract; I adore our *Liberty*, because I believe in abstract *Liberty*; *our* rights, because I believe in abstract *Right*."[70] This epitomises the way in which ideologies harness reason and emotion.

Only in extreme twentieth-century ideologies of the right is emotion exploited as a prime means of mobilising mass support, moving beyond the arational "holy passion" of Maurras[71] to irrational practices such as the Nuremberg mass rally, commensurate with Hitler's portrayal of nationalism as "a driving force . . . of fanatical, even hysterical passions."[72] Significantly, this emotionalism singles out national will, not national reason. It is then let loose to dominate the conceptual morphology, attached only to an unconstrained version of power located in pseudoheroic élites, and the political practice it endorses is violence. Conservatives, on the other hand, recognise the centrality of emotion in human conduct, but seek to contain it as a source of evil as well as good and appeal to moral instincts, to a quasi-mystical national consciousness,[73] and—as with Oakeshott—to the comfort of long-standing temporal proximity.[74] Renan insisted that community of interests alone does not make for nationality; it must be supplemented by soul, by "a heritage of glory and grief to be

[68] Acton, "Nationality," pp. 152, 163.

[69] See Canovan, *Nationhood and Political Theory*, p. 89; M. G. Dietz, "Patriotism," in T. Ball, J. Farr, and R. L. Hanson, eds., *Political Innovation and Conceptual Change* (Cambridge, 1989), p. 187.

[70] Viroli, *For Love of Country*, pp. 149–50, quotation on 152.

[71] C. Maurras, "The Future of French Nationalism," in Dahbour and Ishay, *The Nationalism Reader*, p. 217.

[72] Quoted from *Mein Kampf* in Koselleck, "Nationalismus," *Geschichtliche Grundbegriffe*, vol. 7, p. 402.

[73] B. Schönemann, "Volk, Nation," in *Geschichtliche Grundbegriffe*, vol. 7, p. 356.

[74] A. Aughey, G. Jones, and W.T.M. Riches, *The Conservative Political Tradition in Britain and the United States* (London, 1992), p. 84; M. Oakeshott, *Rationalism in Politics* (London, 1967), p. 169.

shared."[75] The various uses of emotion are methods of locking conceptual relationships into place, preventing or permitting internal morphological flexibility and legitimating certain types of argument.

Many current explorations of nationalist thought are based on a functionalist view of what nationalism does to, and for, the groups it pervades, or on the styles of politics it involves, or on the ethical propriety of its contentions, or on its ideational genesis. When they do relate directly to ideological families, rough and sweeping dualistic categorisations are frequently in evidence. It has been argued here that a morphological analysis of nationalism is a more appropriate aid to understanding both the diversity and commonality of nationalism. The focus of this approach is on the thought-product itself, on the idea-artefacts produced and consumed by a given society, through which we can best appreciate the features of an ideology. Such an analysis allows us to assess whether nationalism is an independent ideology, and to examine the nature of its complex relationships with the comprehensive ideologies with which it intersects. When understood as an ideational phenomenon that displays variegated conceptual configurations, nationalism appears as a plastic structure, reflecting the even greater complexities of its broader host-containers. Only when it occasionally attempts to stand on its own does its ideational paucity come to light. To reduce nationalism to its thin-centred form may well be an effective and forceful political tool in the hands of political actors, but as a general characterisation of nationalism it employs abstractions and truncations that serious students of politics should eschew.

[75] Renan, "What is a Nation?" p. 201–2.

CHAPTER ELEVEN

Political Theory and the Environment: Nurturing a Sustainable Relationship

New Maps for Old?

Consider sitting on a tree. Every year in Oxford hundreds of human beings sit on trees. Most of them are children, often in their backgardens, scrambling over branches, hiding in their tree houses. Some are adults, out for a walk, looking for a view, or a place to rest for a while when the ground is wet. Sitting on trees is a recreational activity, and has been so since time immemorial. Not long ago, one group of adults chose to sit on trees on the site of the Oxford-Business-School-to-be. Was that a recreational activity? I doubt it. The act was the same, but the human behaviour around it was far from routine.

So how do we make sense of such acts? We need to fold up the map we usually use when stumbling across people in trees, and obtain a new one. Political maps interpret practices, which are recurring acts (whether deliberate or not) engaged in by groups of people. If sitting on trees in anger is a one-off event, we may deem it insufficiently significant to map. Yet in recent years the innocuous activity of sitting on trees has been redefined as a saliently political practice, a protest. True, Robin Hood's merry men sat on trees in preparation for ambushing the Sheriff of Nottingham's cohorts. But changing military technologies have marginalised that particular tactic. Now once again we require a new theoretical map in order to realise that, rather suddenly, a set of observable actions no longer inhabits the semantic field in which we have been accustomed to find it. Indeed, even if we define sitting on a tree as a political act, further, competing maps may be necessary to decide what *kind* of political act it is. Political maps are never just descriptive of a terrain, but interpretative and organisational; they are themselves a form of scholarly as well as imaginative creativity. Moreover, the practices they identify may both embody and generate theory.

Some of the ecological protesters claimed to act as guardians of those trees' right to life, perhaps even—if this isn't overstating the case—to dignified life. This argument by analogy sounds more familiar to advocates of natural law, as well as to procedural rights theorists. According to that argument the tree-sitters were, at different levels of articulation, superimposing a set of fundamental philosophical beliefs drawn from current debates onto their actions and the objects of their actions. They were conferring on trees the status of honorary persons, with the entitlements to respect and consideration that personhood entails. And they were justifying civil disobedience in the name of those fundamental principles, because a moral principle concerning one's obligations towards trees had been violated, and civil disobedience is legitimated whenever a higher moral principle is disregarded by a particular political authority. But in the eyes of other observers, the practice in which they were engaging was one of obstruction. These were tiresome faddists who were flouting the law, at great expense to the welfare of the community. The community would therefore have to divert resources from other crucial social objectives in order to remove the protesters.

The map of civil disobedience, however, whether such disobedience is justifiable or not, is a poor one with which to explore the contours of the practice. If it is the only map in town, we may find it difficult to find our way through. The protesters were hugging trees in communion with nature, interacting noninstrumentally with nonhuman objects. Conventional political theory hadn't adequately prepared us for that. In the realm of political obligation, with which civil disobedience is intimately linked, the semantic field has been dominated by concepts such as promising, voluntarism, and consent.[1] But politics is also an arena where strong emotion is expressed, and where group dynamics play a central role. These too need to be incorporated into political theory. One reason that they have been excluded from the remit of many political theorists is that hegemonic models of Anglo-American philosophy have become dismissive of nonrational accounts of human conduct. Such accounts, it is asserted, are irrelevant to constructing the versions of best practice, buttressed by requirements of coherence, that the prevalent notion of the rational, purposive agent requires. Another reason is that manifestations of nonrational theory in the experience of the past century have all too frequently been unpalatable. Theorising about the environment is thus confronted with a choice between extending the category of persons to cover nonhuman objects and consequently incorporating a new domain into mainstream political theory, or seeking alternative conceptual frameworks through which to bestow meaning on its particular foci.

The upshot of this dilemma is to highlight that, if we wish to optimise our understanding of the sociopolitical worlds and the environments in which we are located, political thought needs to take on board a multiplicity of interpretative viewpoints, *many* of which are reasonable, even if not all are equally persuasive. This may upset those philosophers who are looking for consistency, for neatness, and, above all, for decisive cogent

---

[1] See, e.g., H. Pitkin, "Obligation and Consent," in P. Laslett, W. G. Runciman, and Q. Skinner, eds., *Philosophy, Politics and Society*, Fourth Ser. (Oxford, 1972), pp. 45–85.

arguments by means of which to recommend the adoption of certain polit-ical practices rather than others. Political thought is not shaped in the closed laboratory of our minds, but is a result of reflecting, in our various and strange ways, on experiences we have undergone, directly or vicari-ously. Environmental theory and Green political thought are in their cur-rent manifestations relatively new systems of ideas. Unsurprisingly, many of their premises reflect those philosophical ideas that were dominant in their period of inception and early growth. Yet a sustainable political the-ory needs to follow its own maxims in relation to the methodologies it employs, namely, to engage in a continuously critical assessment of those dominant paradigms both from within and from without. A sustainable *Green* political theory needs to identify central values and concepts at the service of the Green family of arguments and to decide which theories and methodologies advance them. Pre-theories always contain method-ological and ideological preferences. There is no view from nowhere be-cause none of us knows where nowhere is.

Wholes, Links, and Patterns

There is, I believe, an interesting interface between political theory and environmental thought. It is common among recent political philosophers to argue that justice is the first virtue of the state, but is it rare for them to add that well-being is the first virtue of the community. Neither of these statements is incontestable, but they serve as good starting points for broadening our view of political theory. I submit that these statements run in parallel, that to assume that societies need to choose between them (on the lines of liberal right versus communitarian good) is a methodologi-cal misconception, and that Green political thought is particularly well placed to utilise both standpoints. To begin with, Green political thought does not have the dual boundary problems constraining much political theory. It does not focus solely on human beings as possessing the only attributes that political theory should consider; nor does it focus solely on political space as constituted by the borders of the nation-state.

The *substantive* reason for the linking of state and community is the interest Green political theorists have in groups, wholes, collectives, or-ganisms, and bio- and sociodiversity, so that, as political sociologists know, the state is merely one aspect of a society, and, as feminists know, the political cannot be encompassed in the activities of the state alone. The *methodological* reason for linking the two is crucial to the very na-ture of political theory itself. Let me put this in a grossly oversimplified way in order to make the point. Anglo-American moral philosophy is profoundly inspired by the power of logic, and its typical manner of arguing is to validate or invalidate particular statements in terms of their consistency with a foundational position, itself formulated in order to promote optimally a moral maxim. Its grammar is cascaded in terms of logical chains: it moves from A to B to C. Thus *if* we wish to pursue justice, *then* we will need veils of ignorance and original positions, and *then* we will arrive at certain distributive rules, et cetera. Much of the debate is immanent: is the path followed coherent, can it be assailed by alternative cascades and—far more problematic for those who insist that there exists clear blue water between philosophy and ideology—does it conform to our moral intuitions?

But political theory is also constituted by its units, political concepts; and political concepts are signified by words, and words are components of language. And language is a structure of interdependency. Words and the concepts they carry only make sense in complex clusters; and by rejigging the pattern of each cluster, we create different messages, apply different meanings to sentences and passages. Political arguments are always configurations of concepts, and competitions over which configuration attains philosophical, or political, or cultural legitimacy. They cannot make sense as isolated concepts linked in linear sequences, unless they serve certain thought-experiments, the purpose of which is to test an argument to the point of destruction under insulated "laboratory" conditions. It all depends on what we want political theory to do for us. And it is here that we can learn from the study of ideology, inspired by Green concerns, and I will table some suggestions in the form of a number of propositions.

Proposition No. 1

The first proposition emphasises the integrity of the environment; it holds that removing political concepts from their natural habitat, from the idea-environment of other concepts in which they are located in actual language usage, is a cruel and often unnecessary act. The battery-farming of concepts, held in relative isolation and often worked to death in order to gratify the intuitions of human experimenters, should rather proceed with sensitivity and under carefully regulated circumstances, at the end of which the concept should be released back into the sustaining community of language.

Green political thought provides a sympathetic framework for regarding political theory as holistically complex. It also offers an opening for a more elaborate conception of community than the one currently employed by many political philosophers. In general terms, the methodological individualism still predominant in Anglo-American political philosophy might have been more generous in making space for explicit notions of group identity and interests implicit in environmental views. Indeed, political concepts are themselves interconnected, in that their separate meanings are always formed through their interaction with, and proximity to, other concepts. Specifically, community in the Green context may be conceptually proximate to a strict species-egalitarianism, in which human beings are subsumed within a totalising view of nature that refuses to accord them special status.[2] Or it may be conceptually proximate to a decentralised bioregionalism that allows for a multitude of distinct and local communities, rather than a monolithic version of community.[3]

Thus to subscribe to the interconnectedness of concepts is not to support a single unified view of political theory. There are many holisms that may be applied to make sense of one series of facts and phenomena; hence there are also many alternative harmonies, not just one. Each holism is constructed through a different internal configuration of the field of concepts it addresses, a different mapping of the same evidence. Some may offer solutions that are inimical to individual rights and autonomy, but that is certainly not a corollary of organicism per se, as anyone acquainted with social liberal thinking in the early twentieth century knows.

PROPOSITION No. 2

This proposition involves the biodiversity, or rather morphodiversity, of political concepts. Political concepts exist in multiple, indefinite forms, conceptualisations, and configurations. Political theory centrally embraces a study of the complexity of political argument, its evolution, internal morphology, and the multiple meanings it accrues. Singling out some concepts and arguments as superior—a practice engaged in by many moral philosophers—is a form of discrimination. Let's call it "conceptism." It has its obvious uses, no doubt, for we wish to make moral judgments, develop our virtues, and improve the world. But it excludes much human thought-creation and is often unreasonably disrespectful of the variety and the quality of other conceptual arrangements. Conceptism may even, deliberately or unwittingly, modify the evolutionary process through which unexpected new combinations of political concepts are created and from which future generations may benefit. Moreover, it is quite unjustifiably contemptuous of ideologies, which are vital and necessary communal resources at the disposal of a society, without which polit-

[2] See, e.g., W. Fox, *Toward a Transpersonal Ecology* (Totnes, Devon, UK, 1995).
[3] For a critical assessment of bioregionalism see J. Barry, *Rethinking Green Politics* (London, 1999), pp. 81–90.

ical decisions simply cannot be made.[4] Political ideologies comprise the actual political conceptual arrangements that people, philosophers included, inevitably construct when they map the social world. Anyone who thinks about politics has to select some meanings rather than others from the indeterminate and contested universe of the conceptions a concept contains. What some philosophers prefer to call moral intuitions, analysts of ideologies may call non-negotiable, decontested core beliefs on which a political Weltanschauung is anchored. And they may then arrive at the shocking conclusion that more than one moral intuition within the same ethic, or within the same semantic field, may be valid; namely, that political concepts lend themselves to multiple combinations, and that a convincing case can be made for quite a few of those combinations. Even when such ideologies are not at their qualitative best (and most ideological families do display great sophistication in the structure of their conceptual arrangements), that dimension of political thought provides a rich source material from which to distil meaning, to understand the consequences of certain conceptual decontestations that, though logically arbitrary, have crucial cultural significance. If ideologies tend to stress difference, their *analysis* emphasises connections and sensitises us to conceptual structure.

PROPOSITION NO. 3

According to this proposition, thinking globally is always a form of thinking locally. Local varieties of political theory require protection from standardisers; indeed, the habitat of political theory is always local. Political theory, like Green practice, is invariably the view from somewhere. Here we find both similarities and divergences with respect to Green political theory. Its very focus on globalism lends itself to universalism and the prospect of single overarching solutions. But that ignores the fact that the possibility of multiple holisms undermines universality. Put differently, every proposal for a holistic viewpoint constitutes a particular reading of universality. On the other hand, one of the great attractions of environmentalism is its sensitivity to the concrete and to the particular, through its emphasis on action and on practices. The notion of practice is elevated, in similar although certainly not identical fashion to its role in Marxist thought, to the status of a core Green principle.[5] Recent trends in political thought argue that the divide between theory and practice is far from clear, that practices are theory-rich and decodable in many different ways.

[4] See M. Freeden, "Ideologies as Communal Resources," *Journal of Political Ideologies*, 4 (1999): 411–17.

[5] See Freeden, *Ideologies and Political Theory*, p. 527.

This does not mean that generalisations are impossible to formulate. First, some generalisation is of course advantageous, as long as we acknowledge its possible contingency, awaiting contrary argument. Second, some strains of political theory itself may spread uncontrollably, rampantly supplanting other local varieties, as Rawlsian political philosophy has done from its Eastern-Seaboard roots, supported not merely by its powerful intellectual appeal but by the capitalist power of American publishing and the Ph.D. factory. The result has been a genetically modified liberalism, in which a spurious neutrality creates the illusion of a suprapolitical stance, though some Rawlsian supporters insist that this fortifies liberalism's immunity to infection by particular conceptions of the good.

The losses to Green theory are sometimes considerable: Even an eminent and subtle ecotheorist such as Eckersley has attributed an historically quite misleading attribute to liberalism—the autonomy of atomistic individualists, which is at best a mid-nineteenth-century feature of liberalism—and ignored others such as tolerance and the recognition of community rights, both friendly to environmentalism.[6] She has fallen into the common trap of ideologically misrepresenting an ostensible opponent's views and thus excluding them from one's semantic field at considerable theoretical cost.

Proposition No. 4

One of the lessons of the above for Green political theory is the precautionary principle. Excessive risk-aversion in political theory should not crowd out risk-taking. Methods adopted by political philosophers and by analysts of ideology often employ parallel perspectives on the same subject matter, and the enthusiasm of either needs to be contained by the legitimate concerns of the other. Some interventions in political thought may be irreversible, some ideas may be irredeemably contaminated and lost to posterity. But some of these losses may be desirable—a view that, incidentally, few environmentalists endorse when it comes to biodiversity, yet is the entire environment equally deserving of blanket preservation just because it is there? Death and decay are just as natural as life and growth. A young discipline is an experimental one and therefore rightly risk-prone, but it should not be risk-averse. Green political theory has developed by provisionally positing certain goods and exploring value systems that may secure them. This trial-and-error process is attractive from the standpoint of a political theory that endorses conceptual poly-

---

[6] R. Eckersley, "Greening Liberal Democracy: the Rights Discourse Revisited," in B. Docherty and M. de Geus, eds., *Democracy and Green Political Thought* (London, 1996), pp. 212–36.

semy and plural paths of valid or justifiable argumentation, and eschews homogeneous universalism.

The problems of universalisation for Green political thought are of course those of holding time and space constant. Theories of justice, some of which rely heavily on universalisation and immunity to change, run immediately into difficulties when made to intersect with theories whose concerns are grounded in an appreciation of the local, the diverse, and the evolving. All ideologies harbour theories of time and change; and all serious theories of ideology respect the contingency of conceptual permutations. Would a space- and time-sensitive theory be more applicable to Green perspectives? Global issues notwithstanding, and recognising the argument for some generalised obligations, we also need to assess the claims of a political theory that argues the parallel case for our responsibilities for the near over the distant, in both space and time. Not all forms of obligation need to be informed by a strict egalitarianism in terms of its objects—that is, allocated to all potential beneficiaries. In social space the prioritisation of the near is commonly practised, and ethically justifiable, with respect to our attitudes to the family, as well as to our interpretations of ethnicity, multiculturalism, and even benevolent forms of nationalism. These put a premium on nonrational aspects of human interaction—bonding, sentiments, pride in group belonging, care—all of which have been underconceptualised in recent political theory, if not eliminated altogether (outside feminism and the revival of interest in nationhood and nationalism).

Localised environments and concrete communities are the arenas of these features. Dare we even suggest that localism, or finiteness, in time are equally comprehensible, so that some of our responsibilities to the near future may plausibly be stronger than to the distant? One asset of Green political thought is its receptiveness to notions of growth, change, and evolution, which allow for graduated conceptions of time and space, unavailable, say, in the static character of natural rights theory. If Green political thought continues to conceptualise such questions in terms of boundary problems and clear-cut categories, as is the wont of some political philosophers, it may not be able to resolve this kind of issue. Instead, it should begin to build on its own strengths, thus assisting in a broader invigoration of current political theory.

In that light we can begin to analyse Green political thought as a particular family of manifestations of thinking about politics. There is no correct Green political thought, nor is there a single Green political theory, nor *can* there be without totalitarian coercion, nor should there be. That is not to argue that all forms of environmental debate are equally attractive, persuasive, or reasonable. But, like all ideologies, the Green family is a multiverse. It is pluralist not only in intent and in its conception of the world, but in the very structure of the political thought-patterns and practices it engenders.

PROPOSITION NO. 5

The final proposition maintains that human beings must abandon their aspirations to control optimally their cultural as well as physical environments. Green political theory contains the perceptive implication that, all too often, excessive control has serious downsides in its invasiveness and its intellectualization of environmental concerns. Three points follow. First, an agency-cum-autonomy-cum-purposive model of human nature is ultimately grounded in the notion of reflective self-control and self-criticism. It is echoed in many philosophers' attempt to control language through logic and persuasive argument. Paul Ricoeur's notion of the "surplus of meaning," however, enables us to pursue alternative routes in exploring political and social thought.[7] The deliberate meanings we intend to convey are always accompanied by unintentional ones; hence, the analysis of political messages imparted by political actors cannot be reduced to examining the purposes of those messages alone. The inevitable absence of complete control over meaning is precisely what a study of ideologies reveals; it opens up a different role for the scholar as one who accepts linguistic usage and linguistic communities as given, though modifiable, rather than threatening or inadequate, just as by analogy ecologists enjoin us to accept nature and to adjust it in a sustainable way. If we want, contra Marx, to change the world through reinterpreting it, we must, as professional thinkers, descend from the Olympus of a specialised moral language and work with our subject matter, human beings, using their ordinary tools of thought and language as well as ours in our professional capacity. Environmental thinking offers us a good example here.

Second, through the very fact that Green political thought, as a family, deals with unreflective as well as with reflective entities, it is well placed to distance itself from the proclivity of some political theorists to dismiss the unreflective altogether. And Green political thought, because it crosses the boundary between the human and the nonhuman, and locates human beings in nature, is well placed to appreciate the physical and emotional attributes of human beings. True, they cannot be treated in the same way as the intellectual and the moral attributes, but they are nonetheless in-

[7] P. Ricoeur, *Interpretation Theory: Discourse and the Surplus of Meaning* (Fort Worth, 1976), p. 55.

eliminable features of being human and acting as human beings, even though we share some of those features with animals.

Third, we, too, are passively conditioned by the manifold communities of which we are members, side by side with being purposive agents. No amount of ideal-type liberal theory can wish that away, nor *reduce* us to our capacity for agency alone. Here is where well-being joins autonomy as a twin value of political theory, but one that cannot be catered to entirely through procedural theories of justice designed to maximise our capacity for informed and considered choice. We do not have to choose between humans as moral agents and as possessing other human attributes. The merit, for Green political thought, of configurational conceptual analysis, or the appreciation of ideological morphology, lies in its mirroring of the environment's holism and antidualism. As noted above, it rejects the cascades of lexical and logical priority and replaces them with a cluster notion of conceptual interdependence. Indeed, this is also the case with the five propositions offered above. They are not sequential but mutually supportive. You can work your way from any one to the others.

A PROVISIONAL BALANCE SHEET

Some philosophers are rightly exercised about *resolving* tensions within arguments. Ideologies, to the contrary, suggest alternative routes of *reasonably avoiding* tensions—and avoid them one must if political decisions are to be made. Otherwise, we get trapped in incommensurabilities or indeterminacy as an argumentational chain unfolds. Studying ideologies helps us to be more modest about our intellectual ambitions, to resign ourselves to the necessity of making path-choices on the basis of cultural constraints, emotional attractiveness, as well as conformity to current scholarly practices.

Green ideology in its various manifestations is, however, thin-centred. It lacks adequate conceptual complexity to address the range of issues that mainstream ideologies have addressed over time. As an ideological family, it does not have a full morphology, containing particular interpretations and configurations of all the major political concepts attached to a general plan of public policy that a specific society requires. Unlike liberalism or socialism, its core concepts do not have sufficient pull to constrain the structure of its adjacent concepts. The relation of human beings to nature, the preservation of the integrity of nature, and an appeal to holism, are shared by all its variants and hence constitute the core of its actual usage of language, but they are insufficient to prevent loose centrifugal arrangements.[8] Some of its arguments are subsumed in other

---

[8] See Freeden, *Ideologies and Political Theory*, pp. 485–87.

ideological groupings: ecosocialism, anarchism, or conservatism. Much of its discourse decentres human action and the overriding value, evident in other ideologies, that is attached to human societies. It needs, therefore, to borrow from other schemes of distributive justice; it does not have a distinctive approach even to democracy. Flying the colours of a progressive ideology, it nevertheless cannot propose a unique decontestation of concepts central to progressive debate: liberty, equality, or rationality.

Does that make it a postmodernist receptacle for all values and none? Far from it. Green thought is imbued with a strong sense of desirable values, among which of course justice is important, but it mirrors the diversity and the interconnectedness of the world it is designed to preserve, and it identifies human beings as possessing attributes irreducible to their mental and moral faculties. For that reason, a political theory tailored to cope with interwoven variance, in method as well as substance, is likely to be a useful tool at its disposal. For political theorists as students of ideology, sitting on trees is more than an expression of moral agency; it offers the elevated vista of multiple routes through the world.

CHAPTER TWELVE

Practising Ideology and Ideological Practices

ALTHOUGH AMONG the categories informing the study of politics there are few as fundamental as those demarcating theory and practice, that distinction is highly problematic when applied to the analysis of ideologies. Many traditional as well as current approaches regard political thought as the area in which issues of moral philosophy pertaining to political entities are aired, with the objective of setting defining ethical and validating criteria that are then to be applied to political practice. A grounding of this view may be found in Kant, for whom individuals were subjected to clear and unequivocal moral duties and were *therefore* also men of affairs concerned with political right. As Kant argued, "Experience cannot provide knowledge of what is right, and there is a *theory* of political right to which practice must conform before it can be valid." Hence, "Not all activities are called *practice*, but only those realisations of a particular purpose which are considered to comply with certain generally conceived principles of procedure." The value of such a practice depended "entirely upon its appropriateness to the theory it is based on."[1]

This position has recently been restated thus: "The major goal of a moral theory is to resolve conflicts arising in moral decision making giving clear guidance on how to act."[2] Building on ancient Greek views, such approaches hold contemplation to be inextricably linked to practical wisdom and virtue.[3] As a consequence, politics—inasmuch as it contains conflict—is seemingly transcended, at least until it encounters a new moral dilemma for which further guidance will be available. More recent hermeneutic accounts are subtler in assessing the interaction between theory and practice, identifying a mutual relationship of interdependence, in which the contingencies of politics continuously batter against the walls of our preformed conceptions. Nonetheless, these accounts remain wed-

---

[1] I. Kant, "On the Common Saying: 'This May be True in Theory, but it does not Apply in Practice,' " in H. Reiss, ed., *Kant: Political Writings* (Cambridge, 1991), pp. 61, 63, 71–72, 86.

[2] "Introduction," I. Shapiro and J. W. DeCew, eds., *Theory and Practice: Nomos XXXVII* (New York, 1995), p. 2.

[3] M. C. Nussbaum, " 'Lawyer for Humanity': Theory and Practice in Ancient Political Thought," in Shapiro and DeCew, *Theory and Practice*, p. 193.

ded to the eliciting of new holistic truths from the multiplicity of time- and space-bound human experiences.[4]

In either case, it is frequently unclear where ideology stands in relation to theory or to practice. Ideology is sometimes conceived of as bad theory—that is, not even "true in theory"—in the sense of its utter separation, through abstraction or dogmatism, from the actual world of contingent conduct and events. It is therefore deemed incapable of guiding political practice that is portrayed as pragmatic, if not opportunist, by its very nature. Standard views of political science in the 1960s articulated such understandings, and they have continued to assert themselves since. One prominent example of that notion of ideology has been promoted by Sartori, for whom ideology is a particular type of political belief system that is closed to action on relevant information. Instead of relying on empirical evidence based on correspondence, it constructs an internally coherent, rational, and deductive view of the political world.[5] More recently, Minogue has continued this line of argument by classifying ideology as distinguished by a specific and impractical monistic logic that is alienated from actual politics.[6]

At other times, conversely, ideology is defined as action-oriented, that is, as political theory especially designed to direct political conduct and practices. Far from presenting a disjuncture with the world of practice, ideologies are thought-phenomena believed to be primarily concerned with controlling and changing political practices. Though some American political scientists see this as a neutral, functional aspect of politics, other scholars, picking up the Marxist conception of ideology, insist that ideology reflects power as manipulation, or that at least it commonly betrays the moral expectations attached to political philosophy. Hence ideology is another kind of bad theory, one reviled as polluted by power relationships that undermine the emancipated reflection required for good practice. Ideology thus reduces the status of political thinking to the level of crass instrumentality, in the service of the interests of the groups who exercise social control. As Minogue, straddling both approaches, sees it, "those who characterize ideologies as 'action-oriented' are no doubt correct but one striking feature of ideologies is that, at their core, they do

---

[4] Cf. H-G. Gadamer, *Truth and Method* (London, 1979); P. Ricoeur, *Lectures on Ideology and Utopia* (New York, 1986).

[5] G. Sartori, "Politics, Ideology, and Belief Systems," *American Political Science Review* 63 (1969): 398–411. These understandings of rationalism have long since been challenged. See, e.g., R. J. Bernstein, *Beyond Objectivism and Relativism: Science, Hermeneutics, and Praxis* (Philadelphia, 1983).

[6] K. Minogue, "Ideology after the Collapse of Communism" (special issue) *Political Studies* 41 (1993): 7–11.

not advocate, exhort, propose or concern themselves with policy except tactically."[7] None of these views is entirely wrong, for they do not correspond to unknown instances of ideological thinking. But if we are to adopt a broader interpretation, we cannot assess ideologies through singling out particular cases as representative of them all. The above perspectives offer unhelpfully restricted vantage points from which to understand the specific shared features of ideologies. Those features are definitely not limited to solving moral quandaries, to illuminating the path of correct conduct, to "rising" above the particular, or to imposing and justifying unassailable élites.

To compound the complexities involved, there is a further sense in which the study of ideologies is torn between Marxist and non-Marxist approaches. Adherents of the former see ideology as a distorting or illusory epiphenomenon, obfuscating material relations and practices. This elicits a critical assault entrusted with the dual role of unmasking that type of political thinking, and concurrently replacing it with true understandings that arise out of unalienated human practice and activity. As Lefort sees it, ideology entails a split between "an order of practice and an order of representation" and occupies an artificially separate domain.[8] The impact of such views has been to perpetuate the aversion to regarding ideologies as deserving analysis in their own right. Instead, they are consigned to metaphysical digressions from, or interventions in, what actually happens in the world.

The non-Marxist approaches are often disparagingly believed to involve mere description, whose very essence is considered to be non-normative and therefore irrelevant to guiding practices. So whereas engaging in normative political theory has been labelled as creative, engaging in the study of ideologies has not. Here the difficulty has been a naive understanding of description, erroneously assuming it to entail a mere correspondence with or reproduction of facts, rather than their reconstitution and reassembly in an act of interpretation and analysis. Whether such an act is simplistic or sophisticated in the hands of its diverse practitioners, it, too, is creative and imaginative. Indeed, inasmuch as Marx announced that "philosophers have only interpreted the world, in various ways; the point is to change it," it could be counterargued that "ideologists change the world by interpreting it in various ways" and that students of ideology identify, reinterpret, and reconstruct—analytically and imaginatively— the overt and covert interpretations that ideologies contain.

[7] Ibid., p.7.
[8] C. Lefort, *The Political Forms of Modern Society* (Cambridge, 1986), pp. 183–85.

POLITICAL THOUGHT-PRACTICES

Three discrete, if supporting, issues require bearing in mind. First, ideologies are themselves political thought-practices and as such have distinct features. Second, ideologies as a group contain a specific category of thought-practice pertaining to understanding the relationship between theory and practice. Third, each of the major ideologies displays different interpretations of the relationship between theory and practice. The third issue is thus central to illuminating the second, and the second constitutes an important aspect of the first.

A practice is here understood to mean the performance of, and participation in, an identifiable regularity of action or thought, one replicated as well as shaped by other such practitioners. It is hence a communal activity taking place in social space and recurring over time. Practices and acts are not synonymous: many acts do not constitute practices, and some practices-cum-regularities of thinking do not constitute acts. On the macrolevel, the phenomenon of ideology is itself a particular yet ubiquitous type of thinking about politics that conforms to the above definition. On the microlevel, ideologies are sets of specific thought-practices whose content and morphology differ from one ideological family to another. To analyse an ideology (as distinct from participating in formulating one) is to categorise, elucidate, and decode the ways in which collectivities in fact think about politics, the ways in which they intentionally practice the art of political thinking, and unintentionally express the social patterns that that kind of thinking has developed. That analysis encompasses a span ranging from what is done to what can be done. It includes an exploration of what *ideologies* claim should be done, but excludes any judgment concerning what ought to be done from an external, absolute, or unitary moral viewpoint.

A major problem then arises: if moral and political theory are ordinarily entrusted to tell us how to act, can an ideology, in its dual role as both theory and practice, do the same? Of course, most ideologies *purport* to tell us how, or how not, to act. But can the status of their recommendations attain theoretical respectability among communities of theory-producing scholars? This points to a disjuncture between the ideologist and the student of ideologies that is absent within the field of political and moral philosophy. The moral philosopher as scholar is indistinguishable from the moral philosophers to which he or she refers. Moral philosophers aim to improve on or elucidate the arguments of their predecessors, but both present and past philosopher are engaged in the same activity of morally philosophising; they are both therefore oriented to recommending certain kinds of practices. This rendition of the activity of moral and political theorists does not fundamentally deviate from the understandings and motives they impute to themselves. Those theorists are thus participants/observers in a joint discourse.

By contrast, there is a considerable difference between the formulators and the students of ideologies. The former focus—as do moral philosophers—on the politically desirable, but their justifications rest on widely differing bases of truth and validity. Their thought-practices do not necessarily occupy the same, or even a broadly common, discursive space. The latter, exploring as they do ideologies as a thought-practice, possess a different starting point. They are neither concerned with advocacy nor with improving the practices and techniques of ideologists (although their knowledge of ideologies may give us insights into what is desirable). Their interpretations may vary from the functional to the contextual or the morphological. The consequence is the production of a different kind of theorising about ideologies, which is not directly and deliberately practice-oriented. It does not participate in the same thought-practices it analyses.

If, then, ideologies are thought-*practices*, can we conversely extrapolate from them guidelines on how to theorise? What would prevent those guidelines from being, in the cumbersome translation from the language of German hermeneutics, "always already" a conservative affirmation of what is? Alternatively, if description becomes an act of reconstitution, and this serves as the measure of the reflexive nature of scholarship, then scholarly findings have an aura of contingency about them. That does not imply indifferent scholarship but an acknowledgment that the architecture of political thinking is overwhelmingly multiform. Inasmuch as ideologies are particular configurations of the actual and attainable meanings of political concepts, the investigation of thought-practices provides an insight into the ways given ideational systems are staked out, into the consequences of the connections among arguments and among conceptual decontestations. At the very least these perspectives open up to the scholar a world of choice emanating from an appreciation of the pluralism of political thought-practices. The analysis of ideologies as practices thus offers tools through which to enrich the conventional relationship between moral philosophy, in which judgmental choices play a vital part, and political action.

Sound political theory is hence informed by three ingredients. First, by the assertion that, whatever else it may be, political thought is a set of socially mediated ideational practices, with their own (multiple and differentiated) regularities. Second, by the claim that all political practices are a crystallisation of norms, values, and interpretations that at least partly account for action-choices, though they are not themselves coterminous with action. Third, by an understanding of the costs and benefits of chains of thought-practices, of what is possible and compossible, and how various semantic fields are defined by certain conceptual configurations. That is one central outcome of the study of ideologies, and may be harnessed by moral philosophers to the end of furthering good practice itself.

ETHICS AND IDEOLOGY: MISRECOGNITIONS AND DIFFERENTIATIONS

What are the particular thought-practices associated with ideologies? To talk about ideologies as action-oriented does not constitute a sufficient boundary line between them and other types of political thought. Ethical theory is clearly action-oriented as well. Let us examine some differences, evident or alleged. One supposed distinction is that ethical theory may be universalised, while ideologies are particular to time and space. Another is that ideologies may be partisan and favour a particular set of practices irrespective of the latter's ethical merit. A third is that ideology has to do with (allegedly unethical) power and control and is therefore essentially linked only to social practices of that nature. A fourth is that ethics in theory and practice must be intentional, whereas ideology can be embedded also in unintentional practices. A fifth is that ethical theory needs be authentic, in the sense of being a creative discovery, in dialogue with others, of the life design of an individual,[9] whereas ideologies mask real thoughts and relationships. These invite further examination.

The temporal and spatial attributes of ideologies become evident when they are explored as conceptual configurations, in which general concepts, often courting universal appeal, and shared by the preponderant membership of an ideological family, are fleshed out by adjacent and peripheral concepts whose main function is to construct a two-way link between the concrete and the abstract. While most ideologies (fascism and some narrow nationalisms are obvious exceptions) are couched in universal terms, on closer inspection most do not meet these aspirations. The particular fails intellectually to attain universal status, even when it seems to succeed in doing so politically, at least in the short term. The contract theory of liberalism proves to be associated with constitutive practices, models of individual will, and rational forms of promising that fall short of boundless acceptability. Dealienated man in the Marxist vision is hampered by an insistence on a liberation from custom that emanates from a world in which material relationships overrule all others. Even the particularisms of conservatives are elevated to a position that, on the one hand, assumes a general fear of inorganic change while evoking the constants of human nature yet, on the other, topples conservatism

---

[9] See C. Taylor, *The Ethics of Authenticity* (Cambridge, MA, 1991), pp. 66–68.

from this psychological pedestal by accepting uncritically the unique experience of particular nations. While ethical theory is typically couched in a universal discourse, on reflection, however, this usually applies only to a few fundamental principles, such as the sanctity of life and the gruesomeness of torture—on their own insufficient to delineate a semantic field. Otherwise, ethical theories themselves do not overcome ideational barriers to universalism.

Like all practices, ideologies are not only located in cultural and social space but exist over time. As a consequence, ideologies tend to be seen both by their practitioners and by their observers as constituting a tradition, whether past- or future-oriented. To conceive of an ideology as a practice is both to embed it in an historical setting, and to internalize history as a necessary dimension of ideology.

It is, however, quite true that ideologies do not always promote ethical ends or—a rather different point—they do not always promote political ends ethically. An appeal to a unitary state may use ethical rhetoric, but have no moral value on its own, or no more value than an appeal to a federal state. The enhancement of some forms of political power may utilise blatantly unethical concepts, as in the revolutionary extolling of terror. And many progressive ideologies have suffered internal rifts when aspects of human welfare have been brought about by coercive means.

To claim disapprovingly, however, that ideologies are about power may have strange consequences. If power is the ability to get things done, then to remove ideologies as frameworks for power would be to disable practice entirely. But if power is merely exploitative and manipulative, ideologies are not wholly about power, and not all ideologies are primarily about power. Ideologies need be no more oppressive than the moral edict "thou shalt not steal," which, presented as a divine rule, is backed up by spiritual as well as secular sanctions. If language constricts the choice of meanings we employ, then ideologies are a normal aspect of political language.

As for intentionality, ideologies clearly are a mixture of deliberate and unconscious thought-practices. The latter have been aptly summed up by Ricoeur's phrase "the surplus of meaning," allowing for an utterance to contain more than its author intended. Of course, moral philosophers may—indeed, will—be "guilty" of a similar surplus, but that would be seen as a deficiency or, at best, irrelevant in appraising their stated maxims. In the analysis of ideologies, unintentional thought-practices deserve to be treated as seriously as intentional ones, precisely because human practices are frequently not the deliberate product of identifiable human will. To restrict the exploration of political thought to its intentional manifestations is to neglect some of its most interesting practices. Liberalism's former blindness to ethnic diversity and its past unheeding endorsement of the nation-state are centrally shared thought-practices, as is Marxism's unawareness of its re-engagement of power through the control over nature.

Nor is authenticity what ideologies are about. Ideologies focus not on the individual, even as a dialogical entity, but on the group in which dialogue or, more appositely, multilogue takes place. Ideologies always are group practices. Their production and consumption occur in a social context and would be indecipherable were the individual to be the unit of analysis. Moreover, when group experience is transmitted in an ongoing process of political socialisation, the conscious self-understanding of the individual is peripheral both to the morphology and the function of ideologies. Besides, the topic of authenticity presumes a reality behind ideological practice that, when contingent understandings are the order of the day, begs the question. It is quite possible to grant that ideologies are less than perfect representations of human political values, while simultaneously querying whether beyond them there exists a world of true values. There is a wide gulf between the good, the useful, and the true, but all may be worthy modes of assessment. Ideologies are dedicated to constructing conceptual configurations of political values in ways that can either be more, or less, intellectually, emotionally, even morally, satisfying. Ideologies may well be all we have, though this does not entail that their content is therefore invariable.

INTERPRETATIVE PLURALISM AND THE IDEOLOGICAL ASSIMILATION OF POLITICAL PRACTICES

Although ideologies share some of their thought-practices with other kinds of political thought they are, from their particular viewpoint, less interested in the clarification of those practices than in providing readily available, applicable, and widely consumable solutions for groups. In that sense both philosophy and ideology engage in informing and reflecting practice, but with different ends in mind. An ideology, however, is itself a distinctive type of political thought-practice. As noted in previous chapters, it effects a decontestation of the political concepts it employs by means of a combination of logical and cultural proximities among them, which prioritise certain concepts over others, and certain meanings of each concept over other meanings. The external manifestation of this thought-practice is a unique conceptual configuration that competes over its legitimacy with other conceptual configurations. This practice arises from and indicates the existence of a plural world of meaning, and that in turn provides a justification for influencing the exercise of choices among sets of meanings. The effecting of such choices is itself a practice within a practice, a form of conduct; after all, we describe it as *making* choices. In sum, the conceptual configurations that constitute the theoretical form of ideologies, and the way we handle them, invoke political competition-cum-action. But the *internal* logic of ideologies directs them to straddle the divide between theory and practice in a peculiar fashion: by reducing the rational, reflective component linking the two; and by problematising, occasionally eliminating, the choice that moral theory claims to offer.

The thought-practice referred to as ideology is a common and ubiquitous one. But ideologies are not simply action-oriented, in the specific sense of providing an agenda for political action. The competitive action may be between different groups of theorists, writing books and pamphlets intended to refute each other's viewpoint, a practice common to all producers of ideology. Often, then, ideologies contend with each other as systems of ideas, and it would be rash to deny these activities—these "wars of words" disseminated through the press and the mass media— their central standing as the *political practice* of influencing the manner through which we impart meaning to our societies.

Ideologies as distinctive thought-practices also interrelate with the world of concrete practices, of practices as regularities of action, in a singular manner. Political ideologies are hence action-oriented in the far broader sense of constituting mapping frameworks through which we can imbue any particular action with political meaning. Here theory itself is simply the imparting of plausible meaning to a set of practices, rather than the determination of correct relationships among facts, or the uncovering of truths. The upshot of this is another central linkage between ideology and practice, observed from the practice → ideology direction of the feedback loop: ideologies identify sociopolitical practices and locate them at the perimeter of their semantic fields, permitting them to assist in decontesting core and adjacent concepts while simultaneously absorbing those practices into their interpretative domains. Crucially then, there is no one-to-one relationship between an ideology and a practice. A practice may be equally comprehensible by superimposing on it different theoretical maps (which is the same as extrapolating such maps from the practices themselves). An industrial strike could, in liberal democratic eyes, be a legitimate expression of an assembly of individuals to alter an unfair contractual relationship and to express dissent, if it conforms to legal and accepted procedures. The same strike may be interpreted as a revolutionary act by a radical socialist, or as a destabilising and extortionist act by a traditional conservative. The theory-cum-interpretation extrapolated from that practice may range from regarding politics as the arena of legitimate procedures, to regarding politics as the exercise of group power against constraining and oppressive structures, to regarding politics as a controlled and directed field of authoritative knowledge and responsible conduct. But an industrial strike also has to be *identified* as a practice, and as a practice that has political import to begin with. Because ideologies can be decoded through the analysis of political practices, there is a case for asserting a two-way flow between practice and ideology. Unlike Kant's view of theory versus practice, neither ideology nor practice has ontological priority over the other.

Those who divorce ideology from practice are guilty of the same fault in their own analysis. Sartori's closed ideology is simply not supported by empirical evidence. There is a world of difference between the "closure" that ideologies effect when controlling the meaning of political language, and insulation from social practices. That sort of insulation is chimerical. Even totalitarian ideologies interact with the political world in which they are located, drawing on existing practices (the Nazis' use of prior anti-Semitism) or adapting them in accordance with vital extraneous needs (Stalin's industrialisation projects); they do not conform to their "formal" or doctrinaire features. Ideologies always contain perimeter concepts and practices that ensure a certain amount of ideational flexibility as these react back on the core concepts. In the cases of nontotalitarian ideologies, such flexibility may be encouraged; in any event, it will result in continuous changes to the core itself. The relationships among the conceptual components of an ideology cannot be contained in abstract logical structures. Such structures would anyhow be unintelligible to most political actors, even including political élites. Moreover, Minogue's proposition that ideologies are only tactically interested in policy neglects the alignment of all ideologies with the promotion and realisation of what they conceive to be fundamental social values, however distasteful some of them may appear to others.

Practice and Its Constraints

We now turn to a discussion of some of the different positions concerning theory and practice embraced by thinkers and scholars who represent a spectrum of ideological positions in the broad sense adopted here. The literature on practice has itself not always been conducive to the study of ideologies and some of it runs counter to the exploration of ideologies as practices with an easily recognisable and theorisable structure. Two illustrations, relating to Pierre Bourdieu and Michael Oakeshott, will point to problems and ways of confronting them. Bourdieu has focused on the sociological and anthropological study of practices. He detects what he terms the "logic of practice," but it is not a logic that suggests the theorisation of designed patterns within practices. Rather, it is a special kind of theorising that practices evoke. Abandoning the harmonising congruity that sociologists have frequently sought to attribute to practices, Bourdieu retorts that the coherence of models, while economical, hides the impossibility of mastering the logic of practice, which is positioned somewhere between the coherent and the incoherent. For Bourdieu, "theory . . . is a spectacle, which can only be understood from a viewpoint away from the stage on which the action is played out."[10] The kind of legitimate theorising about practices such as rites lies in their very identification as activities that have no logic beyond their existence. Hence the interpretation typical of hermeneutics results in misrecognition, for the logic of practice is prelogical. If practices are understood not to be implementations of plans, a way beckons of overcoming the limits imposed on conventional political philosophy by those who insist on intentionality as a necessary component of both theory and practice. On the other hand, by identifying the "habitus" as a system of dispositions produced over time, a system that "is the basis of the perception and appreciation of all subsequent experiences," it is nevertheless possible to stipulate continuities and regularities in practices without being able to account for their schematic nature. Summing up, Bourdieu sees the "habitus" as "an infinite capacity for generating products—thoughts, perceptions, expressions and actions—whose limits are set by the historically and socially situated conditions of its production." It is "a spontaneity without consciousness or will." New practices are neither mechanically reproduced nor reflective, and they contain no "unpredictable novelty."[11]

It is instructive to contrast this with Hannah Arendt's understanding of action as having the character of "startling unexpectedness," because for her action means taking an initiative, beginning something new.[12] The ontological fissure between the two thinkers indicates a different decontestation of the relationship between individual and society. In Bourdieu's case, culture, time, and society themselves are seen to supply the infinite variety of human practice that constrains the individual as an acting corporeal body, in specific situation after situation. In Arendt's case, it is human consciousness itself that operates at the level of the particular, of opinion rather than truth. Human beings are creative conditioners of their own, unique lives and of those with whom they share lives. Freedom is far more central in this scheme, albeit a freedom forged in the public spaces that combine differentiated individuals. No wonder, then, that for Bourdieu ideology is the imposed control of a cultural good, language, the superimposition of an objectivist understanding in which practices are represented and fitted into planned schemes, the symbolic "gentle vio-

---

[10] P. Bourdieu, *The Logic of Practice* (Cambridge, 1990), pp. 11–12, 14.
[11] Ibid., pp. 54–56.
[12] H. Arendt, *The Human Condition* (Chicago, 1998), pp. 177–78.

lence" by which domination is misrecognized as legitimate.[13] And no wonder that for Arendt ideology is an all-inclusive logical consistency in which the status of truth is separated from individual human judgment.[14] Ideology loses out in either case. Both thinkers adopt a narrow conception of ideology as incompatible with proper practice and action.

LOGICAL ARBITRARINESS, INTENTIONALITY, AND CHANGE

How can a reading of Bourdieu apply to a more open view of ideologies? The great strength of Bourdieu's argument is to demystify practice and to show the limits or, alternatively, the arbitrariness of the ideological representation of practices. But arbitrary logic, rather than Arendt's logical consistency, is precisely one of the crucial features of ideology. The brute facts of ideological morphology are the infinite logical relations among political concepts and practices, and the limitless representations of those relations. It does not follow, however, that a particular decoding of logical relations, a particular logical path among political concepts, is devoid of significance. Even if we accept that practices simply exist, ideologies are precisely those devices that attribute meaning to certain practices. The process has two facets. First, through their identification by a political ideology, those practices have themselves already been recognised, or are newly recognised, as political. Second, the attribution of meaning occurs the moment societies enter a stage of reflexivity, however elementary, because it is then that such practices demand or attract cultural legitimisation or delegitimisation. So in one important sense it does not matter that practices may be unthinkingly entered into and unwilled: once they exist, ideologies integrate them into patterns of significance or, to the contrary, ignore them. We are, of course, focusing exclusively on political practices. These are practices that are ideologically identified as public, that are harnessed to compete over collective decision-making processes, and that are pervaded by the justificatory and legitimating processes at the heart of ideological practice. When societies generate their own rules to govern these issues, they are arbitrary in the sense that no *specific* rule is dictated by logic, but necessary in the sense that these issues require cultural solutions for societies to function.

Does Bourdieu's account suggest an intractable conservatism? Not at all. Another merit of his approach is to detach the accentuation of tradition from aversion to human or social change. In that elemental sense all ideologies have a history and are formed by their past. Nineteenth-century

---

[13] Cf. J. B. Thompson, *Studies in the Theory of Ideology* (Cambridge, 1984), pp. 58–59.
[14] See M. Canovan, *Hannah Arendt: A Reinterpretation of Her Political Thought* (Cambridge, 1994), p. 26.

Marxism is consciously a product of the German metaphysics against which it reacts, and twentieth-century liberalism has been closely wedded to ideas of evolutionary change, even regarding itself as a set of beliefs whose essence lies in its being subject to historical processes, processes that ensure the emergence of rational and energising practices.[15] The thought-practice of proffering practices as the quintessence of politics need not signify a distaste for progress or for theorising about progress. Nevertheless, Bourdieu cannot easily include the spatial permeability that is a feature of open ideologies. In complex societies, and with increasing intercultural communications, entire ideologies, as well as ideological fragments, interact across the traditional boundaries of family resemblances, forming new hybrids and displaying plastic morphologies.

One final consideration respecting Bourdieu. In examining the relationship between theory and practice it is important to distinguish between a practice as a deliberate, and thought-out, attempt to change political conduct and processes, and a practice as a "pretheoretical" cultural pattern, which may then be raised to the level of consciousness. This impacts on two issues. The one concerns the question whether theory is ontologically prior to practice, in which case theory might also be accorded superior status in the conduct of research, giving rise to optimism about the possibility of human control over the political world; or whether practice is ontologically prior to theory, in which case we can only operate within the constraints of the existing, perhaps even the known. The other concerns the question whether theory is the product of individual minds, presumably of talent if not genius, in which case political theory would be an aspect of unique creativity awaiting more general acceptance; or whether it is the product of groups (whose collective consciousness is at the very least questionable), in which case political theory would already have some of the features of an ideology and reflect the practices of complex interactions that take place between human beings at various levels of awareness.

Here what Bourdieu has to say on intentionality is acute. Much human practice is automatic and impersonal, for "the habitus makes questions of intentionality superfluous." Crucially, he claims to solve the "paradoxes of objective meaning without subjective intention."[16] The solution lies in the temporal dimension, which permits the emergence of "a sequence of ordered and oriented actions that constitute objective strategies." This insight is central to an appreciation of the workings of ideologies. Although they embody myriad variations, ideologies can be identified at least in part as distinct "strategies" of thinking with patterns

---

[15] Cf. chap. 1 in this volume.
[16] Bourdieu, *The Logic of Practice*, pp. 58, 62.

of argumentation, style and structure. Those strategies are social and cannot be traced back to any specific individual volition: in other words, they do not have a specific beginning.[17] They can only be discovered by tracking them over time and space, embedded as they are in particular cultural histories. In that sense ideologies have an "objective" existence that Marx denied: objective not as transcendental, let alone impartial, but as a series of observable and discoverable practices in the world.

Moreover, even revolutionary ideologies exhibit features parallel to the "habitus." Both are a matrix "generating responses adapted in advance to all objective conditions identical to or homologous with the (past) conditions of its production."[18] Intentionality certainly cannot wholly account for action because, in Bourdieu's version of Ricoeur's "surplus of meaning," "it is because agents never know completely what they are doing that what they do has more sense than they know."[19] And yet one cannot take the analogy between "habitus" and ideology too far. The more flexible the conceptual arrangements of an ideology are, and the more pluralist the political culture that nourishes it, the more it is capable of effecting change through an alertness to "objective conditions" as well as through the volitional and conscious thought-processes of its more animated champions. Pluralism sensitises a culture to the possibility of change, to the role of human will in the act of decontestation, in choosing the logical paths between ideas. Paradoxically, that role has been recognised even by Marxist approaches, though mainly when attached to the ideology of exploitative bourgeois self-interest.

The Space between Theory and Practice: A Conservative View

If Bourdieu's examination of concrete practices does not inexorably lead to conservatism, the same cannot be said of Oakeshott. Oakeshott's early work began with an exploration of experience as the constituting unit of human understanding. Unlike Bourdieu, Oakeshott challenged the barrier between theory and practice from a different starting point, by postulating that experience was thought or judgment, a "world of ideas." Precisely because experience was a totality of facts, it was a truth. Truth and experience were therefore inseparable. Experience itself, however, was apprehended as a continuously changing system, and the consciousness of it being a system was part of the world of ideas. Consequently, experience was not an interpretation of the world, because that would imply a world

---

[17] On the question of the "beginning" of ideologies see M. Freeden, "Editorial: The 'Beginning of Ideology' Thesis," *Journal of Political Ideologies* 4 (1999): 5–10.

[18] Bourdieu, *The Logic of Practice*, p. 64.

[19] Ibid., p. 69.

of ideas removed from and external to experience. There was simply no space between experience and ideas about experience. The significance of an idea related to its necessary place in its world, and emerged from the coherence—coherence in the sense that there was no other way of conceiving it—of that world. In sum, there was only one experience.[20]

Theory (or philosophy) and experience cannot consequently be seen as opposed. Philosophy is unreserved, self-critical, and self-conscious experience, "in which the determination to remain unsatisfied with anything short of a completely coherent world of ideas is absolute and unqualified."[21] As for practice, it, too, was located in the world of ideas as a judgmental aspect of experience, yet as a vehicle for change it was concurrently to be understood as activity. Importantly, the change incurred through practice was not, as is often held, the realisation of an idea in a world external to it, but "always the co-ordination and completion of a given world of ideas." Nor could practice be judged by its consequences, because that would involve an unattainable future-orientated truth instead of the truth of experience, which had to be not only given, but also holistically coherent.[22] Indeed, even practice fell short of that coherence, as it could not effect a final resolution of discrepancies in such a coherence, but only of the particular instances of such discrepancies. Hence practice could not supply an adequate assertion of experience and was irrelevant to the development of a critical philosophy.[23]

In *On Human Conduct* Oakeshott's notion of theorising became far more tentative and conditional, a continual process of furthering understanding, but one always faced with a "not-yet-understood." The theorist is quite distinct from the theoretician. The latter intervenes in human conduct by formulating postulates, rather than exposing, attempting to understand, and rendering conditionally intelligible the contingent "goings on"—the postulates, performances, and practices—in a society.[24] Indeed, the ideologist would be a particularly unwelcome version of the theoretician, as ideology was an abstract, superimposed abridgment of a concrete tradition.[25] Here also is an expanded version of Oakeshott's notion of practice. A practice is there to be understood, not directed. It is a more or less durable relationship among agents, involving observances, customs, principles, and rules pertaining to human actions and utterances. It is also "a prudential or a moral adverbial qualification of choices and performances . . . in which conduct is understood in terms of a procedure." It

---

[20] M. Oakeshott, *Experience and its Modes* (Cambridge, 1933), pp. 27, 28–29, 31, 34, 81.

[21] Ibid., p. 82.

[22] Ibid., pp. 256–57, 259, 264–65, 287.

[23] Ibid., pp., 291, 303–4, 319.

[24] M. Oakeshott, *On Human Conduct* (Oxford, 1975), pp. 1–10, 106.

[25] M. Oakeshott, *Rationalism in Politics* (London, 1967), pp. 123–25.

does not determine the substantive choices and performances of agents, but establishes the rules concerning how to make choices and how to perform. Importantly, no practice "is capable of being participated in except by learning to do so." It appears "as various invitations to understand, to choose, and to respond."[26] Every practice involves the exercise of intelligence, or learned response, however instantaneous; therefore there cannot be a "thoughtless practice." A practice "is an instrument to be played upon," encompassing the understanding of a performer.[27]

Practices cannot be transmitted in the abstract but have to be engaged in by the would-be practitioner. And theory recognises that understanding human conduct involves nothing more than making claims like the one made in the previous sentence. Theory can only generalise about the particular and the specific, through providing a map as an instrument of understanding. The relationship between theory and practice is such that "performances may be theorised by being read in respect of their places upon this map or by being assigned a place upon it." Identifying an action or a performance is a thought process that understands them as relating to practices, a reflective rather than directive relationship.[28] Intelligent thought cannot exist as distanced from practices and other "goings on": theory and practice intermesh. Practices also refer to human association— and that is why human conduct is social, not in any overriding and fundamental sense, but simply in the concrete free involvement of agents in practices—but they are not actions as such. They rather relate to speech and action, and include principles, rules, language, and morality in terms of which to think as well as act. Crucially, Oakeshott sees practices as "compositions of beliefs and sentiments" that are "themselves historic occurrences whose intelligibility is contextual."[29]

Oakeshott's version of the relationship between philosophy and practice remains deeply conservative in its portrayal of any attempt radically to change the world as futile, and in its nonpluralist holism, which lacks even the synthetic tension of opposing elements to be found in much Idealist thought. Despite a superficial similarity with Bourdieu, whose notion of the "habitus" imposes constraints of continuity on time and space, as does Oakeshott's view of experience, and despite the aversion of both scholars to planning, there are important differences. The rough and incompatible edges of Bourdieu's practices, which may account for innovation and variety but can be conceptualised only with difficulty, give way in Oakeshott's writings to an aspiration to contain that rough variety of

[26] Oakeshott, *On Human Conduct*, pp. 23, 55–58.
[27] Ibid., pp. 89, 91.
[28] Ibid., p. 99.
[29] Ibid., pp. 87–88, 78–79, 100.

experience within, and as, a total and coherent framework of thought: the very obverse of Bourdieu's thoughtless spontaneity. As an example of conservative thinking, Oakeshott's collapsing of the space between thought and experience and between theory and practice fashions an ideology that allows little room for human choice and diversity in the face of reality, or for differential experiencing of reality, let alone for the designing of possible futures. Nor, conversely, does Oakeshott accord unconscious patterns a role in understanding human conduct, inextricably linked as it is to agency, though agency without an overall plan.[30] Oakeshott could not entertain the possibility that some practices are discovered by the observer, and that agents may be unaware of them. For even were all practices to be conscious and intelligent, cannot different levels of consciousness and intelligibility offer a possible ranking of practices? Ideologies operate both at the level of the conscious willing of political ends and at the level of expressing unconscious accumulative practices. Conservatism, as much as any other ideology, displays the two levels because conservatives, too, choose to impose specific understandings of the past on the political sphere and work to safeguard them in the present.

We may, however, wish to utilise Oakeshott's view of philosophy as the pursuit of complete coherence by contrasting it with a view of ideologies as devices that establish a *selective* coherence, though we may also doubt whether in that sense philosophies ever surpass ideologies. On the macrolevel, the scholarly study of ideology provides the means to view the world from a range of alternative perspectives, precisely because ideologies are more selective mechanisms of coherence, less ambitious than Oakeshott's philosophy. Conversely, on the microlevel, we may exploit Oakeshott's view of the contingency of occurrences to suggest that different combinations of contingent occurrences may be intelligibly and reasonably offered by competing ideologies. While Oakeshott is suspended between an unattainable totality and a limited contextual understanding, the flawed creativity incumbent in the practice of ideologies offers the far superior tools.

IDEOLOGY AND THE PHILOSOPHY OF PRAXIS: A MARXIST ADAPTATION

Although early Marxism was replete with references to the distinction between theory and praxis, later theorists within the Marxist tradition, of whom Gramsci is a striking example, recognised political theory itself as a thought-practice. Through Gramsci's extraordinarily perceptive discussion of the philosophy of practice one can clearly appreciate how polit-

---

[30] Ibid., p. 72.

ical thought is both illuminated and obfuscated by its association with the critical thinking of the Marxist tradition. Western moral philosophy may well fall short of the radical critique demanded by Marxism, inasmuch at it fails to challenge some of its own categories or to internalize the centrality of material and historical relationships. Though ideology undeniably includes uncritical because unconscious components, it is not, however, therefore devoid of a critical dimension both in its practice in the world and in its practice in scholarship. In their practice in the world, some ideologies shape their conceptual configurations through disputing alternative existing ones. In an open society they also offer the experience of rivalry with its implications of choices between better and worse ideologies—a choice that is, after all, central to the rhetoric of ideology itself. In the practice of the study of ideology, as we have noted, the uncovering of ideological morphology offers a structured and explicable indeterminism that may be put to sceptical or creative uses but, either way, allows us to question any given conceptual arrangement.

Gramsci's contribution lay in the sociological and cultural exploration of the ways in which philosophy penetrates the world of social action, thus overturning the apparent denigration by Marx of (German) philosophy as metaphysics. Leaving aside the more common focus on Gramsci's notion of hegemony, it is of particular interest to explore the intricate way he grappled with the three-way relationship between ideology, philosophy, and practice, arriving eventually at a new understanding. His espousal of the unity of thought and practice is evident in the following passage: "The majority of mankind are philosophers in so far as they engage in practical activity and in their practical activity (or in their guiding lines of conduct) there is implicitly contained a conception of the world, a philosophy." In a signal departure from Marxism, philosophy is demystified and concretised by Gramsci, as well as reintegrated into the normal thought processes of individuals qua organic members of social groups. Studying "the history and the logic of the various philosophers' philosophies is consequently not enough."[31] Here then is a further gloss on Marx's final thesis on Feuerbach, which could now read: "Most philosophers change the world through their activity in it."

Gramsci was particularly alert to the tension between philosophy as an expert activity, often pursued in transcendental and idealist forms, and as conceptions *of the world*, a term akin to Weltanschauungen, and emerging from real human activity. He did not entirely subordinate the first to the second, however. The disjointed and unformed thoughts of the masses could, and had to, be led by élites entrusted with imparting the dual attributes of coherence and critique. On the other hand, a comprehensive,

[31] A. Gramsci, *Selections from Prison Notebooks* (London, 1971), p. 344.

total philosophy was both an historically concrete and a collective activity, a view thatt conformed to Marx's own notions.[32] At this point ideologies tentatively enter the interpretative field. For conceptions of the world exist in an embryonic and fragmentary manner in broader social groups, among the masses: "A conception which manifests itself in action, but occasionally and in flashes." The philosophy of praxis may be glimpsed crudely in mass understandings of political activity; indeed, that is so because of the historical and social nature of thought. In fact, the philosophy of an age exists on three, not two, levels: as individual philosophies (or philosophers' philosophies), as conceptions of leading groups (an articulated philosophical culture), and as popular "religions" or faiths. And here Gramsci crucially informs us: "At each of these levels, we are dealing with different forms of ideological 'combination.' " The role of intellectual élites is to modify the "ideological panorama" of the age, not to dispense with it.[33]

The divide between the philosophical and the ideological thus begins to evaporate on some dimensions. Gramsci was torn between the view, culturally inherited within the Marxist tradition, of ideology as doctrinaire and abstract, and the recognition of ideology as an historical phenomenon within the framework of the philosophy of practice, which needed to be freed from its negative connotations. Societies exhibited ideology-cum-common sense, which incorporated a healthy nucleus of good sense. Hence ideology "in its highest sense" was "a conception of the world that is implicitly manifest in art, in law, in economic activity and in all manifestations of individual and collective life." Yet concurrently even the much-vaunted philosophy of praxis tends, when it is confused with vulgar materialism, "to become an ideology in the worst sense of the word, that is to say a dogmatic system of eternal and absolute truths." Ideology in Gramsci's hands is a slippery phenomenon that, as he put it, is situated between philosophy and day-to-day practice but that displays the attributes of both and neither; that sometimes goes unnamed, or by other names, and at other times is explicitly identified; that in some of its forms is relegated to the unacceptable margins of social thought and at other times retrieved as a fruitful political force for positive change, sharing features with the philosophy of praxis, and located at the very point where practice and theory merge. Once the starkness of the Marxist dichotomy between truth and illusion is alleviated, there emerges a provisional and historical status of truth and its practical origins that, according to Gramsci, "is valid also for the philosophy of praxis itself."[34]

[32] Ibid., pp. 329–30, 326, 324, 321.
[33] Ibid., pp. 327, 345, 340.
[34] Ibid., pp. 328, 406–7, 427.

In some important features of his thought, Gramsci's analysis of ideology remained well within the Marxist tradition. If human thought cannot be perfected, it can at least be improved considerably. Gramsci was still wedded to the belief that ideologies can be refined when their concepts become more universal, and that they can then become more effective weapons in the struggle to achieve an autonomous and superior culture. Specifically, ideological unity and coherence are attainable within a given social bloc. But the process does not stop there. Only a totally unified system of ideologies, attached to different structures and superstructures at a particular historical period, "gives a rational reflection of the contradiction of the structure and represents the existence of the objective conditions for the revolutionising of praxis. If a social group is formed which is one hundred percent homogeneous on the level of ideology, this means that the premisses exist one hundred percent for this revolutionising: that is that the 'rational' is actively and actually real."

When Gramsci argued that only mass adhesion to an ideology was the "real critical test of the rationality and historicity of modes of thinking," he was conceiving of the mass in that special sense. That total ideological system would be "true" specifically and historically, and would therefore constitute a fusion of theory and practice. This rather naive Marxist reworking of Hegelian philosophy significantly—and unlike with Hegel himself—disavows the values ideological pluralism might contain. Nor can one fail to be struck by a Mannheimian undertone in the possibility of objectivity arising out of the total juxtaposition of the prevalent ideologies of a society. Ultimately, then, this method not only locks theory and practice into a fused unity, but decrees that a sole and singular manifestation of this unity expresses the social world in toto.[35]

Notwithstanding those reservations, Gramsci's analysis takes us considerably further down the road towards understanding the complexity of ideology. First, because it refers to a structure combining continuously varying levels of political articulation, style, and argument, the concept of ideology can be applied to arenas of commonplace as well as rarefied political thought, and be assigned to concrete rather than metaphysical and remote guides to action. Second, this approach begins to indicate that ideologies are not as monolithic as the promoters of "ideology as illusion" or "ideology as dogma" would have it, but rather display diverse features. Third, the notion of an ideology as a collective structure suggests that it is a product of social activity and requires to be analysed as a form of human interaction, as historically and socially concrete. Fourth, when Gramsci claimed that for the masses philosophy could only be experi-

---

[35] Ibid., pp. 388, 328, 366, 340.

enced as a faith,[36] he had in fact recognised the important and perhaps necessary emotional appeal of ideological argument. Fifth, Gramsci paid tribute to the organisational function of an ideology, implying that a specific form of practice was forged. Ideologies were no longer allocated to the realm of fancy. Rather, they "create the terrain on which men move, acquire consciousness of their position, struggle, etc."[37] Ideologies were central to practice in delineating semantic fields, providing political and social maps, and identifying points of ideational competition, all of which enabled action. Mapping, as with Oakeshott, becomes a central property of theorising. We may take this further, by regarding mapping as a major interpretative, not representational, feature of ideologies.[38]

LIBERALISM'S DESCENT FROM OLYMPUS

Liberal theory and ideology are often thought to view the relationship between theory and practice as one of applying universal and abstract standards to concrete cases. In earlier centuries, that had much to do with the appeal to natural law, via a theory of natural rights, in order to determine rules of right conduct. By the nineteenth century, a more anthropocentric perspective encouraged the search for such standards in human proclivities, although with similar ends in mind. As J. S. Mill asserted, whether or not one subscribed to intuitive moral principles, "for the remainder of the practice of life, some general principle, or standard, must still be sought." For Mill that general principle, "to which all rules of practice must conform, and the test by which they should be tried," was the promotion of happiness.[39]

Twentieth century liberalism has demonstrated a more convoluted connection between theory and practice. Hobhouse continued to subscribe to the postulate of decisive guidelines in the structuring of practice but, as noted in chapter 1, was emphatic in insisting that the philosophies that have driving force behind them arise out of the practical demands of human feeling, and are not based on deduction from abstract truths. This took Mill's utilitarianism into more complex territory. For Hobhouse, "the impulse to establish harmony in the world of feeling and action . . . is of the essence of the rational impulse in the world of practice."[40]

---

[36] Ibid., p. 339.

[37] Ibid., p. 377.

[38] Cf. C. Geertz, "Ideology as a Cultural System," in Geertz, *The Interpretation of Cultures: Selected Essays* (New York, 2000).

[39] J. S. Mill, *A System of Logic* (London, 1970), p. 621.

[40] L. T. Hobhouse, *Liberalism* (London, 1911), pp. 51, 130.

That assertion was explained in greater detail in his book *The Rational Good*, subtitled "A Study in the Logic of Practice." Here Hobhouse introduced two considerations. First, theory did not influence practice from an external fulcrum but was itself at least in part the product of human characteristics. The world of human practice was that of values supported by feelings; indeed, rational intelligence had its roots in prerational impulse. Second, human emotions were themselves a legitimate object of the study of social conduct. If reason as knowledge was divorced from experience, and reason as conduct was divorced from feeling, that would be "fatal to a true understanding." Nevertheless, Hobhouse did not deviate from a view of principles as the test of practice. Even if theories "owe their ready acceptance to a favourable emotional prepossession" the choice among them was still rational, logical, and evidential, and judgments about values and emotions could themselves be assessed in terms of truth and reality. Practical reason was "in permanent operation within the emotional field."[41] Coherence, compatibility, mutual adjustment—these were central to the harmonious meeting of theory and practice.

British liberalism in particular found itself confronted with the ubiquitous suspicion of ideas embraced by British political culture. Practical reformers, who swore by piecemeal, eclectic and improvised policies, were taken to task by advanced liberals. Hobson accused them of shedding theory and abandoning intellectual principles entirely. This "revolt against ideas" encompassed the opinion that great national issues turned "upon the arts of political management, the play of the adroit tactician and the complete canvasser." By contrast, Hobson invoked the liberal faith in the "conscious play of organised human intelligence." Between a "half-intellectual, half-emotional" utopianism and a "crude empiricism," Hobson advocated the "practical utility of 'theory' and 'principle,'" middle principles that emerged from "legitimate generalisation out of past experience."[42]

Of course, such generalisation was posited on the liberal belief in progress, a core concept that significantly underpinned the movement of theory and assisted in structuring practice. Reason combined with progress was itself a theory of social development, enhanced by the evolutionary ideas of the time. It ensured that human intelligence emerged through political practice to increase both individual welfare (which included the liberty necessary for flourishing) and the collective regulation of goods in the interests of social justice. In this new liberal interpretation, the role of theory was to accelerate progress by transforming it into the "conscious

[41] L. T. Hobhouse, *The Rational Good* (London, 1921), pp. 27–29.
[42] J. A. Hobson, *The Crisis of Liberalism: New Issues of Democracy* (London, 1909), pp. 114–16.

expression of the trained and organized will of a people not despising theory as unpractical, but using it to furnish economy in action."[43] An ideology in which change was endemic, and was furthermore inextricably linked to the augmenting of coordinated rational intelligence over time and space, had to subscribe to privileging conscious over unconscious thought, directive over reactive thought, and patterned and adjustable practice over timeless or mechanical practice. Indeed, one of the pivotal liberal practices is a continuous reassessment of one's own interpretative standpoint. It is the general practice of deciding whether a particular practice should be discontinued.

Many recent versions of liberalism remain linked to conventional views of the relationship between moral theory and political practice, according to which the general rules of the former instruct the latter in formulating correct solutions to concrete cases. Yet an alternative version has emanated from British and American liberal traditions in which collective social life is seen as the source of social wisdom, or at least understanding. British new liberalism was the more influential in providing an account of the social, even organic, base of society. American liberalism, especially through Dewey, insisted on a pragmatism that searched for meaning in the concrete world of human practices.[44] For Dewey, liberalism had originally cultivated a belief in two spheres of action, that of the individual and that of political society; and those spheres only began to converge in the latter half of the nineteenth century. Utilitarianism was one factor in that process, Dewey argued, because "it greatly weakened the notion that Reason is a remote majestic power that discloses ultimate truths. It tended to render it an agency in investigation of concrete situations and in projection of measures for their betterment."[45] Liberalism began to be understood as a type of political practice, involving governmental action for the purposes of social justice, and defined "in the concrete." That practice arose out of a "spirit of reasonableness, fostered by social organisation and contributing to its development." It was also a form of the vitalism explored in chapter 1: the component of activity as the dynamic driving force of societies, a prevalent theme of twentieth-century liberal thought.

All this demanded that "the method of inquiry, . . . of test by verifiable consequences, be naturalised in all the matters, of large and of detailed scope, that arise for judgment." Thus liberals appraised actions by the results they brought about, in the light of the already existing capacities of individuals. But they also appraised actions as historically situated, as

---

[43] Hobson, *The Crisis of Liberalism*, p. 132.

[44] A. Ryan, *John Dewey and the High Tide of American Liberalism* (New York, 1995), pp. 126–27.

[45] J. Dewey, *Liberalism and Social Action* (New York, 1935), pp. 5–6, 20.

occupying temporal and spatial points. Liberalism in the concrete was seen as related to the particular, not the universal. The recognition of concrete social conditions is a recognition of the locus in which these conditions occur, a community of human relations, an arena in which external conditions penetrate "the internal make-up and growth of individuals," and a field of a practically "experimental and constructive intelligence" counterpoised both to intuition and to custom. And experiment in the social sphere always implies planning; it was no longer an individual prerogative, as past liberals had regarded it, but a social activity. Dewey insisted that cooperative social intelligence was clearly both thought and practice. Moreover, social and historical inquiry were themselves organised practices, "a part of the social process itself, not something outside of it." Thought in action involved the understanding and judgment of meanings and these entailed the "conversion of past experience into knowledge and projection of that knowledge in ideas and purposes that anticipate what may come to be in the future and that indicate how to realize what is desired."[46] The rational modification of habits and practices is yet another challenge to a simplistic dichotomous relationship between the "ought" and the "is." Because ideologies tend to interweave the two, this indicates one of the main areas where ideologies have a salient role. They are not merely recommendatory devices but interpretative ones of a peculiar kind: they are a thought-practice that claims, through decontestation, to describe the world, yet does so through recommending or denouncing the values contained in that very description.

What implications and limitations does this pragmatic liberalism have for understanding the interplay between theory and practice? As Anderson has noted, on this interpretation liberal principles become contextual tests of product, techniques, and performance, but they are also themselves discovered in the process of creative practice and deliberation. Hence they are unencumbered by the rigidity of formal liberal philosophy and unhampered by the classic rational search for a single answer to problems. The relevance of this method to studying ideologies lies in its celebration of the flexibility of the interaction between principle and context and in its recognition of the malleability of political architecture.[47] It therefore leads—from the observer's viewpoint—to a conceptualisation of the internal morphology of all ideologies as consisting of temporally and spatially bound understandings that are configured into culturally contingent wholes. It also centres on individual initiative and the capacity of coordi-

---

[46] Dewey, *Liberalism and Social Action*, pp. 31, 39, 43, 45, 50.
[47] C. W. Anderson, *Pragmatic Liberalism* (Chicago, 1994), pp. 19, 43, 46, 156–58, 184.

nated social conduct to make a political difference. On the liberal understanding ideologies are, to borrow Bell's phrase, "levers for action."[48]

While pragmatic liberalism offers insights into the nature of political thinking-cum-ideologies, it is, however, unmistakably a *specific* ideological variant. Morphological flexibility happens also to be a conscious core component of most *liberal* practitioners. It reflects the readiness of liberals to organise their key concepts, employing a reflective commonsense that permits a modicum of pluralist adaptability, and that is prepared to contain a variety of views within the family of liberalisms. In parallel, and quite expectedly, pragmatic liberalism displays the *general* characteristics of ideologies as well—their ultimate refusal to recognise their own decontestations as preferences rather than indomitable truths. Anderson mirrors this in his concern to render best practice commonplace in the social sphere: "To make the exemplary case general and routine."[49] True, pragmatic liberalism cannot disguise the ideological feature of best practice as metapolitical and universal, as do many philosophical schools, because it derives best practice from reflective understandings of particular contexts. Its decontestations do not seek refuge in "unassailable" political language. Nevertheless Anderson rejects the ideological status of pragmatic liberalism in typically ideological terms. Liberalism is not a matter of choice to be offered alongside other systems of political belief, but "the foundation of our system of political understanding" and should be taught as such.[50]

Conclusion

The juxtaposition of the concepts "theory" and "practice" is a compressed surrogate for a number of complex and disparate issues. The tightly assumed flow between given theory and advocated practice no longer obtains, and this view of the political world is bound to strengthen the status of ideologies vis-à-vis some forms of political philosophy. First, for those scholars who deny that theory can be solidly grounded in moral postulates, a major sustaining reason for considering ideologies to be inferior theory has been removed. Indeed, ideologies are grounded in rationally meaningful ways of understanding the world, in that their features are now acknowledged to be central to the process of contextual thinking itself. Second, the aspiration of theorists from Marx to Habermas to overcome distorted communication may be queried by students of ideologies not because communication and dialogue are impervious to standards of

---

[48] D. Bell, *The End of Ideology* (New York, 1962), p. 400.

[49] Anderson, *Pragmatic Liberalism*, p. 26.

[50] Anderson, *Pragmatic Liberalism*, p. 198.

assessment but because "undistorted" communication is unknowable. The question revolves rather around the kinds of communication presumed to be inevitable or even functional in political thinking. Third, ideological morphology dictates the existence of multiple routes from a given theory to a range of given practices and from a given practice to a range of possible theories. The metaphor of an open grid rather than a one-way channel seems more apt. Fourth, it is at least as plausible to link ideology and practice as it is to link theory and practice, because practices, like ideologies, are the product of groups and social intercourse, whereas theory may be the speculative product of individuals and hence not directly connected to practices. Fifth, if one *is* inclined to employ the language of truth, even an imperfect political thought-practice contains its own truth in two different senses. On one dimension, it demonstrates that societies simply *have* such thought-practices, just as the particular practice of permitting and encouraging political philosophers to prescribe political norms exists, and is itself an ideological practice worth examining. On another dimension, even were we to accept that ideologies involve distortion, misrecognition, or rhetoric, there are contextual reasons for those features, and they, too, evince ideational patterns that may be decoded. They therefore make sense in a particular society; indeed, they may be essential for the transitivity necessary for collective political action.

As for ideology as a distinct political thought-practice, we may borrow Oakeshott's understanding of a practice—without subscribing to his broader purview—in attempting to explore the properties of ideologies. For they, too, are not only substantive sets of beliefs but a particular set of conventions, of procedural, or adverbial, conditions for thinking about politics: the conscious and unconscious decontestation of language through statements held, or masquerading, as truths; the forceful and purposive assertion of the legitimacy of concrete practices; the bestowing of political recognition on some patterns of human conduct; the marshalling of emotional support for certain practices, among others through the simplification of the issues on which such support can focus; the choice of specific logical paths linking political concepts through which cultural interpretations are sanctioned; and the semantic competition over the high ground of politics. These are the distinct features constituting the thought-practices of ideologies.

Index